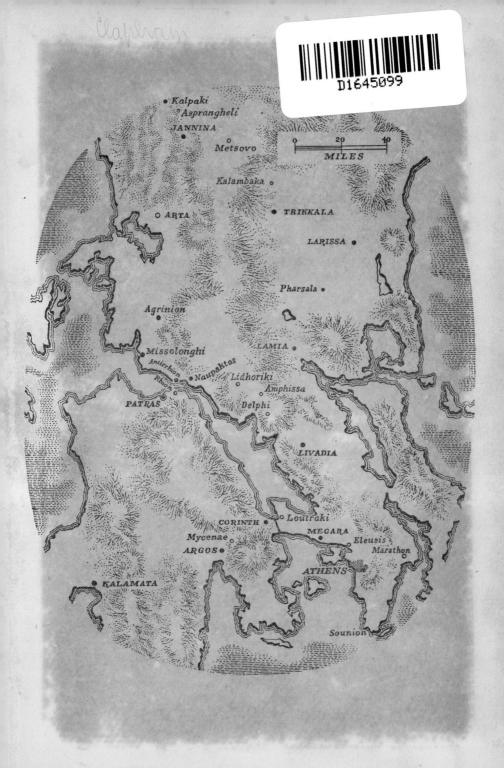

An Affair of the Heart

DILYS POWELL

An Affair of the Heart

◊✳◊✳◊✳◊✳◊

LONDON

HODDER & STOUGHTON

DESIGNED BY JOHN LEWIS, F.S.I.A.
AND PRINTED IN ENGLAND FOR HODDER AND STOUGHTON LIMITED
BY W. S. COWELL LIMITED AT THEIR PRESS IN
THE BUTTER MARKET, IPSWICH, SUFFOLK

For Leonard

Author's Note

My special gratitude is due to Viscount Kemsley, Editor-in-Chief of the *Sunday Times*, whose generosity made it possible for me to travel in Greece in 1953 and 1954.

I should like to thank also Mr Sinclair Hood, Director of the British School of Archaeology at Athens, and all the members of the Emporio party of 1954.

My spelling of place-names makes no pretence of consistency. With familiar places I have generally used the familiar English spelling; occasionally, with less-known ones, a transliteration more nearly approximating to the Greek original.

Some of the people in the pages which follow appeared in a book about Greece which was published during the war; to avoid confusion I have kept the disguised names which at that time I thought it best to employ. But though a few of the names may be false all the characters are real; and all the incidents are true.

Contents

First Sight

I

Nowadays when I look back on my acquaintance with the village I think of three episodes, or three days rather. A day in December 1945; in October 1953; in June 1954 – each time I went back life there had reached a fresh stage, and in the candid eyes of my friends I saw the changing directions of my own life. But the beginnings were years earlier, and if I am to give the flavour of the relationship I must first look farther back still, to the early part of the 1930s, when the English were digging out the treasure of the temple by the lighthouse.

It was at the end of 1929 that my husband Humfry Payne, then newly appointed Director of the British School of Archaeology at Athens, searching for an ancient site to explore, first came to the place. From Corinth, if you look across the Corinthian Gulf to its northern coast, you distinguish the little town of Loutraki. A mountain leans over it. To the left of Loutraki a peninsula, separating the Corinthian from the Halcyonic Gulf, drives westward in diminishing waves of rock until at last it rears a crested headland with, at the extremity a lighthouse. This desolate and beautiful triangle of Greece is known as Perachora, which means the country beyond. Inland, hidden by Loutraki's mountain, is a village called also Perachora.

The ancient Greeks too, looking across from Corinth, spoke of the district as the land beyond: beyond, that is, the sea. The headland, point of the triangle, was fortified in antique times, and a Heraion was set up, a sanctuary of Hera, wife of Zeus. History records a skirmish there between Spartans and Corinthians. And the place has been touched by legend as well as history. In the past, scholars have suggested (though today the theory is brushed aside) that here it was that Medea, when in Euripides's play after being deserted by her husband Jason she killed her children, brought their bodies for burial.

All this was known to the learned when Humfry Payne came walking down to the lighthouse looking for potsherds and ancient walls. Yet nobody had thought the Heraion worth excavating. Remote, difficult, waterless, the promontory held off explorers. But not this one.

I must explain the system under which archaeological excavation by foreigners is carried out in Greece. A number of countries – France, Italy, Germany, Britain, the United States of America – have established in Athens Schools or Institutes for archaeological study or research, most of them endowed with at any rate some government support. A School may have its own official expedition, or an individual archaeologist may dig under School auspices; in either case the Government of Greece must be asked for a permit. There was an unwritten rule before the war – and I daresay there is one still – that no foreign country should carry out excavations at more than three places in any one year. A site, its exploration once begun, became under Greek sanction the temporary preserve of the exploring nation, which had the right to publish the results of excavation.

Thus certain ancient cities came to be thought of as, say, German hunting-ground, or French. The Germans had excavated Olympia, and the names of German scholars were always to be associated with the great sanctuary. Delphi and the island of Delos, birthplace of Apollo, were French sites. The Americans had, one might say, dug themselves in at Corinth, and were making ready, at the time of which I speak, to bring their learning, their enthusiasm and their genius for engineering to the heart of Athens, where much of the ancient city still lay hidden under the old Turkish quarter at the foot of the Acropolis. In Crete, Sir Arthur Evans, a formidable scholar-explorer from the nineteenth century who still commanded awe in the twentieth, had not merely uncovered the palace of Knossos, lair of the Minotaur, but had reconstructed a good deal of it to a height of two storeys, leaving it in the earthquake-haunted island a British liability in more ways than one.

The English had been digging for some years at Sparta. But with the advent of a new Director the Committee of the British School decided to break fresh ground. Humfry was convinced, against the belief of earlier visitors, that there were important remains at the obscure Heraion of Perachora. He asked for a permit to dig, and in 1930 he began work.

The excavations lasted four seasons: 1930–33. Each year as spring uncurled the fists of winter the English arrived, a party of half-a-dozen or so, to pitch their tents on the headland; they stayed until mosquitoes, flies, heat and seasonal difficulties with labour drove them back to Athens. The workmen came from Perachora village, six miles away in the hills. On Saturday night they tramped home with their wages, to return at dawn on Monday. The rest of the week they camped beside the English tents, or found a lodging in the lighthouse; and for nine hours a day they hacked, dug, sifted and carted. And they found; every hour of the day they found. In many parts of Greece an archaeological expedition is a commonplace; not here, not in Perachora village. Everything was new; a golden world opened before these uncorrupted peasants, owners of a few pines, a stony field, a terrace of struggling vines. Years afterwards – a life-time afterwards, if one were to judge by what had passed between – I was, as I shall later describe, a visitor at an excavation in the island of Chios. The discoveries seemed satisfying enough to me, but the director felt that he should excuse them: You must not, he said wryly, expect the wealth of a site like Perachora, you know. And indeed I did know. I am not an archaeologist, but I have seen what it is like to search day after day and find nothing, I am aware that spectacular success is rare. The exploration of the Heraion was the chance of a lifetime.

I was not present for the 1930 season, and I did not see the first astonishing finds of bronze and ivory and pottery. But the next year and every year until the work finished I was there, an onlooker at the exhumation. Briefly, the Heraion proved to be the site of a small but well-to-do Greek town with temples and altars, market-place and colonnade, roads, watch-towers, an elaborate system of

15

water-storage. The foundations of a temple from the ninth century B.C., of another from the eighth, of yet another from the sixth; fine architectural remains from the classical fifth and fourth centuries and the later, the so-called Hellenistic period of Greece – the discovery of these alone would have been great reward. But it was the amassing, season after season, of beautiful and precious small objects, gifts offered to the goddess Hera in gratitude for favours or in entreaty for help, which brought distinction to the Perachora expedition. Little bronze statuettes of men and animals, birds and mythical creatures; ivory seals, ivory pins, little couchant animals of ivory; jewellery and scarabs; hundreds of bronze bowls, hundreds of terracotta figurines, fragments of exquisitely painted pottery to be counted not in hundreds but in hundreds of thousands – only the most famous sanctuaries had yielded so much miniature treasure. That it should now be found in an unregarded corner of Greece was a kind of miracle.

II

THE PEOPLE OF Perachora village had, as I say, never before seen an archaeological excavation; more important, they had never enjoyed the advantages of having a well-known ancient site in the neighbourhood. Foreigners in Greece take their custom, naturally enough, to the famous places: Mycenae, Olympia, Delphi, Epidauros, Sparta, Mistra; to travel off the roads, though to my mind it is a magical experience, needs knowledge of the country and occasionally some small hardihood. The Perachorans, shut away behind their mountain, saw none of the visitors who are drawn to Greece by her monuments. In the early 1930s the Perachora peninsula had no motor roads. Above Loutraki in the side of the mountain a long score showed where the road to the village had been begun and for the time being abandoned; the journey had to be finished on foot. To the lighthouse and the Heraion there was no road of any kind, only the mule-track down from the village or a faint and stony path, a three- or four-hour walk, along the shore from Loutraki. The lighthousemen, the captain and two adjutants, lived under the eye of solitude.

Now, year after year, the wilderness hummed with voices. There was employment in the village. Rich Athenians arrived in yachts to visit the excavations, anchored off the lighthouse rock and swarmed ashore with cries of admiration. Foreigners came, and to a Greek peasant all foreigners are rich. The Perachorans, like the people of other villages in the peninsula, are Albanian-Greeks, and to this day the older of them still speak Albanian among themselves. Race, language and geographical isolation had given them a habit of ironical aloofness. But they were not too aloof to feel proud of the Heraion dig, a success in which they all shared. A success, what is

17

more, with money in it. Archaeology, they realized, could feed mouths.

The women, when on occasion they came down from the village to visit their menfolk and see what was afoot, always asked me why we were digging up the Heraion. I would take out yesterday's finds; old Aspasia, better used to winnowing grain or trenching vines, would pick up a delicate little ivory ram and hold it awkwardly askew in leathery, uncomprehending hands.

'Is it valuable? Is it valuable?' she repeated.

'Yes,' I said haltingly, 'it is a rare thing.'

'What will you do with all these things, will you sell them? Will you sell them?'

'No,' I said, 'we cannot sell them, they are not ours.'

'Then why do you dig them up? Why?'

I turned over my handful of Greek and selected a word. 'For history,' I said; and the phrase ricocheted through the group of women: 'for history, she says . . . for history . . . for history . . .'

'But where will you put them? Where?'

'In Athens,' I said, 'they must be put in the museum in Athens; it is the law.' And so indeed it is. The antiquities of Greece, no matter by whom they are discovered, very justly remain Greek property and must not be taken out of the country. Greece has many local museums. The great sanctuaries have usually kept their treasure; Delphi and Olympia, though today they are no more than villages, still house their own august sculptures. Lesser sites, too, often possess a modest museum. Where no museum exists the finds must go to the nearest town which can shelter them. Even where there is a museum the precious small objects often have not been deposited in it, but can be found instead in the National Museum in Athens. And it was to the National Museum that the finds from Perachora were sent. At the end of each season a caïque, a sailing ship with auxiliary engine, anchored by the lighthouse rock; cases filled with bronzes, ivories, terracottas and vase-fragments were taken aboard; and the boat set off on a summer night's sail to Piraeus, the port of Athens. From Piraeus the cases were taken by lorry to Athens, to be unpacked in a workroom of the National Museum and the contents to be cleaned, sorted and mended; some day to be exhibited.

As far as the Perachorans were concerned the finds might as well have been in Greenland. Many of the villagers had never travelled as far as Athens; many of the women had scarcely moved beyond their village and their fields. 'To Athens I have not been,' some wrinkled mother of many sons would say. Then she would point towards the town which from the lighthouse we could see ten miles away across the Gulf: 'But' (as if the experience set the seal on a lifetime of globe-trotting) 'I have been to Corinth.' And yet the relation between the village and the world outside was changing. Now the life from beyond the mountain and the sea was beginning, it seemed, to seek out the life of the peninsula. It was not simply that the English came every summer and invited visits from other archaeologists. Sometimes an unheralded foreigner appeared in Perachora village and asked the way to the Heraion. Even when the English were not there hardy walkers now and then traced the path to the headland; the lighthousemen watched them rummaging amongst the antique walls, and felt the hot breath of the world's traffic.

The Perachorans were profoundly affected by the appearance of these transitory figures. Those of the villagers who knew only their own peninsula watched the visitors with a curiosity which had in it a shade of naïve hope. Those who had stirred about in Greece, seen perhaps some ancient sanctuary haunted in spring by flocks of tourists, began to scheme how to snare for themselves some of the migrants. True, even the most optimistic recognized that there were gaps in the local amenities. The motor-cars which, when a cruise arrived, brought the visitors from the nearest harbour to Delphi or Mycenae or Olympia, could not drive along the path to the light-house; they could not even get all the way up the unfinished road to the village. Could they have reached Perachora village the material rewards were small. Tumbledown walls and sagging roofs, a rill from the spring running down the middle of what passed for the main street, a single fly-infested café, no shop that I can recall, precipitous ankle-cracking paths – even for an unfrequented Greek village, even for a poor Greek village, and Perachora through no fault of its own was poor, the place was in those days totally lacking in the elegances. I would not myself, except in goodwill to its inhabitants, have wished a stone moved. But to the stranger from Western Europe, and still more to the touring American, Perachora must have seemed an unmitigated dump.

In the face of these handicaps the Perachorans counted their blessings. They had good, pure, cold water, and in Greece drinking-water is a positive pleasure, not something taken for granted. They had wine from their arid, stony hillsides, and from their pines they had resin with which to smear the insides of their wine-casks; for the Greek countryman likes his drink thus flavoured. They had a road, incomplete though it might be. Now suddenly they had the sanctuary of Hera and its treasures. Resilient amidst their poverty, the villagers began to dream of the future. Their very remoteness from the world, their ignorance of material comfort, gave their hopes extravagance. Perachora, they said, would be famous. Visitors would come, droves of them, English, French, Americans, Germans, Italians, Russians, from all over the world they would come to see the discoveries at the lighthouse. They would come by car, they would stay in the village, they would eat and drink, they would bring wealth to Perachora. In the imagination of my friends the cluster of ramshackle cottages was turned into a splendid modern town; along the boulevards roared an endless line of glittering motor-cars; while the cafés on the pavements were crowded with citizens who all wore new shoes and could afford to eat meat every day.

My friends, I say; in those days they were my friends at second-hand. With the women of Perachora I had fairly quickly established some kind of communication. I was struggling to write a book; morning and afternoon I sat under a tree at my typewriter. Taking no share in the archaeological work; blinking out of my tent for breakfast when everybody else had been at the trenches for two hours; not even doing the cooking – to their eyes I was a mysterious sluggard, an object of ceaseless curiosity; and with them I somehow stumbled into speaking Greek. With the men's world, however, the world of affairs in the village, I had few dealings. It was through Humfry that, at the time of the Heraion expedition, I knew the Perachorans. I watched, I listened; I felt myself as close to them as if I had no intermediary. But with Humfry there to interpret I was glad to be an observer and nothing more. Not until several years later when I came alone to the village was I driven back on my own conversational resources.

In any case I had a struggle at the start to make up for the time I had lost by missing the first season. The routine of field archaeology was foreign to me. I had to learn the faces and the names; I had to learn the place itself. The pattern of the relationship between the Perachorans and the English was already drawn. But when I arrived the attitude of the Perachorans towards the discoveries at the Heraion was still uncertain. The villagers had not yet given themselves over to optimism. After all they could not have been sure that the dig would continue. But now here were the English back with their tents and their packing-cases. The scope of the work was clearly growing. The season began earlier and was to go on later. More workmen were needed. The village earned more pay. The Perachorans began to boast of their triumph to the people of other villages. And while we watched the hope of prosperity took hold.

My first season at the Heraion, then, coincided with the birth of the dream. Perhaps that is why my feeling for Perachora is so deeply affected by the contrast between the fantasy and the reality. Even now I see the Perachorans forever, in their rickety village, constructing some visionary Empire State Building. And I linger with especial affection over the passages in their communal story in which this dogged and touching optimism can be seen in action. For instance, the plan to keep the Heraion finds for the village by building a museum.

III

WHEN I SEARCH in my memory for the forms of the past it is as if I were leaning over a sea-pool among rocks. The water is sunlit, and there are clear shapes beneath it. The outline of pebbles and rocks is sharp; I can see life moving. But there are dark grottoes too where the seaweed drapes its curtains; and as I fixedly look the edges blur and quaver, the weeds toss in a flow of water, and now I can distinguish with certainty nothing.

The beginning of the Perachora museum is hidden from me in one of the grottoes. I thought I could remember as if I had heard of it this morning. Indeed I often feel that the months when, sheathed in sun and wind and the endless susurration of the sea, I lived at the Heraion belong to my present, so close do they seem. And if I am content to accept what memory freely offers, everything is clear; I can see the faces of my companions round the camp-table, I can hear the voices of the workmen calling from the trenches by the harbour. But when I try to fill in the details I notice the caves where forgetfulness sits.

So it is with the museum. I have the image of a patch of baked fawn earth, its surface powdering, dry thistles hissing together at its edge; a group of men are measuring out a square with string and rough wooden pegs. Humfry and his friend Alan Blakeway, who for a short summer was to succeed him as Director of the School, are among the group; Humfry, his eyes bent gravely on the ground, is pacing the distances. But who are the others? I strain to see, but their faces are turned away from me. I fancy I can distinguish the foreman of the dig and the village doctor. But I cannot be sure; and now the group fades, the patch of earth grows indistinct, the whole picture is without shape or colour.

That Humfry and Alan were enthusiasts for the idea of the village museum – this at least is certain. I recall long debates on the subject: the site, the cost, the nature of the building; though again I do not remember all the figures who were spokesmen for the village. The site was chosen; so far my picture is accurate enough. The ground was bought, and bought with Perachoran money. The village lacked everything, but not imagination; and amidst their struggle to exist these necessitous, self-reliant peasants found the means to secure, as they hoped, a famous future.

It was the year 1931. The world looked stable enough. True that in England there were portents which did not pass unnoticed in remote Perachora – for the Greeks with their unrivalled political awareness do not need to be persuaded that they are part of one world.

' "My Virgin!" ' cried Niko the lighthouseman, describing his emotions on reading the newspapers: ' "My little Virgin," I said, "the pound has fallen!" '

But that England should have gone off the gold standard, or even that America should have suffered a financial catastrophe, did not in those days, or did not to the unthinking, mean earthquake weather. For a few more years we could go on living our lives. Not until the second half of the decade did we become conscious that we were living history.

The Perachorans, then, could cogitate their museum. They were on fire with enthusiasm. Already in their fancy a handsome edifice was rising; a keeper, all in gold braid, sat behind the ticket-desk, selling picture postcards by the dozen; already the first car, loaded with rich foreigners, was pulling up at the door. And since we felt ourselves their friends we shared their excitement. We longed for them to draw some perennial benefit from the excavations at the Heraion. We admitted the justice of their desire to house their own antiques. Against our reason we even began to believe in their vision of wealth. At any rate we believed in the museum.

All the same when we came back the next spring the thistles, green now, still rattled together round the square of earth by the village.

There seemed to our disappointed eyes no reason why, a first step having been taken, the Perachorans should not have taken a second and a third. Nor was there a reason, I think, except the unchanging, perhaps the unchangeable circumstances of their country.

When I first went to Greece it was common to see an unfinished road. Sometimes the bends were expertly banked up, and the intervening straight passages not yet attempted. Sometimes, with the road from Loutraki to the village for instance, the builders seemed to have lost heart before they reached their journey's end. Various reasons were offered. Those of us who were entering the first phase of a besotted, a lifelong passion for Greece were apt to advance the national temperament as cause: fecklessness, we said, lingering over the word with a lover's indulgence. If we asked a Greek countryman he usually insisted that the contractors' dishonesty was at the root: 'They ate the money.' I now incline to believe that the lovers were half-right: national temperament, but not fecklessness. The English have never been poor. As a people they do not know what it means to live from hand to mouth; two frightful wars, the second fought in their own skies, have not even now broken their faith in their right to prosperity. The English, when they build, begin with the conviction that they can finish without interruption. The Greeks, inured to invasion, occupation, earthquake and political upheaval, always struggling to lift themselves from some unmerited disaster, begin with enthusiasm and finish when they can. The Perachorans began their museum with enthusiasm. We ought to have known that though in a year's time there would still be optimism, there might be nothing else.

Affectionately disposed though we were, we could not hide a shade of English censoriousness. But I have to admit that I never heard the Perachorans' side of the story. For once nobody could be accused of eating the money. The simple truth, as I see now that I know my friends better, must have been that there was no money to eat; all there was had been spent on that naked plot of ground. But whether this was ever admitted I do not know. I remember only time passing and nothing done. For a while some kind of demarcation of the site, I fancy, was visible: vestigial foundations, or perhaps no more than a flimsy enclosure. Once, trudging up the path to the village, 'Is that the museum?' I asked, pointing ironically to a waste lot where a goat was tethered; and 'Yes, yes, the museum!' came the rueful reply. Soon we accepted defeat.

Not that the Perachorans had abandoned the dream of prosperity. Long after our camp on the headland was struck for the last time the old men were still talking of the purity of the water, the excellence of the wine and the general suitability of the village as a resort for tourists. Once or twice Humfry and I made an excursion to Perachora and to the lighthouse; and on the instant our friends were weaving their bright fantasies about the crowds of visitors who would appear some day – or the crowds of visitors who had already appeared.

'Of course people come,' cried Vasili of the lighthouse. 'Many people come. Last winter, December it was, three Americans walked down from the village to the Heraion, two boys and a girl. And in the spring a German came, a professor, an old man riding a mule from Loutraki. Of course people come!'

But nothing was changed. At the Heraion the same solitude, the same unfrequented paths; in the village the same poverty. By the middle of the thirties we were losing touch with the Perachorans. Soon we should be looking for another site. But in 1936 we were to spend one last season at the Heraion. A few weeks before work was due to begin Humfry fell ill; early in May he died in Athens. A year later I went alone to the village and the lighthouse. Then came a time when none of us could travel. The war had cut us all off from the land beyond the sea, from Perachora, from Greece itself. The world's weather had broken.

Estrangement

I

It WAS DIFFICULT in 1945 to believe that I could go to Greece again. There had been a time when I promised myself that I would go back every year. But that was before the landslide of history swept over personal memorials. I was in one of the Aegean islands when the first rattle of stones bouncing down from the heights was heard, when in fact in August 1939 news came of the Russo-German pact. Between my husband's death and the outbreak of war I had spent every summer holiday in Greece. I had kept in touch with the friends Humfry had made in Athens; every year I had visited the village graveyard at Mycenae where he was buried. But amidst the roar of approaching war the size and aspect of individual life altered. A personal loss, accidental in the midst of order, gives a feeling of isolation, as if heaven had chosen its victim with spite; that the world should go on with the day's business seems injurious. Time alone can itself put the egotism of grief to shame. But such a cataclysm as war can change even the quality and proportions of memory.

At the end of August 1939 the danger to Greece seemed to me to be minuscule, and I was irritated by the nervousness of my Athenian friends, who, more far-sighted, feared entanglement. The English, I felt as I waited for a berth on an airplane home, were the ones who had the right to be anxious. Athens is at the best of times acutely sensitive to the breath of international affairs; even its most popular papers have a range of foreign news unimaginable at the English breakfast table. Now, in the lunatic days before the explosion of war, there was reason to be sensitive. The Athenians sat by the hour over their radio sets. The newspapers shrieked. And the rumours flew. Mussolini had intervened; Roosevelt had intervened. England, a taxi-driver dolefully assured me one morning, had backed out, let Poland down; he had just learned it from a friend who had heard it over the wireless. Anybody who has been abroad at a time of crisis will understand my disorientation, my craving for today's English paper, however insular, to put things in their familiar English perspective. And every night I looked up at the rich, deep, glittering curtains of the Mediterranean night and wondered if at that very moment London was being bombed. The personal ties which I had thought bound me to Athens seemed to be fraying. My devotion to Greece persisted. But when someone at the British Embassy suggested that there might be work for me if I stayed, I was startled to find with what passion I desired to be in my own country.

But now in mid-November, 1945, with the war in Europe ended only six months earlier, I was on my way back to Athens. In 1943 I had married again; I was lucky, I was happy; my life had been reshaped. Yet after all I had not been quite separated from Greece in the years since 1939. In 1941, soon after the fall of Crete had clenched the German hold on the Balkans, I had begun working in London for a Government organization, the Political Warfare Executive. My concern was with Greece, and for the four remaining years of the war I had a private view of what was happening under German and Italian occupation.

At first the private view did not differ much from the public view. Everybody who could read a newspaper knew that Greece was starving, that people were dying of hunger, openly, in the streets of Athens. The major feats of resistance and sabotage were reported: the dynamiting, for instance, of railway bridges between Athens and Salonika. But as time went on the news grew too complex to be readily grasped without some personal knowledge of Greece. War is an abbreviator of titles. The parties, the guerilla groups, the underground organizations into which the Greeks formed themselves were known by their initials; and how was the English reader, himself not without preoccupations, to tell ELAS from EDES, or to master the connection of the first of them with EAM and the Communist Party, the KKE? Looking back now, it is easy to see what was happening in Greece between 1940 and 1944. It was not so easy then. War gives the opportunity for national self-esteem. The Greeks rejected Mussolini's ultimatum in October 1940; they drove back the invading Italians; they can be proud of it. But war gives also the opportunity for revolution. In war conspiracy collects itself, violence gathers its forces. The Germans invaded Greece in April 1941; in May they descended on Crete; by June all the mainland and all the islands were occupied. And in June Hitler invaded Russia. All over Europe, Communists knew now what they had to do. In Greece certainly the Party, the KKE, knew. I remember seeing, about the end of 1941, a bundle of Resistance pamphlets published by a group calling itself the National Liberation Front, or briefly by its Greek initials, EAM. The pamphlets were full of jargon: fascist lackeys, hyaenas, cannibals; and though the style of the propaganda was not as familiar then as it became later, there should have been little difficulty in recognizing EAM as a Communist-controlled organization. But nothing, in those days, had clear edges. There were plenty of voices insisting that EAM, though it might have Communists among its leaders, was made up largely of patriots with no political colour. And EAM, it seemed, operated in the towns only. Presently in country districts a body of guerillas, andartes as the Greeks called them, appeared with the title of the Greek Popular Liberation Army, or, familiarly, ELAS. Optimistically, many of us tried to persuade ourselves that it was not a Communist creation.

We did not succeed for long, if at all. And a time came when anybody could see that ELAS was simply the military wing of EAM. But those were days of general sympathy for Russia, and not sympathy merely for an Ally. The British were going through a phase in which the left, politically speaking, was always right. And the andartes of ELAS were protected by this sympathy, as they were sustained by the Allies' military need to vex, sting, unnerve and scatter the forces of Europe's Occupiers. They were armed by the British; they were financed by the British; sometimes, when they allowed it, they were organized by the British. As I look back I do not believe that the military need justified the risk taken in Greece, and I am sorry now that I should ever have thought it did. Not only was the resistance in country districts during the war extravagant in lives, in hostages shot, in villages wiped out in reprisals. There were other consequences as terrible. Briefly, the Communists were able to use the opportunity of war for their own political ends. Among the fighters of ELAS there certainly were patriots who risked everything for their country. There were also ambitious schemers who turned their arms not against the Germans but against their Greek rivals. The British had supported and equipped other bands of andartes. With the largest of these ELAS kept up a desultory civil war; a minor group they succeeded in wiping out altogether. When Greece was liberated in October, 1944, ELAS were the dominating force in the country. They were armed, they were ready for revolution. And two months after the first British troops came in, they struck.

My concern is with historical events only so far as they explain the situation I found when I returned to Greece, and thus affect the story I have to tell. Perhaps it does not seem necessary even to recall the insurrection. But memories are short, and at the time the English, many of them, were told a false story. Amiably infatuated with the word democracy, they had not listened to the rare voices which warned them that EAM used it in a different sense. They were still without experience of Communist tactics. In December, six months before the end of the war in Europe, they were offered a lesson.

There had been a long wrangle over the disarming of the andartes. Suddenly it came to a head, the EAM members of the Greek government resigned, and EAM called for a demonstration and a general strike. The Cabinet, what was left of it, forbade the demonstration. EAM were defiant. All night the church-bells rang; the faithful of the left collected; in the morning crowds began to move towards the centre of the city. It was a Sunday, in Athens traditionally the morning for public ceremonies, for parades in the square called Constitution. The propaganda had been efficient, and there were women and children among the demonstrators.

Exactly how the shooting began I cannot tell. Some stories declare that the demonstrators struck first, but this, since I was not there to see, I must not maintain. A journalist whom I trust says that they advanced taunting and threatening. What is certain is that the police, understandably on edge, fired on the crowd and that there were deaths, some at any rate innocent: some deaths even of children.

The British took no part in this day. But they could not ignore it. They had been invited into Greece. The war in Europe was still being fought. And not six weeks earlier an agreement had been signed by which the guerillas of all parties had undertaken to place themselves under the orders of the British Commander in Greece, General Scobie. The day after the shooting in Constitution Square, then, Scobie ordered ELAS to withdraw from Athens and its port, Piraeus. Immediately EAM and ELAS moved to seize the city.

The Greek Government could call on only a tiny body of their own troops, veterans of the Allied campaign in Italy. The British forces numbered no more than five thousand. Everywhere outside the capital the rebels were in control. In this crisis Churchill, intervening, gave his personal authority for the order: Athens must be defended.

The British had scarcely counted on a battle. On the contrary, they had been encouraged to expect friendliness. When the liberation of Europe began, troops moving into a foreign country were given a pocket guide to manners and customs. Those who landed in Greece arrived with a booklet which began (I know; I wrote it): 'You are lucky to be going to Greece.' Yet here they were, fighting for their lives within a perimeter which at the start shrank to enclose only the centre of the city.

To realize how narrow the escape was the English must imagine themselves in the Athenian situation of December 1944. In a London just freed from enemy occupation, then, an internal revolt breaks out, obliging us to accept – no doubt to our exasperation – the help of our liberators the Americans, who hold Piccadilly and Mayfair, Trafalgar Square and Whitehall; military headquarters have been set up in the old Carlton Hotel. Everywhere else the tide is against us.

St. James's Park and Buckingham Palace are still ours, but not the South Bank. We are cut off from the East End and the docks, which are in rebel hands. Watney's Brewery at Victoria is an insurgent strong-point. Where Oxford Street meets Tottenham Court Road, no-man's land begins, and there is fighting round the British Museum. Small detachments of the Guards still hold outposts in Whitechapel, in Croydon and in Roehampton, and the Americans are fortunate enough to occupy the heights at Hampstead. But reinforcements are slow in arriving; Pentonville, where police, Guardsmen and Americans have been fighting to save political prisoners from lynching, is in flames, and at Highgate the American Air Headquarters is overrun.

'You are lucky,' the British soldiers, fighting to save Athens, said to one another, 'to be going to Greece.'

The Greek Government had evidence that a *coup d'état* had been planned. But it was a long time before people in England believed it. At the time all they understood was that the British Army and the Greek andartes, allies of yesterday, today were fighting one another. And in the political temper of 1944 the tendency was to think that the andartes must be in the right. With a few exceptions, newspaper correspondents gave the impression that the British were shoring up a reactionary government against the will of the people. To be fighting on the wrong side, and into the bargain to be fighting what seemed at first like a losing battle – it was too much. It must be somebody's fault: probably Churchill's.

Churchill went twice to Greece, the first time when the danger was the greatest, on Christmas Day 1944. He went to see for himself; to bring both sides to a parley; to judge the chances of pacifying anti-Royalist feeling through a Regency. A parley was held; plans for a Regency were laid; the visit began a change in the fortunes of Greece. Two months later he paid a second visit to Greece, this time in triumph, when ELAS had withdrawn from Athens and the surrounding province of Attica and peace with them had been signed. Greek friends have told me that he saved their country. Yet I know educated Englishmen who still do not understand that the battle of Athens in 1944 was the first shot in the Communist battle for Europe.

For the time being, then, the Athenians had won. But in their minds they were still fighting. I was quite unprepared, when I went back, for their mood.

II

It was not the first time I had seen the capital disturbed. In the first part of the thirties, when for several months each year I had lived at the British School of Archaeology in Athens, there had been political uproar enough: in 1933, when a party of assassins with tommy-guns set on Venizelos and his wife as they drove home one evening; in 1935, when there was a Venizelist insurrection, with mutiny in the Navy and the Army and fighting in the streets; in 1936, when Metaxas, who four years later was to reject the Italian ultimatum, made himself Dictator. Now in 1945 I knew what the capital had undergone since I last saw it. But I could not rid myself of my romantic ideas. I still thought of Athens as a place of sun, friendly, elegant, cosmopolitan; a place of chattering cafés, smart parties and sophisticated argument; a place to sit on a summer evening amidst the murmur of crowds and the glimmer of bright dresses. Intellectually I recognized that Greece was living with savaged nerves. Yet I could not bring myself to look on it except as the easy, welcoming country I had known before the war. When I thought of Greece I thought of swimming off hot, voiceless, deserted bays, rousing at dawn to walk all day through mountains, coming at night to a village with the scent of charcoal braziers. I thought, to be honest, of Perachora.

Now everything was changed. I came back to a country full of rage. After the long, cold, hungry war, after the relief of liberation, the Greeks had found themselves in the trap of another battle. And it was not their fault; they were sure of this. As a matter of fact, said some of my old friends, it was the fault of the British. The British had armed the guerillas; the British had paid them, and in gold sovereigns; night after night the B.B.C. had praised their exploits

– and all the arms, all the money, all the glory had been lavished on EAM and ELAS, with not a gun or a coin or a word for anybody else. At this I faintly protested, for I was well aware how desperately British policy had struggled to encourage andartes of other parties, and at what risk and cost British Liaison Officers in the field had fought to dissuade ELAS from destroying their rivals. But it was useless to protest: night after night during the Occupation, my friends repeated, they had listened at their peril to the B.B.C., only to hear EAM and ELAS, praise of EAM and ELAS, hurrah for EAM and ELAS! And I shrank from arguing about Greek affairs with Greeks, and Greeks who had such good reason to be bitter. To reflect on their experiences during the years since our last meeting was enough to silence me. And their anxiety to dissociate themselves and their country from the ferocities of ELAS was heartbreaking. I have said that there were brave and honourable men among the fighters of ELAS; and so there were: simple men deceived, patriots who would presently discover that patriotism was not the policy of their leaders. But even those in England who at the time took ELAS for a liberal army could not overlook the atrocities it committed: murders, mutilations, the carrying away of the innocent as hostages. The Athenians a year afterwards were still urgently disowning the cruelties. Never before, they said, had Greeks done such things; impossible that they should be doing them now; the criminals were not Greeks, they were Germans left behind after the retreat, they were Bulgarians. Again I forbore to argue, for this grieving and angry shame was to be respected.

And yet I found it increasingly difficult to keep silent. The Greeks I knew were mystified by the political obtuseness, as they saw it, of the English. Liberals themselves, they could not understand a liberalism so easily misled by phrases about freedom and democracy. But some went further than complaining about the Englishman's vague ignorant sympathy with EAM and ELAS. In their mourning and their anxiety they wanted action. They wanted the British to destroy ELAS; especially they wanted the British to stop conciliating the Russians.

'Yes, monsieur! Of course, monsieur!' they cried, mimicking a fancied Foreign Office; 'But certainly! With pleasure!' (lifting an imaginary homburg and bowing respectfully). 'Thank you very much!'

These were not the former right wing of Greek politics. They were the old anti-Royalists, the old, dogged Venizelists from whom before the war I had taken my political prejudices. Now they looked at me accusingly, with angry bewilderment, even, as it seemed to me, with hostility, and 'Why?' they shouted.

Right or wrong, they were not practical; not at that moment, not as the British then thought and felt. In any case I could not publicly agree with them. I was still employed by a Government Department; I had been given leave to come to Athens to lecture for the British Council. In England I could say what I liked. But in Greece it was not form to acquiesce in criticizing my own Government, nor indeed to join in opposing its policy, which in 1945 was bent, laudably though I fear inanely, on uniting the Greeks. I confess that I had unworthier reasons. I was beginning to feel childishly aggrieved when my friends argued against me as if I were an ally of the Communism which had so nearly destroyed them. Often enough in England, struggling to do work for which a deep disinterest in politics fitted me poorly, I had been accused of partisanship; but then the accusation had been that I was a Royalist, a Tory, one of the Red-bogey brigade. Years later I met an English diplomat whose toga I must once or twice have twitched in the war.

'I could never make out,' he said, 'which side you were on.'

'I was,' I answered, borrowing I fancy someone else's phrase, 'on the side of the Greeks.'

And so I was. But to the educated, sophisticated Greek, politics is a sixth sense, and the senses do not recognize neutrality. Now the people I knew, the liberals whose opinions I had remembered when, separated from Greece, I had struggled to judge EAM and ELAS fairly, were treating me as a Communist dupe. There were times when I found myself shouting as angrily as they.

Not all, of course, were liberals. Sometimes I encountered the fanatics of the right wing, dangerous because the violence with which they spoke obscured what was just in their cause; listening to them, the moderate, lethargic English began to sympathize all over again with ELAS. The right wing had its hooligans too. One heard of villages where massacre by one side had been avenged with massacre by the other; murder echoed back and forth. What astonished me at first was to find how nearly forgotten, in this fury, was the war itself. The last of the Prime Ministers under the Occupation had organized a rural force, anti-Communist, German-armed, to protect, he said, the villages against raiding guerillas. From London the Greeks had been warned by the B.B.C. and by their own Government in exile against joining, and when after the war collaborationists were on trial, responsibility for the Security Battalions, so-called, was a major charge. I wanted to know what patriotic Greeks thought about the Battalions. But my questions were brushed aside; nobody seemed interested; I had the impression that nobody really cared any longer when I asked whether so-and-so had not been pro-German during the Occupation. For the Athenians – and I do not mean only the middle class, the elegant, the rich – everything, invasion, hunger, the odious presence of the enemy, had dwindled beside the huge fact of the December battle: the siege of Athens, one might call it.

When I walked about, or went into houses I had once familiarly known, I saw and felt the shrinkages of war. Difficulties with electricity; water turned on for a day or two a week, and baths frugally used as storage tanks; people thinly dressed in the chill weather; food a monstrous price – all these were the material results of the Occupation. There were other reminders. The building in the well-to-do street – near the pastry-cook's where ten years earlier I used to shop – had been Gestapo headquarters. But the smashed houses and the rubble at street-corners near the Museum were nothing to do with the war against Germany and Italy. They were the débris of the December battle. As I tried to reconcile the bleak view with the remembered magic of Athens, perhaps even tried in a sentimentalist's self-deception to feel a magic no longer there, I became half-conscious of a threat. There was nothing to which one could point. Occasionally a sullen face, perhaps; sometimes a blank instead of the old eagerness of manner; but when one looked again, nothing. Yet when one neither looked nor listened, it was there. It was, if I must try to describe it, like a faint drum-beat in the air.

My friends could hear it; they could hear little else. I was staying in the house of Shan and Roxane Sedgwick. Shan, correspondent of the *New York Times*, alone among the American journalists in Athens had understood the truth about ELAS and the December battle. But it was not recognized yet as the truth, not even by the *New York Times*. Shan argued in vain. And the inextinguishable generosity of my hosts could not keep out a chill of anxiety.

'What has happened,' I asked, 'to your maids?' I remembered the loyalty with which before the war the Sedgwicks had been served by an island family. 'Ah,' I was told, 'they are for EAM; the brothers, all the family are for EAM.'

A nervous vibration ran through the household. And every evening at the masticha-hour, the cocktail-hour, the drawing-room was filled, in the informal, hospitable fashion of cosmopolitan Athens, with visitors arguing in Greek, French and English: about the Communists, the KKE – the koukouedhes, as in the Greek pronunciation of their initials they were colloquially called; about the latest Government changes; about the errors of British policy – for the Americans had not yet made themselves felt in Greece. I was humiliated by the slow-wittedness which the soft-talking English feel in the presence of the ironic Greeks, by inability to speak any foreign language at the pace even of my halting thoughts, and by my own political innocence.

Only when I turned to Greeks quite withdrawn from politics did I find it possible to ignore the differences in experience. In the thirties I had come to know a girl whom I will call Frosso. I could talk with her about the war; I too had seen war, though of a different sort. The bleak rations of the English, I learned, would have made feast-days for an Athenian family, even a well-to-do one, under the Occupation.

'What did you live on?' I asked. 'What did you eat?'

'Oh,' said Frosso, 'beans sometimes, dried peas, things like that.'

There had been a day, she went on, when the household promised itself a square meal; by good fortune and at great cost a piece of donkey-flesh had been bought. But even in their hunger they could not eat it. The family, the servants, everybody shrank, sickened; the meat was left on the plates.

Frosso spoke of the griefs as well as the miseries. On the day when the Germans hoisted the swastika over the Acropolis, she said, her father sat at table weeping; I could understand that. But what she told me of the dissensions between Greeks was foreign. She had been a nurse in the war, and after it in the December battle when the casualties of both parties had been brought to hospital. The ELAS wounded, many of them, were fine country Greeks, she said, simple, grateful, stoic, friendly. But every so often the 'enlighteners', the Communist propagandists, went round the wards. After each visit the friendliness had vanished; the men were silent, sullen, resentful. It was a fortnight before they were themselves again.

Yet in this thundery climate her own actions remained always collected and serene. After the siege, when ELAS had withdrawn from Athens and Attica, the victors had turned on the raggle-taggle of the defeated. Some of the fugitives were as guilty of atrocities as any obscure Nazi war criminal. But there were innocents too among the pursued, and one of these, a boy at fault, she said, only in being a member of EAM, came to my friend. Her upbringing, her class, her situation might have made her an enemy. But she took him in; with the indifference to authority of a Greek who disagrees with it she sheltered him. She hid him in the kitchen quarters of her own family; she fed him; and with the amiable and touching connivance of the servants she managed to conceal his presence until with the cooling of political tempers it was safe for him to go home.

III

Frosso's story reminded me of the old Greece, wilful, generous, resourceful, and brought a desire to escape from Athens and the complicated smell of hatred into the society of the villages. I longed to see Perachora. But it was almost impossible, at the end of 1945, to move about Greece. Outside Attica the greater part of the country was still controlled by ELAS. In any case the Germans when they withdrew had dynamited as they went; roads and railways, embankments and bridges, everything down to the smallest culvert was wrecked. The country, I heard, was full of unexploded mines. An ordinary car could not move on the ruined roads. Certainly there were no buses. I had left England with a foolish notion that somehow or other Greece would be hospitable to her lovers. Somehow or other I should be able to get about, I should be able to go to Perachora. Soon after I arrived I was given a demonstration of the difficulties.

I had been brought to Greece to lecture not only in Athens but also in Salonika, at normal times a day's train journey from the capital. But there were no trains. The road from Athens north through the centre of Greece is the main route to the Balkans, but to take it was out of the question; stories were told of travellers who had spent a week struggling with mud, potholes and détours. People on official business went to Salonika by air. My business was counted official. I made ready to travel by air.

In Athens the weather was sepia-coloured, and storms slanted in from Phaleron Bay on the morning I was driven down the long gritty road, past the dumps of wrecked lorries and the barbed wire enclosure marked Mines, to the airfield. I spent the morning watching the rain. No airplane came in that morning from Salonika, and none left. I went back to Athens.

'We expected you,' said the Sedgwicks.

Next morning the vaporous skies had cleared: luckily, for I was to lecture in the afternoon. We flew; I did what I had to do – lectured, talked, dined, retired to the officers' hotel to which my errand entitled me, drew some blankets from store and went to bed. Before dawn, army blankets returned to store, I was ready to leave.

The airfield at Sedes was warm in the sun. But no airplane came in, and none left. We waited till dusk. Then we drove back to the hotel in Salonika and I collected some blankets.

Next morning I returned my blankets once more. The sun at Sedes was hot that day; I could feel its faint sting on my arms. It would have been pleasant, sitting there in the clear landscape, had one not been anxious – and hungry; for military airfields made no allowances for civilian frailty. We talked, those who were waiting; we watched the sky; we looked at our watches. Abruptly I stopped grumbling when an officer in the party said, mildly, that his trip to Athens was of some urgency – he was getting married there next day. Early in the afternoon a buzz in the distance grew to a bellow. An airplane circled, banked, landed on the other side of the field. We waited for it to taxi across to the rudimentary buildings. It did not move. Nobody got out. Is it the airplane from Athens? we asked; but there was nobody to answer. An hour passed; the sun swung on its hinge; a rumour ran that the plane was a military plane and would as an act of charity take a passenger. One berth, one obvious candidate. About three o'clock the engines broke the stillness with a snort. Silently we watched the machine dart irritably forward and take off, almost vertically as it seemed. The bridegroom would have a jaunty trip, but at least he was on his way. An hour or two later we turned back again to Salonika, the hotel and the game with the blankets.

The chances of reaching Perachora before I went back to England grew more wretched every day. My companions were as impatient as I was. That evening, I remember, in our frustration we began to consider other and disapproved ways of getting to Athens. Should we risk the journey by road, and perhaps spend days fretting in some half-way shack? Should we buy ourselves aboard a trading-boat and toss round by sea? We grumbled, we vacillated, we chafed.

Yet in the end I was glad to have been halted. The few days in Salonika filled in a corner in my picture of the bewildered, shattered country. From the window of my bedroom in the hotel I could look out on the harbour. Trading-caïques, ships both masted and engined, smelling of oil and brine and tar, crowded by the quay; baskets of tangerines, mounds of golden tangerines from the islands, glowed on the decks. But elsewhere the funnels of sunken cargo-ships jutted from the water. Every activity wore the air of improvisation and impermanence.

In a kind of desperate willingness I had agreed, one of the evenings of my incarceration, to broadcast in Greek from the Salonika station. I would write in English. The script must be translated for me into, I insisted, the simplest, the easiest, the most colloquial Greek. Anything else was beyond my powers of speaking. And I must be given time to master it.

Twenty minutes before the hour I was handed two foolscap pages of high eloquence. It struck me afterwards that this may have been a political move, for in Greece even the forms of language are political, the right wing favouring an archaistic, literary tongue, the left wing defiantly writing in the colloquial Greek which everybody speaks. Perhaps the translator was using me to express his opposition to EAM. At any rate I had on my hands a speech which I could scarcely read, let alone deliver. I went to the broadcasting station in a condition of desperate composure; nothing, I knew, could save me. But instead of the glacial officials I had feared I found a Greek engineer and a boy both of whom clearly regarded the whole business of radio as a fascinating experiment. A kitten sat on the table by the microphone, purring enthusiastically. I stuttered through the script. At last I stopped. There was a silence, and the engineer looked at me enquiringly.

'Is that the end?' he asked in tones which must have been audible throughout Macedonia and Thrace.

As I stumbled away from the building a figure sprang at me in the darkness, and for a moment I wondered if my borrowed words had concealed some political indiscretion. But it was only an agricultural expert who wanted me to read his paper on the reafforestation of Macedonia.

It was easy to cause political mischief in the Salonika of 1945. Every phrase uttered was quoted on behalf of one or other of the parties, and after a lecture in which, remembering the loyalty I owed when abroad, I had spoken with respect of the policy of the Labour Government then in power in Britain, I was startled to find myself hailed as a supporter by the Communist newspapers. Once again I was out of my depth in a savage political current. Not that I was treated with anything but kind warmth; and since it was the first time I had been in Salonika there were no old friends to blame me for their troubles. But the bleakness I had felt in Athens was stronger here. The Macedonians are said to be a more dour race than the southerly Greeks. But something other than geography was affecting the people I watched in Salonika. In the streets, on the quay-side, the eyes were hostile. In Greece faces light up readily. Men and women have an unquenchable interest in their fellows; they smile back. Nobody in Salonika smiled back. The men unloading the golden tangerines from the caïques, walking gracefully on bare feet up the gangplanks, stared with dead eyes. For the first time in Greece I felt I was taken for an enemy. The drum-beat in the air grew louder.

At last the floods on the Athens airfield which had prevented our journey abated; transport airplanes could take off once more. In brilliant light we hummed southward past the crocus-coloured snows of Mount Olympos. It was none too soon for my time-table. To reach the lighthouse, I realized now, would be impossible, and I was beginning to doubt if I should reach Perachora village. But I still hoped to make the journey to Humfry's grave at Mycenae. Even without this duty I should have felt the desire to go into the country. The preoccupations of a Greek village restore the perspective of life, and I wanted to collect myself. Most of all I wanted to find the people I had known – if they were alive. Often in the war I had looked at the secret reports from Greece and wondered if I should see the name of a remembered village. I was sure enough that I should find the names of Englishmen I knew. Among the former students of the British School of Archaeology in Athens, Greek-speaking, acquainted with the terrain, accustomed to rough travel and frugal living, there were liaison officers almost ready-made; and as I sat safe, warm and to tell the truth bored in my office I was shamed by reading the account of some young scholar and Philhellene who had parachuted into occupied Greece and was now living a danger-haunted life with the guerillas. Soon the familiar place-names were recurring. Bands of andartes on the slopes of Mount Parnassos; fighting at Arachova on the road to Delphi; German reprisals at Lidhoriki in the hills north of the Gulf of Corinth, a village on the road from Amphissa to Naupaktos which Humfry and I had planned to visit – and never saw; Kalavryta, beginning and end of many of our walks across Arcadia, now burned to the ground and the inhabitants massacred – reading, the heart turned over. But though I searched day after day the name of Perachora was never there. The war ended, the young heroes came home, some of them, but they were not of the group which had camped with us by the lighthouse, they could tell me nothing of Perachora.

With Mycenae I had better luck. Mycenae lies just off the main road and the railway line going south from Corinth. It is in a strategic neighbourhood; there was news of Mycenae. I had asked, when I could, about the inn, the Fair Helen. The peasant couple who set themselves up there years ago had christened their children with a flourish; beginning quietly with Constantine for the eldest, they came presently, taking names from the fabled heroes of the region, to Agamemnon and Orestes. Yes, I was told, the inn had survived, the three brothers were still there.

I had been satisfied with these naked facts in England. In Greece I wanted more. And as I say I still hoped, even while we were chafing in Salonika, somehow to make my way to Mycenae. But without transport and with no more than a few pounds in Greek money the hope was lunatic. I could hardly believe my good luck when it came.

Suddenly everything was easy. The Department for which I worked had by now its heart in Athens. I was a visitor among colleagues who were also friends, and the senior among them – I still feel grateful – without fuss stirred himself to help me. I had thirty-six hours with no lectures, no engagements; I was lent a jeep with a Greek driver.

'Where shall we go?' said my driver.

The road I had so often thought of runs westward through Eleusis and Megara and along the northern shore of the Saronic Gulf to the narrow Isthmus which joins northern and southern Greece. To go to Perachora you turn right when you have covered about three of the four miles across the Isthmus and, after passing through the little spa of Loutraki on the northern shore of the Gulf of Corinth, take the way scored above it in the mountain-side. The road to the village had been finished before the war, but whether it was open I did not know. The other way crosses the bridge over the Canal through the Isthmus, then goes south to Corinth and climbs through hills into the Argolid, the province of Argos and Mycenae. This road I knew was open, and it was said by the standards of Greece in 1945 to be passable. The whole journey should normally take about three hours.

'Where shall we go?' my driver repeated.

'Let us go to Mycenae,' I answered.

We set off in the afternoon, a Saturday afternoon late in November; I know, because in my diary there is a pencil scratch: Dep. 3.30 p.m. It was a fretful afternoon, and later, in darkness, it rained. My driver was a smooth-faced, fresh-coloured young man who began the trip in a silence learned, no doubt, in employment with the British; that I remember, for I had time, sitting hour after hour beside him in the jeep, to persuade him to talk. And I knew that I wanted to incise everything on my memory. I was going back after a long tunnel of time to revisit a scene which had formed much of my life. I was going in search of people who might no longer be living, or who if alive were so by virtue of lasting out the indignities of war and murder. And I was travelling across a landscape every mile of which had romantic associations for me. I expected to be powerfully affected: to feel again, and more piercingly, the excitement as the road comes in sight of Salamis and the bay of Eleusis, or darts round the bends beneath the cliffs where in the legend Skiron waylaid the traveller. I tried to feel; I almost deceived myself. But the emotion which belongs to time and place is capricious. Some sunny idle afternoon will unaccountably take on the quality of ritual; for no reason the world stands still in holy silence. And some trivial moment will be remembered. I can recall now, after more than twenty years, pausing for breath on a road in Arcadia on the way to Nemea. But of this November drive, which I had imagined as so momentous, to Mycenae I remember nothing. It must have been dark when we reached the Isthmus, and I have a smudgy recollection of crossing the Canal by an improvised bridge at water-level, the high bridge over the deep cutting having of course been wrecked. But I cannot be sure. I am sure only that it was wet and cold when we started on the second part of our journey and that as we bounced southwards from Corinth the rain, driving in to the exposed front seat of the jeep and splashing up from the broken roads, chilled me from feet to thighs. Everything else is empty until the moment when, in the hissing night, we banged at the door of the Fair Helen Inn at Mycenae and Agamemnon opened to us.

'Good evening,' he said. 'So you have come.'

Perhaps I ought to have guessed that the report of an Englishwoman's arrival in Athens to lecture, strenuously spread by the propagandists, would reach those outside Athens who knew her. But to suppose that I should be recognized under my professional name, and at Mycenae, seemed extravagant.

Ancient Mycenae has some of the most silencing monuments in Greece – the gigantic walls guarding the lost palace on the acropolis, the citadel-hill; the huge beehive-shaped tombs on which legend has set the names of King Agamemnon, of Clytemnestra his wife and her lover Aegisthus who together killed him when he came home from Troy and who were in turn killed by his son Orestes. A few miles away across the plain you can see Argos, famous among the cities which sent ships and men to fight for Helen at Troy: the plain, the mountains which shoulder round the plain, all belongs to the ghosts of heroes. But the Mycenae of today is on another scale. The living world makes only a shallow mark on the haunted soil. You get down from the train at a wayside station and walk nearly half-an-hour up the road to the village which has taken the ancient name of Mycenae. All is humble, obscure: whitewashed village houses, bare-foot children, goats tethered by the road, everything conspires to enlarge the grandeurs of the past. It is hard to believe that a news-paper ever reaches the place.

But in a country with the political temper of Greece every man reads the newspapers. I ought, as I say, to have guessed that the brothers at the inn would learn that I was in Greece. What I could not guess was that they would expect me to visit Mycenae. No trains, no buses, roads passable only by military transport or jeep and with tedious détours – they were acquainted well enough with the obstacles. And yet with absolute certainty they waited for me to turn up. Cold as I was, wet, tired, stiff, hungry, I had a feeling of triumph as I stood in the doorway of the Fair Helen. I looked for surprise, even felicitation.

'So you have come,' said Agamemnon, standing there with a lamp, and kissed my hand. I might never have been away.

At first I thought nothing was changed. The same big, bare room which, running the width of the house, used to serve in winter as dining-room and reception hall; the same naked wooden stairs; the same boards underfoot in the upstairs passage between the scrubbed bedrooms; the same rough mattresses waiting, rolled on the iron bedsteads, for the next visitor, the same enamel wash-basins, the same towels damp from laundering. It was half-past eight when I arrived. Not a light showing from the houses anywhere, for November is no time, nor indeed was 1945 the year, to be sitting up of nights in a Greek village. But it was not only from the outside that the lights were muffled. The inn was dark. A single lamp went from room to room. There was silence in the shadowed corners, and the shutters, instead of enclosing light and warmth, seemed to be holding off an enemy outside. And as I sat at supper the talk told me, though perhaps without using precise words, that someone was still there, in the darkness, in the hills.

At the Fair Helen the family serves the visitor, takes him to his room, waits on him as he eats; then, if he is a friend, the men will sit down with him and talk while the women, sometimes the children too, cluster in the background. That night there was no crowding family in the circle of lamplight. Food was brought, and Agamemnon sat with me; yes, he said, the household were alive and well. We spoke of common acquaintances. He had seen a friend from Oxford who was later to become professor of ancient history, but who in the war, having parachuted into Greece and lived for two years with the guerillas, had been concerned with making present history. The family had tried to look after Humfry's grave; the oleander bushes, Agamemnon said, were growing round it: I should see in the morning. Once or twice, he added, Germans had gone to visit the grave, Germans who knew the name of Humfry Payne. I thought of days before the war when that name indeed had been known to German archaeologists. In 1945 the old honourable relations between scholars seemed to belong to another world, another life. And now I could hear Agamemnon talking of difficulties and dangers survived. The inn lacked everything, he said, blankets, fuel, everything; and again I had the feeling of a danger still waiting. Yet they had not doubted that I should come to the inn. Much had changed, but not the welcome.

'Which is my bedroom?' I asked. I had not spent a night at Mycenae since Humfry's death in 1936.

'The same one,' said Agamemnon, as if astonished that I should ask, 'the one you have always had.'

Next morning when I walked up the hill the rain was gone, and sun painted the drops of water hanging on grass and trees and the humble ornaments of village graves. I had always seen the plain of Argos in fair weather. Mycenae was the first place to make me feel the august presence of the past in Greece: the ruined palace walls, still powerfully alive, the mountains unchanged by time. I was glad to see it again in the same light. But for once I did not stay to look at the monuments. The road which passes the village and the inn climbs between mountains; on the right there is a valley, on the left a shoulder in which the beehive tomb sometimes called the Treasury of Atreus, sometimes the Tomb of Agamemnon, is hewn; at the road's end you pass through the Lion Gate, beneath the heraldic lions carved in stone, to enter the citadel; and then you stand on a rock-plateau; a mountain stoops over you, ravines plunge beneath you; far away down, the pacific plain. But after the little walled graveyard I turned back. I had no time for the twenty-minute walk to the acropolis and the palace. The day was before me. There was the jeep, there was the driver; we could at least try to reach Perachora village.

I was to have company. Of the three brothers of the inn, the eldest, Kosta, was still absent that morning. But the house was coming to life: women bustling about, children crying to one another in fife-voices – 'Hector, where is Hector?' 'Come here, Ajax!' And the third brother, Orestes, had reappeared. Orestes had business in Athens: could I take him with me? Of course, I said; but we must try first to reach Perachora. Was the road open? He believed it was. My driver came out shaking himself; the family gathered to wave; Orestes hunched himself in the back of the jeep. Once more we bounced on our way down the road between the pepper-trees to the station, then northwards along the plain to the pass between the mountains, to Corinth and the Gulf.

It was a more talkative trip than yesterday's, for the driver after his proper initial hesitations had decided that the Englishwoman could be treated with something less than military etiquette. Orestes, with long experience of innkeeping, of visiting foreigners and the niceties of respect, belonged to the sophisticated rustic Greeks. For Orestes I was the formal 'you', I was the lady, the *kyria*, though it must be admitted that, in a country where Humfry's name was so familiar, he found it difficult to remember my new married name. At Mycenae, as at Perachora, for years to come I was to be greeted as the kyria Payne.

The driver was not so smooth.

'What is your name?' I told him. 'Is that your little name?' – for the unlettered call one another by their Christian names, and a foreigner can know a working Greek for a long time without learning his surname. The Greek letter *d* is pronounced like *th* in *the*; the English sound is rendered by *nt*. 'Nteelees,' he repeated after me; 'Nteelees: that is good, now we are like brother and sister.' And he addressed me with the familiar 'thou'.

On the drive down I had observed nothing of the state of the villages. On the way back I was more attentive. The landscape of Mycenae, for all its violence, is severe. Under its cyclops-gaze, life settles into proportion, and I was cured of expecting romantic reactions to the occasion. The road climbing northwards out of the plain of Argos passes through a gorge where in the War of Independence the Greeks won a victory. Near by there is a hamlet; we stopped for a glass of wine. A man came to talk. He had been a prisoner of war, he said. He had not come back empty-handed, for on his left arm he wore three wrist-watches – at that time the equivalent of money in the bank. But his clothes were scarecrow: patches, shreds, tears; and as I looked about I saw that he was the well-dressed one. The other figures which stood by the road or stared from the doors of hovels wore rags and sacking cobbled together; flesh, in the wintry weather, showed through the rents. To Orestes and the driver the company of misery was a commonplace. But though I was used, from long days spent with Humfry exploring remote valleys, to the poverty of Greek villages, I had not encountered destitution. In the poverty I knew there had been a kind of heroism. This time I wondered if I was seeing a people for whom poverty had at last been too much.

At Corinth I looked, as so many times before, across the Gulf to the crested headland of the Heraion. There was the lighthouse, ten miles away as Medea might have flown; to me that day, I knew, inaccessible. But when we asked we were assured that there was no difficulty in going to Perachora village. The route was undamaged, perhaps because it led nowhere else. Between Athens and Corinth the Germans had wrecked as they retreated, but Perachora was the terminus of its road; no lines of communication here.

'Let us,' I said, 'go to Perachora.' We crossed the Canal, and this time instead of turning eastward, back towards Athens, we drove on across the desolate Isthmus, through Loutraki with its hot springs and its hotels, deserted then, and up the road in the mountain-side above the sea.

IV

To arrive by day in a Greek village is to be welcome. From the cafeneion, the café, a few lounging men may stare, but it is a stare of interest, and there is nearly always somebody to come forward and talk. To arrive in a Greek village where you are known is to be enveloped in welcome. Yet I was not sure of Perachora. So much had altered; so long had passed. I had not seen the place since 1937, when, a year after Humfry's death, I travelled there from Athens by train and bus, sat talking for an hour in the house of Niko the light-houseman, and walked down to the Heraion. Perhaps the Perachorans had turned sour. It might be that outside their doors too the enemy waited; it might even be that nobody remembered me. I would, I thought, ask for Niko. Or I might ask for Vasili, Niko's friend and partner at the lighthouse, or for Yanni, Vasili's brother, who when we were digging at the Heraion had been our postboy, riding to the village every day on his donkey to fetch our food and our letters.

The jeep came round the last bend in the road. There was the plateia, the square – the village green, you might say, except that no green thing ever grew on that ochre blank of trodden earth. It was deserted: not a soul in sight.

'Stop,' I said. 'Stop here.' The jeep pulled up and I began to get out.

What I had not counted on was the rarity at this time of visitors of any sort in an out-of-the-way village. Mycenae is a celebrated site; every visitor to Greece goes if he can to Mycenae. Nobody who has not some archaeological quest or some personal attachment goes to Perachora. And at the end of 1945 the war was still near enough to turn the arrival of a foreign visitor into an event.

Almost before I had put my feet to the ground we were surrounded.

Dazed at first, in a few moments I began to distinguish among the faces, among the hands which stretched to take mine, the faces and hands of those I knew. There was Niko of the lighthouse, small, dark, nimble, with his firm squared features and quick smile. There was Vasili with his air of indolence, his wide, fair-stubbled face, eyes a little bleared by sea and wind. There was Spiro his brother, whom I remembered as a good-looking, dark-eyed, round-headed little boy, now broadened and roughened into a man. And there, unchanged, durable as rock, was old Aspasia, ferocious leader of the village gossips, my mentor, years ago, in the local jollifications.

'I came to see you all. I could not leave Greece without seeing you.'

'But we were expecting you!' cried Niko. His words went off like a rifle.

'You were in Greece, naturally you came to Perachora.' Vasili's voice grated as I had heard it grating in my imagination.

'You were expecting me?'

'But of course! Did you think we should not expect you?' Niko's dark eyes opened wide.

'In these times it is difficult to travel in Greece. I was afraid I should not be able to come.'

'Bah,' said Vasili, laughing a little. 'For you it is easy. For us who are poor it is difficult.'

'Poor, are we?' Niko broke in ironically. 'But see what a fine village we have. It is like Athens. Is it not like?'

'But certainly,' I said, answering in kind, 'the same. That is why I had to see it again.'

'Why did you not come sooner?' cried Niko, the words volleying.

The party of us, and many more, had moved to the cafeneion, which was also the village restaurant; it was now the property of Yanni, who had followed the lines marked for him by temperament and liking. As our postboy at the Heraion he had seemed more sophisticated than the men who dug for us: smoother than his brother Vasili and the other lighthousemen; readier to talk of politics in general terms; better able to look on the poverty of his

55

village as part of his country's dilemma. I believe that after his employment with us he had worked for a time as a waiter in Loutraki, thus beginning a move which he was not to finish towards the black-coat class. Now he was back in the restricted, harsh existence of the village, living a life not quite of the soil: a business man, you might say. He had not altered. Fine, dark eyes under black eyebrows; the face drawn down a little, melancholy; black moustache over the small sensual mouth; the walk deliberate, thoughtful – only the manner had developed, turning more assured, measuring the world.

'Welcome,' he said in the traditional greeting.

'Well have I found thee,' I responded.

'It is a long time since we have seen you.'

'A long time. What you have been through, all of you!'

'Well we have passed it, well,' said Niko sardonically; then, half-aside, 'What we have been through, ts, ts, ts!'

It was not, I think, in the cafeneion itself but in some adjoining room that we settled down to talk, eat and drink: Niko and Vasili, Orestes and my driver, Yanni, Spiro and myself and a crowd of others. I had brought food with me, for in 1945 the British could not and would not live off the country. As an official visitor I had my rations. When at the beginning of my stay I arrived at the Sedgwicks' flat a British orderly brought a sack of provisions, and I had set off on my trip to Mycenae and Perachora with tins of meat, fish, I no longer remember what. 'We have our food,' I said now, holding out one of them. I had reckoned without Yanni's new authority. 'It is not needed,' he said with dignity, and there was no resisting him.

I like to think that the Perachorans, hidden behind their mountain, following their own lights, living on the road to nowhere, may have fed better than some in the war. After it they had at any rate the sea; whatever prohibitions there may have been under the Occupation, in 1945 they could go fishing. And that day we ate fish, good fresh fish cooked in the oil that was still so scarce and so dear. I struggled to hide my appetite. Orestes and the driver showed no such delicacy, and I daresay they were right; the Perachorans wanted to see us eat with gusto. And they wanted to talk. They wanted to take out their experiences and hold them for someone else to see. I wished that I had been alone, listening to them. Had they been telling their stories only to an Englishwoman they would have spoken for her to understand. With two of their visitors Greeks of their own kind they spoke much indeed only for me, but much for all the company; and Greeks with village Greeks talk a language too quick for me. But the women who crowded into the room looked with especially curious and friendly eyes at another woman. It was for me that the women told their stories.

'I travelled in the war,' said one girl, half-laughing amidst her anger and horror. 'The Germans took us, from many villages they took girls to work for them; a year and a half I was away.'

'Where didst thou go?'

'To Austria they took me; a year and a half I was in Austria. And cold, how cold it was thou hast no idea. Snow there was, snow up to here!' She held her hand at the height of her thigh. 'All day we worked in the snow, from six in the morning we worked; thou hast no idea of the cold.' She was wearing no headscarf, and in her excitement a strand of her long hair dripped forward over her animated face and dark-stained eyes. 'And how hungry we were! Nothing they gave us; in the morning soup made of vegetables and a little piece of bread, nothing else!'

'In Albania,' said young Spiro, 'we were hungry.' He spoke with deliberation, as if to reassert a masculine freedom from exaggeration.

'Thou wast in Albania? When didst thou come home?'

'In '41 I came home, in the summer. We were fighting with the Italians, as you know, but when the Germans came everything was changed, it was the end, the generals had to surrender. Those of us who could, as best we could we went home. I came out of it, lucky I was.'

'And you, kyria,' said Niko, imagination as well as good manners pressing him to ask, 'in England how did you live?'

'So-so,' I said, 'we came out of it. The Occupation we did not have, but we had the bombs.'

'The bombs,' said Niko. 'Heegh, ts, ts, ts,'; and his voice rose and fell in respectful exclamation. 'All the same, you came out of it. I heard, is it the truth? that you are married again.'

'The truth,' I said, 'two years ago.'

'Thy husband,' said one of the women, 'is he good? Is he a good man?'

'He is good,' I said, 'good he is.'

Old Aspasia, her face with its deep vertical wrinkles full of gloomy interest, leaned towards me; she was doing her best, I could see, to satisfy her curiosity without being rude to a visitor. She pointed at Orestes, sitting across the room in his peasant's town-going suit. 'Is that one,' she shouted in my ear, 'thy husband? Thy husband is he?'

As the glasses of wine were emptied and filled again the talk came round, naturally enough, to politics. Ever since I first knew them the Perachorans had been Venizelists, followers of the great liberal statesman who in the First World War had been the opponent of the King – though afterwards he made honourable peace with the royal house. In the first half of the thirties they had watched with disapproval the coming to power of royalist governments. 'What do you say to So-and-So?' one would ask; and 'Thieves, all thieves!' the Perachorans would grumble back. In their fastness they preserved an incorruptible loyalty to their leader, and safe in the distant lighthouse his photograph looked down from the whitewashed wall. But Venizelos was dead now, and his party had split and re-formed into new groups; everything was altered. In Athens I had found the political landmarks moved; with former Venizelists on the right wing now, united in horror of Communist savagery with their old Royalist opponents, I no longer could find my way. Outside Athens I was more uncertain still. Salonika with its sullen looks had confused and disturbed me. At Mycenae I had found an unexplained reluctance to enquire into political allegiances. Perhaps Perachora would have changed with the times. But somehow I did not think so. And this stubborn, independent community seemed to be free of the bitterness which had seeped into many of the families I knew. At any rate I had no hesitation about asking questions.

'And with EAM, with ELAS,' I said, 'how did you come off?'
The faces round the table were watchful but not shuttered. 'Here,'
said Vasili, 'we have had peace.'

'Not like Athens,' I said, 'in Athens ELAS did evil things.'

'So they say,' answered Yanni. 'And you' – he looked at me with
an air of challenge – 'what do you say of EAM?'

'For me,' I said, stumbling, 'it is difficult. Only the things I hear
can I say, and for me it is difficult to say them in Greek. But it seems
to me that EAM amd ELAS have done wrong. They have killed
people, they have taken hostages, great damage they have done, and
none of it really for freedom, for their country.'

'It was not for freedom, do you say?' A man whom I did not know,
with smooth oval face, lively brown eyes and the eager, leaning
movements of a Greek who wants an argument, was speaking. 'But
it is the others who do not want freedom. Three months in prison
they gave me because I was with EAM.'

'In prison? But why?'

'For nothing; I had done nothing; only with EAM I was. Those
are the ones who do not want freedom. For us poor Greeks they
care nothing, all for money they are. Capitalists they are, like the
English.'

'Capitalists you say the English are? But I am not a capitalist, I
work, I am a journalist, you know it.'

'You perhaps not, kyria, but . . .' he smiled; 'why did the English
come to fight against us? Why?'

It was the first time I had met a country Greek infected with the
dogma of EAM. I felt ill-equipped to answer him, not because I was
in any doubt now of the proper responses, but because my rustic
Greek is unequal to any argument which strays outside the state of
the harvest, the quality of the local wine or water, or some simple
exercise in recollection.

'But,' I began, hoping that the words would come, 'the English
did not fight against the Greeks. The English came to Greece to help
you to drive out your enemies . . .'

'Why then,' the stranger broke in, 'did not the English leave when the Germans and the Italians had been driven out? Why did the English fight us in Athens? Why?'

Had the question been asked of a Greek every man within hearing would have flung himself into the argument. But respect to a visitor, and perhaps curiosity to hear a foreigner's views, held the room embarrassingly silent and attentive.

'Certainly you know,' I struggled on, 'that the war had not yet ended. And how could we have gone away when everywhere in your country there was no peace? We stayed to help your government, they asked us to stay. And we fought because there were Greeks who wanted to take power by force instead,' I ended weakly, 'instead of by democracy.'

'I have heard that in England there is no democracy, thus they tell me; is it not so?'

'What sayest thou?' I cried, in my agitation forgetting formality to a stranger. 'Of course we have democracy. What lies have they told thee?'

But at this the restraint of the room snapped. Everybody shouted. 'Here in Greece have we democracy?' said Yanni. 'EAM would give you democracy!' said the stranger. 'All talk, all words!' Vasili yelled. And cracking through like gunfire came the voice of Niko; eyes blazing, he was shaking his fist in somebody's face: 'Nothing dost thou know, nothing?'

Thankful for the uproar, I sat silent until the glasses were filled again. 'At least,' I said then, 'we can drink to democracy, to yours and to mine.' 'To democracy!' cried the disciple of EAM, and owlishly we clinked glasses and drank.

'Do you think of us sometimes in England, do you think of us?' said Niko.

'But certainly: all of you, and the lighthouse, and the village. How did you get on at the lighthouse in the war, did the Germans worry you?'

'Bah, it is too far to the lighthouse, they could not walk like us Perachorans.'

'And the Heraion, what happened to the Heraion, to the excavations? Have the antiquities been damaged?'

'Nothing. A few boulders have fallen, and with the rains earth has collected. The antiquities need cleaning, they need sweeping, nothing else.'

'On my journey from England I thought of you all,' I said. 'I came by airplane, we passed over the lighthouse, I looked down, I saw the rocks and the harbour, in my mind I said: Is Niko there, is Vasili there?'

Niko's eyes bulged with delight. 'You saw the lighthouse,' he shouted, 'if I had known you were up there I would have waved a towel, like that time when Vasili and I stopped a ship, a benzina, for you and they took you and your husband to the Isthmus, do you remember?'

'I remember; well I remember.'

There was much to remember, sitting among the Perachorans I had known when, a dozen years before, we had camped by the light-house. And yet as the talk went on, roughening with wine, it was as if a jungle of time separated us from the days at the Heraion, and in crossing it we had all been changed. At the Heraion I had been con-tent to take life as it was offered to me. Chance, it seemed then, had brought me to Greece, and I had fallen under magic; I had watched, I had listened; not for me to speak, to act. My relationship with Greece had been as if through an interpreter. Humfry's death left me to make my own terms with a country which, I suddenly discovered, I could never divorce. Now I had become the seeker, the pursuer; still after the years, after the war, after all the changes in my own life, still the pursuer. And Greece, so easy with the silent, passive friend, might elude now the hunter. Even in Perachora I was not certain. I felt none of the anger which had put barbed wire between me and the Athen-ians. But the Perachorans too looked different, as people who have existed in deadly danger must look different. They were warier. They knew, I suppose, that peace had not settled in Greece yet. They too could hear the drum-beat. And they were still living with their experiences.

'Perhaps,' Yanni said when at last I stood up to go, 'you know this name, an American name?' He held out a piece of paper. I still have the name, and the address too, for I copied them as I stood: the name of an officer who came from across the world, from Oregon. 'If you should ever hear news of him,' said Yanni.

'Who is he?' I asked. 'Is he a friend?'

'There were two of them,' said Yanni, 'Americans from an airplane. They were in the woods up on the mountain. We brought them to our village, we hid them for a few days. Then they went away, and we do not know what happened to them. If you should ever hear news . . .' He might have been speaking of an acquaintance to whom he had offered a cigarette. Yet twenty miles away among the mountains which fall down to the northern shore of the Gulf men had been shot for far less than hiding an airman. I looked at Yanni. He wore his usual air of dark composure. The faces round him smiled, strained in interest; nothing was new in them except the look of experience: a settled look. The village itself, I thought as we went to the outside stairs, was a little more tumble-down, more poverty-stricken, a little bleaker in the November afternoon; the margin between life and existence was narrower.

'How much,' I said, standing at the door, 'do we owe thee?'

Yanni glanced at me with infinite reproval. 'This is not a restaurant,' he said, 'it is a house.'

A group collected to see us go. 'I will leave you the tins of food we brought,' I said, 'we shall not need them in Athens.' Some Greeks, I learned later, believe that tinned food causes cancer. And country Greeks, like country people everywhere, are suspicious of the un-familiar; when relief first came men and women who had almost starved would look askance at the American cans of soup and milk, and ask for oil instead. My offer was accepted politely but without enthusiasm; clearly the Perachorans did not care for tinned food. Old Aspasia stood turning over in her hands a can, unpromising I admit, of pilchards. 'When the Effendi thy husband died,' she screamed in her weather-beaten voice, 'his clothes thou gavest away. Hast thou none left for me?'

'Goodbye!' cried a dozen voices as we drove off, and 'Goodbye!' I called to Niko, to Vasili and Spiro, to Yanni, to the defender of

62

EAM, to the group of scarved women with old Aspasia waving in the forefront. In a few seconds we had turned the corner, and when I looked back the village was out of sight. We drove on in fading grey light: down the mountain-side with the Gulf of Corinth appearing on the right, through Loutraki again, across the Isthmus and, our way now racing beside the railway track, eastwards along the northern shore of the Saronic Gulf towards Athens. The jeep buzzed along détours, bounced over potholes in the road under the railway embankments. Ribbons of wrenched steel bunched on the track. On the stony slopes of the embankments locomotive-carcases sprawled beside the rusty skeletons of coaches; the fields deserted, empty the olive-groves, everywhere desolation. Excited by wine and argument, Orestes and the driver were singing: to them a companionable song, but melancholy to me, watching the glooming landscape jolt by and reflecting on the alterations of time. Perhaps after all the Perachorans were lucky in their isolation. The village was bruised by war. But it was not assassinated: no houses burned, no hostages murdered. The remoteness which long ago had denied Perachora its share of tourists had also spared it the worst attentions of the Occupiers. Perhaps it was conscious of its advantages. The people as I remembered them had always lived apart, observing with a shade of irony the passage of great events. For a little while they had nursed a dream of inclusion in the prosperous world. But even their dream had been proud. I do not think they imagined any surrender of their aloofness; the world was to come to them. Now the bright fancy had floated away: the tourists, the traffic, the museum. The solitude had deepened. And in my mournful mood I doubted, as we came over the pass at Daphni and in view of the lights of Athens, whether I should see Perachora again. Perhaps it was time for me to get Greece out of my blood.

Reconciliation

I

It was eight years before I saw Greece again. A few months after
I came back to London my work with the Political Warfare Executive was at an end. I was free, if anyone was free just after the war;
that is to say I could, at least within a year or so, travel as far as the
currency allowance would take me. My friends wrote from Athens.
'Why don't you come to Greece?' they said reproachfully when I
talked of holidays in Mediterranean France. But the texture of all
our lives had shrunk since the travelling days of the thirties. To be
busy had become a habit. Time, that noble commodity with which
we were once so free, had vanished; nobody had any time. And to
go to Greece for two or three weeks was the prerogative of the rich,
for travelling cheaply meant travelling slowly, and as I say none of
us could afford the time.

But there were other reasons why I did not bestir myself. I am
ashamed to think that among them was a feeling of estrangement.

It is easy for the English to fall into the trap of romanticising
Greece. The serenity of the landscape, the contrast between the ever-
lasting monuments and the fragile tenure of the people living in
their shadow; the dignity of the poor, the informality of the rich
– everything draws the idealistic traveller. Just as in the nineteenth
century the roaming English dreamed of visiting Italy, between the
wars they longed for Attica or the Cyclades. And when they went
to Greece they found the mountains inviolable, the traditional names
gratifyingly preserved. Some of the visitors were faintly indignant
to find at the foot of the Acropolis of Athens a city with hotels, buses,
cinemas and business men in lounge suits. But hastily they averted
their eyes, hastily brushed aside the thought that Piraeus is a modern

port or that Macedonian Greece has a tobacco industry. They saw only the landscape and the monuments. That was all they wanted to see.

For me the temptation to look only at a timeless Greece was especially strong. In Athens during Humfry's lifetime I had been surrounded by people who talked and thought all day of an antique world miraculously and splendidly surviving in word and stone. And the pursuit of its relics had taken us both into the untrodden country. We knew the welcome of the villages; we resented any development, any encroachment of amenities which, as we thought, might destroy their innocence. With the lover's selfishness we wanted Greece to remain a simple, pastoral country, difficult of access for others but not for us. Personal associations deepened the egotism; and when Humfry died in Greece the whole country was fixed for me in romantic colours. I did not think of it as a complex of people and work, cities and soil, but as the frame of my own experience.

The war forced at gun-point a change of view. Impossible with a people fighting for life to look on through a sentimentalist's loop-hole; and presently the news of starvation, massacre and fratricide insisted that Greece was the setting of a classical, a Sophoclean tragedy. And yet I was not cured of my romanticism. The tragedian shows the nobility of suffering which has a term; he does not show how long-drawn suffering, maggot-like, corrupts. I went back to Greece after the war prepared for heroic tragedy, but not for misconceptions, not for vindictiveness, not for destructive rage. It was the moment in an affair when the lovers recognize the unlovable in one another, when each comes face to face with the irritating, the unsympathetic, the uncomprehending. I am aware that it was also the moment when I should have made an effort to comprehend. The trouble was that I came ready with the wrong kind of sympathy. I even came looking for escape. After a war shadowed by Greek politics to hope to find in Greece itself, of all places, a rest from politics may seem absurd; it was a mark of my romantic infatuation. The disappointment was my own fault, but that made it no less painful. And it seemed to me suddenly that I was running a risk. I have always shrunk from political argument as I shrink from firearms; politics too can go off and kill. In Athens in 1945 I was horrified to find myself beginning to dislike my friends.

In London when I came back: 'What is going on in Greece? Which side is in the right?' I was asked; for by then the ferocities of ELAS and the Communists had shaken the liberal English out of their assurance on Greek affairs. And sometimes I answered: 'Both sides are in the wrong.' It was not only that the violence in argument of some of my friends had been apt in my ears to defeat itself. I thought of the harmless boy sheltering from pursuit in Frosso's kitchen. I thought of the few reactionaries who by their indifference to the wretchedness of the poor had helped to bring murder into Greece. Perhaps it is true that even in civil murder there are often two to blame, the victim as well as the assassin. This time at any rate I suspected that the balance was likely to tip too far against the attackers. And I remembered that in Athens many to whom I spoke had railed against the peace with EAM and ELAS which to us had seemed equitable and desirable. They wanted not peace but the finish of the enemy. They wanted the final destruction of ELAS, and they blamed the British for denying them its achievement.

Soon enough it grew clear that they had political reason on their side. In the summer of 1946, after a plebiscite which had recalled the King to Greece, a new guerilla war broke out. The bitterness I had felt in Athens, the moroseness in Salonika, the watchful disquiet in the country were not, as I fancied at the time, the aftermath of events. They were a prelude. And just as in the days before the outbreak of war in 1939, what I had taken for hysteria was the anxiety which comes of knowledge. The Greeks were the far-sighted, the far-listening ones. The drum-beat I had apprehended in the air was a warning, and they knew what it meant. This time the rebellion lasted three years.

A rebellion: I do not think the word is the right one. Certainly to call the three-years' struggle a civil war is to enrage many Greeks. It was a war, they say, against a foreign power. It was an invasion planned and equipped on foreign soil. And though the guerilla army was at any rate mainly Greek it is not difficult, looking at the movement of the long battle, to see what they mean. The heaviest and most persistent fighting was in the north of Greece where the frontier touches Albania, Yugoslavia and Bulgaria. A rebellion nourished within the borders might not have lasted long; for though at first with the country war-broken and the defences unprepared the Government was hardly ready for a campaign, little by little a National Army was shaped, trained and armed. An enemy with bases beyond the border was another matter. The Greek Government respected the frontier; they invited neutral observers to see that it was respected. Greece's neighbours would admit no observers. But there can be no doubt that the guerillas drew their strength and their inspiration from outside Greece.

Whether at the outset the Greeks were united in enthusiasm for the campaign against the Communists I doubt. In parts of the country there probably was sympathy for the guerillas; for instance in the north, traditionally anti-Royalist. In 1945 my own encounters outside the capital had not convinced me that Greeks everywhere looked on ELAS as the enemy. In Salonika, I feel sure, the Communists had at that time a considerable following. And when the talk was about the andartes country people sometimes drew back cautiously. Perhaps they were afraid. Some of them, perhaps, were uncertain; they were not yet sure of their mind. During the three years of the battle I often wondered what were the feelings of the Greeks. This time I had no private view. Occasionally a letter from Athens would speak of hospitals full of wounded. For the rest I could know only what I read in the newspapers, and though most foreign correspondents had changed their song since the siege of Athens – for in the late nineteen-forties it was no longer fashionable to dote on the Soviet Union – I had learned to be sure of nothing in Greece which I had not seen or heard for myself.

All the same it was difficult to doubt, as time went by and the intentions of the guerilla army became clear, that the Greeks had grown angrily determined to have done with the whole affair. The realization that the attack came from outside it was which in the end united the country; that, and the misery brought on the poor by their supposed defenders. The refugees – at the worst moment of the war there were 700,000 of them, one-tenth of the whole population – clustered round the towns and round Athens; they had lost their homes, their animals, their ploughs; many of them had lost their children, carried off to the Balkan Communist states. And though the weight of the attack lay in the mountainous belt at the north-west corner of Greece, during the three years of war the whole mainland lived in fear.

It was not only that Macedonia and Thrace, setting of the tobacco industry on the borders of Yugoslavia and Bulgaria, were pillaged, that Salonika was shelled, that the towns and villages in the rich plain of Thessaly to the south of Macedonia were raided, that to the west all Epirus was threatened. Attica itself, very centre and heart of Greece, was in danger. The Pindus range which splits the northern mainland drives south-east from Albania between Epirus and Thessaly, throws up the huge complex of which Parnassos is a peak, and declines into the lesser mountains which ring Athens. The Parnassos region, during the Occupation a stronghold of ELAS, during the guerilla war became a fastness of Communist bands which held the hill people trembling; and from Parnassos groups made their way along the diminishing heights into Attica, where they descended on villages within a day's march from the capital.

Even the Peloponnese, southernmost third of Greece, which is joined to the northern mainland by only the four-mile-wide Isthmus of Corinth, was a battleground, with garrisons isolated, the railway from Athens into Arcadia repeatedly cut, the ports of Kalamata and Patras again and again attacked. And once more I can grasp what the war meant only by imagining a tracing of Greece laid over the map of my own country. I must picture Scotland a hostile state to which a rebel army entrenched in the Cumberland Fells can withdraw unpursued, where it can leave its wounded, re-arm and re-form. Flame-throwers are used on the border. Liverpool is under artillery fire; there are battles for Newcastle, Durham and York; Manchester is raided; bands of outlaws control Derbyshire and make their way south as far as Tring. Trains are blown up between Birmingham and Rugby; in Wales hundreds of villages are burned, children disappear, flocks of sheep are driven off; it is impossible to gather the Worcestershire fruit crop; fighting breaks out in Southampton, the main railway line to Plymouth is cut, and rebels hold Corfe Castle unchallenged for twelve months. And all this goes on for three years in a country already exhausted by war and by three and a-half years of enemy occupation.

Sometimes Greek right-wing bands took vengeance into their hands, and called massacre justice. Sometimes the law itself was violent; on the Government side there was some ruthlessness in the pursuit of the rebels. I doubt whether in such peril we should have been more lenient. That Greece should have survived at all as an independent nation was miraculous – and without help, I suppose, she could not have survived. In December 1944 the British defence of Athens had been watched by America with lofty disapproval. But presently mistrust of the Russians altered American policy. When it was at last understood that Greece might be lost the military supplies began to pour in.

Yet in the last resort it was not on equipment from her friends that Greece had to rely, but on Greek lives. The danger was not in the numbers of the enemy; probably the guerillas never had more than 30,000 men in the field at the same time. The danger lay in the apparent indestructibleness of the enemy. 'The hospitals,' Frosso wrote at the end of 1948, 'are full of wounded who feel that they, and those who were killed, have sacrificed themselves for nothing. Soon the very strategic points they fought to capture are recaptured by the andartes, who seem to grow out of the ground.' The guerillas had their conscripts, peasants who had been forced into the fight against what they were told was Western fascism, and who deserted when they could. But there were the solid ones who, because they could not be prevented from crossing and re-crossing the frontier, seemed unbeatable. The Government troops stood, and fell where they stood.

At the end of 1947 there was an attack, which Greece will remember, on the little town of Konitsa near the frontier with Albania. Three thousand attackers, a thousand defenders, a battle which lasted eleven days. When the besiegers withdrew, of the garrison only four hundred and sixteen remained alive. Konitsa never fell. But in the Grammos mountains which surrounded it on the Albanian frontier, campaign after murderous campaign was fought. The story is half-lost now in the press of history. Yet it was no trifle. By the spring of 1949 the rebel losses were 70,000 killed, captured or surrendered, the Government losses 38,000 killed, wounded, missing. Tragedy on both sides, tragedy from either point of view. And there seemed no reason why the war should ever end. When in 1949 the Communist leader Markos, protesting that he did it to save bloodshed, announced a cease-fire, the country had almost forgotten what peace was like.

Certainly Tito's break with the Cominform a year earlier had contributed to the rebel failure. It meant one enemy the less on the Greek frontier, one route of escape the less for the guerilla army. Perhaps, too, Russia was finding other preoccupations. Certainly Russian backing was failing; and America's generous help was having its effect. For the second time, then, Greece was saved. In December 1944 few people understood that the battle for Athens was not merely a local political tussle. The war which was fought between 1946 and 1949 could not be minimized; anybody could see that it was a battle for Greece. The Greeks knew that it was something more. 'Why cannot you English understand,' one of them said to me once, 'that we are not fighting only for ourselves, we are fighting for all of you?' So they were; and this campaign at least in the battle for Europe was won.

Clear: today it all seems clear – the enemy not even scotched, the long battle of intervention, the Greeks dying for us. Then, everything was obscure and troubled. 'Why don't you come to Greece?' But Greece was not Greece for me unless I could see the country, and even had I been given the chance to visit Athens I could not during the years of the guerilla war have had any freedom to travel. I was even beginning to think I had lost the desire for the old ways of going about. So many years had passed since I had enjoyed them

– for there certainly had been no freedom in 1945. A great river of events separated me from the green romantic days of camping at the Heraion. Some of the Perachorans might still remember me. But even they, surely, were altered by experience, altered again, and more deeply, by what had happened since 1945. Everything was changed. Greece was changed. I myself was changed. I had married again; my new life now possessed me. No longer reminded every day by my society or my work, I was losing touch with both the Greek past and the Greek present.

Even when the guerilla war was over, then, I made no effort to go to Athens. Had I gone I could have travelled in the country; there was no longer that excuse. But I felt a kind of lassitude, a reluctance to expose myself once more to the emotional violence of Greece. I no longer wanted, I said, to return to what was over. I thought of the Heraion riding the waters of the Gulf, the village spinning its cocoon of work and gossip. I would let the past, I told myself, be past, un-affected by the present. At last, I thought, I was getting Greece out of my blood.

But when in 1953, four years after the end of the guerilla war, the chance of going to Greece was offered me I suddenly felt the old passion. There was no question of refusing.

II

I<small>T WAS THE</small> last week of September when we arrived, a delegation of five to discuss with five Greeks the implementing of an Anglo-Greek Cultural Convention. Our meetings and the accompanying junketings were to last for the best part of a week; at the end I should be free to spend another week in the country.

Dusk was falling that first evening when we landed at the airport by the sea where eight years earlier I had waited in the rain all morning for a plane to Salonika. Lights sparkled along the coast, and as we drove towards the city there was the smell I remembered of sea, baked soil and the sweet night. I telephoned to Shan Sedgwick and gave him messages from Roxane, who was in England; and we dined together in a taverna, an open-air restaurant where we sat in a walled courtyard over plates of black olives and stuffed aubergines, cheese and fruit and glasses of rhetsina, remembering. Or I should say that I remembered. This was a part of the Athens I had once known: the physical contentment, the nervous excitement, the waves of talk, the ready running waiters, and over everything, only a little way above the hum and the movement, the night breathing quietly. But I was pale and stiff from my northern exile. 'I feel,' I told Shan, 'as if I had shrunk.'

Next morning I looked out of my hotel window to watch, by the memorial to the Unknown Soldier in front of the old Royal Palace, the Constitution Square Sunday morning parade, the changing of the guard. I had seen Athens in the winter, in the spring, under the scimitar of summer, but never at the turning from summer to autumn. I was not sure what to expect, what temperature, what skies. But the sun gripped the city, the women were hatless in summer dresses. A Sunday morning it was when in December 1944 the calamitous battle of Athens had begun. But this morning the square was gay with crowds and music and the euzones, the Greek Guards regiment, marching in ceremonial braided jackets, scarlet caps, white kilts and full-sleeved white shirts; as the flag went by, men in the crowd took off their hats. There was no meeting of the delegation until late afternoon, and Shan drove me to the coast near Marathon to bathe. The wind blew steadily across the strait from the island of Euboea, the surge sucked at the rocks and flung itself back on them in curled hissing waves. The brilliant, violent day belonged to the Attica of my visits to Greece before the war. Still I felt a stranger to the physical joy which had once been my companion. I leaned timidly into the water, and could hardly scramble out against the thrust of the breakers.

During the days which followed I looked, in the intervals of work, for signs of the battle. Sometimes I saw walls pitted with gunfire, and near the National Museum there were still street corners with rubble and battered houses. But Athens was full of vitality. Streets were being widened, the old tramlines taken up and new buses used. Restaurants were full, crowds loitered in the cafés. The Museum itself was being newly planned, and in the few reopened rooms the pottery and marbles and bronzes – among them a dozen or so familiar, exquisite pieces from the Perachora Heraion – were splendidly displayed. The city was losing its touches of the old-fashioned. I saw fewer little boys with shoe-shine gear; the shops, obliging as ever, had more to sell. Though there were not many Americans to be seen, the influence of the United States was visible in a new kind of smartness. The old taxis had been replaced by American cars. The ways out of the city led along wide modern boulevards.

Above all the faces in the streets had the lively look of a stirring people. The changes had not been imposed; however assisted, they belonged to the resilience of the Greeks. And I was amazed to find my friends, even those who had spoken the most bitterly, now behaving as if the miseries of the battle for Athens and the guerilla war of 1946–49 had never been.

'You will agree,' said one who had railed against what he took for British subservience to Russia, 'you will agree now that I was right about the Communists?'

'Yes, yes, you were right.'

He waved the past away. 'It is all finished now, quite finished. No more symmorites.'

Symmorites – I had come across the name several times. In 1945 another word had echoed through every conversation; 'koukouedhes', one had heard, and again 'koukouedhes', and knew that the talk was about the members of the Communist Party, the KKE. Now I caught at the new currency – new to me at any rate.

'Symmorites, what does that mean?'

'Symmorites – it means members of a band, a gang, conspirators, it means gangsters.'

I was to be glad later on that I had asked, for nearly everywhere I went in the country the word was the accepted title of the Communist guerillas; scarcely anybody spoke of andartes. But in Athens the war with the symmorites was as old-fashioned as, in London, an anecdote of an air-raid. The delegation met daily with its Greek colleagues; we debated education, scholarships for students, the exchange of books, plays, films. Some of us gave lectures on pacific subjects; all of us were jovially entertained. On the last day there were literary speeches in the university; to mark the dignity of the surroundings and, perhaps, the approaching end of summer, all the women wore hats: all, that is, except myself; having struggled day after day in the heat to show that I was taking my duties as a delegate with respectful seriousness, on the final occasion, the only one, as I discovered too late, when formality was appropriate, I gave in and turned up bare-headed. Afterwards the English party dined at a taverna. In the traditional fashion we went into the kitchen to order. Then we sat out of doors, listening to a singer with a lute and eating, drinking and laughing immoderately. At last we strolled away in the warm night, down some jagged-paved street in the old quarter of Athens which is called the Plaka, until we found one of the resplendent new taxis.

77

It had been a week of reunions. Shan and K. and Frosso; Christos on the taxi-rank; Thalia at the travel agency; Madame S. begging me to go and see her famous collection; Semni at the Museum – with so many friends, so many acquaintances it seemed as if I had only to take up where we had left off, not in 1945 but before Hitler's war. But the work of the delegation had not left me time to settle down. I talked in the hot hours of the afternoon, snatched a visit late at night. I had ceased, from the moment the Viscount came sliding down at dusk to the airfield by the sea, to feel alienated from Greece. All the same I still felt strange. There were things I had forgotten and there were things I had never known. There were new buildings, re-named streets; my friends frequented tavernas which were unfamiliar. Once or twice in the very middle of Athens I had to ask the way.

It was still not late when the taxi put us down at the hotel. That in itself made for strangeness; I remembered summer parties which had lasted to dawn. But I had a great deal to put in order before I set off to the country, and only next day to do it in. I went up to my room.

But I could not sleep. Beneath my window the city trembled and murmured with pleasure; the shadows of passers were thin in the bright lights. At last, giving way to my own restlessness, I put on a cotton dress and sandals and hurried down into the street. I knew where I had to go; and up hilly side streets, over dark cross-roads I went until I came to the British School. It was fourteen years since I had looked with any attention at the house where I had lived in my first years of falling in love with Greece, for in 1945 personal memorials had been muffled by the general anxiety, like sheeted furniture in an untenanted house. In the street on Lykabettos, the hill which overlooks Athens from the north-east, the gate was ajar. I pushed it open and went down the steps, past the front door of the Director's house, through the garden sloping towards the students' hostel. Outside the garden there were the sounds of an Athenian summer night: distant traffic, a singing voice, a tango played over the radio; inside not a stir. I walked stealthily for fear of rousing someone at the late hour, but my feet knew the path as if they had never left it. The bushes had the same solid reticence, the trees cast the same unfathomable shadows, the moon, I could have sworn, hung in the same heavenly place above the cypresses at the end of the road. And now, uncalled for, the emotion came which I had expected vainly on the road to Corinth and Mycenae eight years earlier. Here I had learned to live. I stood with constricted heart looking at my own past.

III

W~HEN THE TELEPHONE~ rang by my bedside at a quarter to six I could not remember where I was. I had not slept until after two o'clock. A nervous indecision had seized me at the thought of once again travelling freely about the country. I was to visit a part of Greece which I had never seen, where I knew nobody. Afterwards I could return to the familiar places, but first I wanted to look without prejudice at the aftermath of the guerilla war. Before I went to bed I must have spent an hour absurdly debating with myself what I should pack in the rucksack which was to be my only luggage for nearly a week.

All the same I came to with a speed which would have been impossible to me in England, and at six-thirty I was on the way to the bus station in Chateaubriand or, as in Greek it is pronounced, Satovrian Street. My plan was to make my way westward along the northern side of the Gulf of Corinth; turn north through Aetolia and the ravaged province of Epirus; go as far as I could towards Albania; climb east over the Pindus Mountains; then finishing the circle, face southwards over the plains of Thessaly and return to Athens. First I had to go to Delphi, and my friend Thalia in Ghiolmans, surely the most accommodating travel agency in Europe, had reserved a seat in the bus. Nearly all my journey, it seemed, could if I wished be covered by road. Travel in Greece had changed since the war. Comfortable new buses would take you now wherever there was a road, and cheaply too; the four and three-quarter hours' journey to Delphi, a distance of a hundred miles, cost less than twelve shillings.

At seven o'clock we were away. The young woman next to me was seen off by her husband; a Greek Army Officer, he looked fondly at the baby in his wife's arms and asked me if I had any children. 'No', I said, coldly I fear, for I was out of practice with the regular conversational exchanges between strangers in Greece. The baby gripped my shoulder and struggled to fling himself in my lap. Behind me I could hear English voices, and when I turned to look I recognized acquaintances from London. They did not at first recognize me; later I was gratified to find that they had taken me for a Greek. And indeed I felt at home as we bowled along the road I had so often travelled: past Daphni and Eleusis, over the mountain pass to Thebes where Oedipus was king, on to Haliartos and Livadia and past the Schiste, the road-fork where he killed his father. At Livadia I took advantage of a ten-minute stop to buy a tin of DDT – unnecessarily, for I was never to use it; Greece, it seemed, had been rid of bugs and fleas as well as mosquitoes. I was able, too, to serve my English friends by discovering for them the municipal lavatories, a row of wooden shacks guarded by an old man and insecurely poised, with a hole in each floor, over a rushing stream. Then we hurried on, leaving behind us the cotton and maize fields of the Boeotian plain and climbing into the foothills of Parnassos. An old man in the front seat began to sing, and presently the young mother beside me uncovered her breast and hummed quietly to her baby as she fed him.

It was nearly midday when we drew up in Delphi, in the single street on the steep mountain-side. Over twenty years had passed since I had come this way. But the place looked unchanged. A little smarter, perhaps, as befits a village bearing a name among the most famous of the ancient sanctuaries of Greece: the road better, the houses more newly painted. And the Castalia hotel, which I remembered as friendly but modest, had moved up in the world: waiters in white coats, a wine-list, and a five-course lunch – which I ate gratefully at the expense of my English friends.

I was to travel farther that afternoon, but I could not bear to leave without visiting the Museum. It was the one I knew best of all the collections in Greece. The first time I saw Delphi was in February weather. We were poor that year and lived on dried salt fish; the mist swam low, it was so cold that I slept in all my clothes, including my mackintosh, and all day while Humfry worked I loitered round the Museum, from case to case, from statue to statue, from frieze to frieze. Often since then Humfry and I had come to the village, wandered round the sanctuary with its complex of foundation walls, the stadium and the huge remains of Apollo's temple, and climbed the cliffs to the cave of the Nymphs on Parnassos. I had never seen Delphi more august than on this October day in 1953. Yet, as I was reminded when I went into the Museum, Parnassos and the westward ranges which I was to skirt in the next day or two had been a guerilla stronghold; battles had been fought over this ground.

It was the custodian in the Museum who, standing amidst the offerings and thank-offerings of war and peace centuries before the birth of Christ, first put into my mind what the Communist revolt had meant to ordinary people living in the provinces. The Museum was being rearranged and remounted after the disorder and destruction of thirteen years. A carpenter was hammering at a base for a broken marble; the sphinx set up by the people of Naxos was in place, and the frieze and pediment from the Treasury of the Siphnians; the bronze Charioteer, still holding his broken reins, had been set on a revolving stand. The splendid things glowed in the reflections of the autumn light while the custodian told his story of terror.

'The symmorites', he said (it was the first time I had heard the word spoken by someone who used it with personal acquaintance), 'the symmorites were worse than the Germans, far worse. They did nothing but kill and burn and steal – your house, your animals, your goats, nothing was safe. Here on Parnassos they collected, up in the mountains where nobody could hunt them, then they came down to the villages and took everything, animals, chickens, corn, everything.'

'Were there any from Delphi among them?'

'A few, not many.'

'What happened to them?'

'Some were killed in the end, some escaped and went to Russia and Poland.'

'But how do you know they are in Russia and Poland?'

'They write; they write through the Red Cross. On forms they write, they say nothing, only that they are well. One of them married a girl from the village, a Communist she was, and took her with him to Poland. Through the Red Cross we know it.'

'And you, were you here in Delphi all the time?'

'I? No indeed, I escaped and went to the mountains.' The custodian laughed grimly, as one laughs at the recollection of pain. 'They were after me, if I had stayed they would have cut my throat. For months I was in the mountains.'

As I paid for my postcards of the Sphinx I watched him: a steady-looking fellow in a countryman's dark suit; not the man you would think of as a fugitive on Parnassos. 'I wish,' I said, 'I could stay in Delphi. But I must go on to Amphissa tonight.'

'You must come back,' he said. 'Next year you must come back. There will be a fine new hotel when you come, the Tourismos has built it behind the village; you will see it as you go. Baths it has, and showers, quiet it has, everything; only the water it has not got yet. Next year you must come back and stay, two or three nights you must stay, and go up to the summit of Parnassos; I myself will take you. But you must stay two or three nights. I shall expect you.'

IV

IN THE AFTERNOON the bus took me down the winding road above the gorge of the river Pleistos, through groves of olives, to Amphissa. I had never stayed there before. I had travelled alone in Greece since Humfry's death often enough, but always to familiar places; this time I was setting off into strange country. A little conscious of my own absurdity – for a solitary woman roving about Greece for the fun of it is still, in spite of the example set by scores of archaeologists, a spectacle slightly bizarre in Greek eyes – I got out of the bus with my rucksack and asked for the best hotel. It belonged, I found, to category E. In the early days of my travels with Humfry the categories were not stated; E, however, was a class with which our small means had made me uncomfortably familiar. Now I welcomed the simple; I know this, I said to myself. I was wrong. I did not know it, for the rough sheets on the iron bedstead were washed, the primitive lavatory had electric light, the tin suspended from the wall over the enamel wash-basin was full, as I found when I turned its tap, of clean water. And when I asked for the bus-station the hotel-keeper himself appeared to show me the way. 'Don't stand in front of the lady,' I heard him saying to a young man in the queue, 'she is a foreigner.' Afterwards I discovered a shop which sold mineral water and bought a large bottle; I did not know where my journey might take me, and in any case I had not been inoculated against typhoid for years.

It was still too early to eat, and in a restless curiosity I began to walk about the streets. Amphissa is an ancient place, a town of perhaps six thousand inhabitants; it is a bishopric; it is the centre of a rich olive-growing region. But few visitors come to it, except to wait for a bus on their way elsewhere. It has never acquired the habit of foreigners. And no doubt in the light cotton clothes, headscarf, socks and tennis shoes which I find comfortable for hot rough travelling I looked a foreigner indeed. Every man's head in every café turned as I passed; women rushed to windows with their babies in their arms; I could see the police taking counsel with one another. In the last of the afternoon light I went into the cathedral. Antiphonal voices chanted, a hieratic figure in white stood at the altar; a priest went by swinging a censer, an old woman in black peasant's clothes crossed herself in its aroma; it was a passage from Tolstoy. I lit a deferential candle and came out into the blue dusk and the scent of charcoal. It was Saturday night, and life was pressing into the streets: shops opening, men strolling and laughing together. A priest in his tall hat and long black robes was buying meat at a butcher's shop; figures waited inside the barber's: on the pavement a man was cooking offal, bound up in long batons, on a spit over charcoal embers; a baker took his flat loaves from the oven with a long-handled shovel. Lights flickered through the cracks of shutters, from cavernous shops, through the half-open door of a café-ouzeri, a bar for coffee and the spirit called ouzo. I walked and listened in the whispering streets. At last, unable to bear my lonely perambulations any longer, I went into a restaurant. This time I was not mistaken. This I did know; it was the true copy of all the restaurants in little provincial towns where, on my first journeys in Greece, I had sat before food I could not eat. I felt almost affectionate when I was served the well-remembered bone – an elbow, I have always supposed – with a fragment of fat floating in a stew of tomatoes and hot oil. Even the cheese with its reek of old goat was familiar. But there was nobody to remember it with me. I looked at the other diners: two Air Force officers; an Army officer sitting by himself; a young man with a bold-looking girl, bare-headed in city fashion; another officer with two priests, one of them, I was interested to hear, complaining about the meat. As I drove the flies away from the congealing stew I noticed a party of children with their faces snubbed against the window, watching me. Violently I felt a foreigner, a stranger, and alone.

It was still early and I had time to kill. If I went to bed I feared I should not sleep, and in my parsimonious luggage I had brought nothing to read except a pre-war *Guide Bleu*. Once more I set to walk round Amphissa: to the cathedral and back, to the bus stop, up and down the streets with the open shops: shops with watches, with bales of cloth, with fruit and vegetables. In the darkness I went almost unnoticed, or perhaps it was that by now I was taken for granted. Once or twice I stopped and looked into a window. An old man in shirt-sleeves was sitting on a chair outside a clothier's, and when I went by his eyes met mine and he said Good Evening.

'Are you American or English?'

'English, from London; it is the first time I have stayed in Amphissa.'

'Welcome! Please come in. I will call my sons.'

A chair was fetched, I sat down, from behind the bales of cloth two young men appeared and greeted me. 'You will allow us to offer you something? A sweet perhaps?' 'No, no', I protested, I had just dined; but seeing that I was offending their hospitality I accepted; 'A sweet, if you will be so kind.' One of the young men ran across the street and returned a minute or two later with the ritual spoonful of jam and a glass of water; the three watched respectfully as I ate and drank. 'You are staying long in Amphissa? Ah, you are going on to Lidhoriki; there you will see what damage the war has done.'

'Burning and killing, all burning and killing,' said the old man. 'Here in Amphissa too we have suffered, with the symmorites and with the Germans. Hard hearts the Germans had, savage they were. But thanks be to God that it is all over now. We have peace.' He looked at me solicitously. 'Where will you stay tonight? If you would like to sleep in our house . . .'

'Thank you,' I said, 'you are very kind, but I have taken a room in the hotel.'

'You are sure?' he persisted. 'If you would like to sleep in our house, it is a clean house; do not mistake me, I would not ask you to a house with no women; there are girls in the house, they would look after you.'

'You will come back next year?' said the old man and his sons as I left. 'In our house you would be welcome. Next year you will come back and stay two or three days?'

I walked back to the hotel ashamed of my moment of complaint.

V

UNDER A DEEP soft drift of forgetfulness I slept until half-past five next morning, when I was brought three brick-like rusks and a cup of tea stiff with sugar. It was dark, and as the bus climbed out of Amphissa two or three lights winked in the town. But work was beginning; men and women drove their mules up the hill with urgent cries, and shy-eyed donkeys minced home with loads of fodder. On our left cloud piled so solidly that I took it for a mountain with spires and long flanks, until the dawn wind frayed and shredded it, and behind us the sun came up, a pink neon light glistering through grey scarves. We drove through desolate hills to a plain where the dried stalks of the gathered maize stood in the fields, and sheep grazed by a waterless stream-bed. Drinks and Cold Water, said the notice at a wayside café; goatskins, stiff and dead, were stacked in the dust by the road, and outside a solitary shanty a peasant was pressing his grapes; his harvest waiting in two tall baskets, his trousers rolled to his thighs and his legs stained purple, he stood in his one-man vat, trampling, trampling.

Lidhoriki stands under mountains at the head of the valley. At half-past seven, when we arrived, it was still in shadow, and the witnesses of war were veiled. When day lightened, ruin edged forward: blackened walls, disembowelled houses, houses with their eyes put out; ruin more deliberate than the wreckage of an air raid, and more malignant. But the village on this Sunday morning was full of life: homes being rebuilt, masons and carpenters at work. I went into the confectioner's, which was also the dairy, and ordered coffee and a saucer of crema, a sweet which is served everywhere in Greece.

Why, I asked the proprietor, was the destruction in Lidhoriki so terrible? The Germans burned the village in reprisal, he told me, half in Greek, half, with a courteous but mistaken hope of making himself clearer to me, in Italian. There was a battle in the district; the andartes fell upon the Germans and killed three hundred of them, only one escaped; so the village was burned, and those who were too old to move were burned in their houses. There was an Englishman with the andartes, he added: an Englishman whom they called Geoff.

As I walked along the stony paths between the dead and the living houses a group of women working in a doorway greeted me, and I stopped to talk.

'Where were you,' I asked, 'when they burned your village?'

'Here,' said one in the total black of the old, 'they drove us out.'

'What happened, where did you go?'

A handsome, deep-breasted girl with shining red cheeks and brown hair streaking from under her scarf answered me. 'To the mountains!' she cried, laughing, 'we went to the mountains!'

'But when you came back?'

'We had nothing, no clothes, nothing!' For a moment her voice hardened, then, seeing the question in my face, she laughed again. 'If you have no animals you cannot carry anything with you. Nothing we had, no houses, nothing!'

'Where did you live, then?'

'Here!' She pointed to the doorway. It led into a mud-floored shed where in the darkness hens were picking at the ground. In many Greek villages it is the practice to stall the animals underneath the living quarters, and I realized that this had once been the stable of a house. 'Here we lived!' And she roared with laughter.

By half-past eight the village was full of sun, and two buses were making ready to leave, one towards Amphissa, one onwards in the direction I should presently take. But I wanted to walk at any rate a little way through the country between Lidhoriki and Naupaktos. It was a region strange to me, for Humfry and I never achieved the plan we had made to cross it on foot; a region haunted once, I knew from the reports I had read in the war, by guerillas; a secret region too, walled in on the north by the bastions of the Pindus, hidden from the Gulf of Corinth on the south by the vertical mountains of the coast. Instead of taking the morning bus, then, I sat watching the movement in the plateia: the donkey swaying off with suitcases and bags brought in on the early morning trip, the piles of sacks, packages, boxes collecting for departure, the men in Sunday suits with a bundle of hens strung together by their feet, the women screaming to the driver as he hoisted a netful of vegetables to the roof.

Presently a middle-aged man wearing a suit more sophisticated in stuff and cut than the rest came across to the café outside which I was sitting and addressed me in my own language. He introduced himself: Timbelis, he said, was his name. Was I not English? Would I allow him to sit down and offer me a cup of coffee? I congratulated him on his English. Ah, he said, he had lived in America; he had a married daughter in Missouri; but in 1927 he came back because he loved his own country.

Lidhoriki, I said, has suffered much; in England we heard of what you had been through. Lidhoriki, he rejoined, has had a long, famous history: 'When I came back from America, an old man, a hundred and four years old, told me that Dhiakos – you know Dhiakos, whom the Turks roasted alive at Lamia? – used to come to Lidhoriki.'

We sat drinking our coffee, and my new friend, with the gift for story-telling which heaven has bestowed on the Greeks, held me with tales of the hero of the War of Independence: Dhiakos firing his gun at a wedding and accidently killing a man; Dhiakos imprisoned in a house, now destroyed, near the bridge I could see from where I sat; Dhiakos in his prison refusing an invitation from the Pasha, who had heard of the young man's good looks ('I am ashamed to tell you this, but the Pasha was how you say anomalous'); Dhiakos, as water-carrier for a band of patriots, seeing one of them fall, dropping the water-skins and rushing into the fight. Lidhoriki, it seemed, was among the hero's favourite villages; he used to sit under a tree in the plateia – 'You see the plane-tree? There he would sit and talk, not under that tree but under another one which used to stand near it'. Indeed he wanted to open the struggle for independence by freeing the Lidhoriki district and making it the headquarters for a general rising; like the guerillas of the 1940s, he understood its natural advantages, its command of the defiles to Amphissa and Naupaktos.

'But the others refused, so he took his gun and went off. Under the same tree he said goodbye to his friends. "Well, boys," he said, "I am going now . . ." '

The voice wavered and stopped, and I saw that the narrator was affected by the story he was telling. His face flushed, tears stood in his eyes, and he struck himself lightly on the throat with the back of his hand to recover.

'Pardon me,' he said presently, 'I have always been how you say tender-hearted. If I listen to music, Beethoven or Schubert, it makes me cry. And to think of Dhiakos here in Lidhoriki . . .'

'You are from Lidhoriki yourself?'

'No, I am from another village, but I have property in the valley. My daughter, who studied law, is in Larissa.'

'But you were here during the war?'

Yes indeed, he was working for the Allies, he was imprisoned for five months by the Italians. One day a guard came to him secretly: 'There is something terrible, I cannot tell thee.' 'But what is it? Tell me, whatever it is I can bear it.' 'Then I must tell thee that in the morning thou art to be shot, and eight others as well.'

'But,' Timbelis went on, 'I had fifteen gold sovereigns, I had them hidden, I gave them to the guard and I escaped.'

'You were working with the British?'

Yes, he said, and with the Americans too; he had found clothes for them, he had helped them to hide and get away. And from his wallet he took out with fond fingers two letters, photographically reproduced with type in white on a black background, thanking him for his services to the Allied cause; one was signed by an American general, one by Field-Marshal Alexander.

The buses had driven off with their loads, the square was quiet in the sun; the story of death and conspiracy murmured like a fairy-tale in my ear. There was a memorial by the bus-stop, and before setting off on the next stage of my journey I went to look. It was a war memorial, a cenotaph with dates and names. Fallen in war, said the front face; the dates were of the wars Greece has fought in this century: 1912–13, the Balkan wars; 1920–22, war in Asia Minor; 1940–41, against Mussolini and Hitler; 1944, the liberation; 1946–49, against the guerillas – for to the Greeks, as I have said, the internal struggle with Communism was a full-scale war. On the right-hand face, nine names: Fallen in Lidhoriki, 1947–49. On the left face: Executed by the Germans and Italians, eleven names, nine of them civilians; Executed by the Symmorites, eleven names, all civilians. Death on foreign soil, death at an enemy's hand, and now death at the hand of a brother; war, resistance, reprisals and the division of a whole people, village against village, family against family. The history of Greece for half a century is written in Lidhoriki.

VI

IT IS THIRTY MILES from Lidhoriki to Naupaktos. Starting late as I did, and with the days shortening, I could not expect to reach Naupaktos on foot, nor had I much hope of finding anywhere on the way to spend the night. There was nothing for it but to trust in the day's second bus, which, I had been assured, would pass in the afternoon. I set off, then, to walk along the road, stopping now and again to ask a passer-by the name of the next village, and how far off it was.

'Stenó,' said an old man on a donkey. 'Thou wilt pass Stenó, my child' (the phrase is used in Greek familiarly, or between friends, or sometimes in speaking to someone younger or less expert than oneself). 'It is a long way, an hour on foot.'

The sun was hot, but there were springs by the roadside with stone basins where, to conserve my Loutraki water, I drank; and with the bottle clanking against the small of my back I trudged on to Stenó, which means Narrow. Indeed the hills and cliffs drew in here, so that once I had passed the bend of the road I came into another landscape. A mile or two farther on a woman was grinding maize outside a hut; a shepherd was sitting by her, and his dog stood up to bark at my approach.

'He does not bite,' said the woman.

'Welcome,' said the shepherd. 'Villages? You will find no villages on the way.'

'The villages are all high up,' said another man to whom I spoke, 'you cannot see them from the road.'

'Why? Why are they all high up?'

'Long ago the people built up in the hills because they wanted to keep out of the way of the Turks.'

Whether this is the true reason I do not know, but indeed there are no villages by the road, which winds along the valley of the river Mornos: no villages, and at the season of my visit few people were working in the fields. I spoke to a little girl riding a donkey who clattered after me and asked for a hundred drachmae – it was, I think, the only time in the Greek country I have been asked for money; to a grizzled old peasant who complained of something I could not understand; to a boy who, overtaking me, said he had seen me in Lidhoriki and offered, as far as we went together, to take my rucksack on his mule; and to a ragged man who came out of the fields carrying a striped bag and answered my questions about the crops. 'The maize is good this year, good. But here there is poverty, great poverty. God does not want us to live!' And he laughed loudly.

When I had gone about ten miles I came on a dozen goats and a girl of nineteen wearing brown woollen stockings under her short skirt and knitting as she herded. She looked at me sullenly at first, but after a few exchanges smiled and asked me to sit down. 'Very well,' I said, 'I have not eaten yet; I will sit and eat and drink while we talk.' And I took out my biscuits and chocolate and the bottle of Loutraki water.

'Why hast thou that bottle, why?'

'I did not know if I should find water on my road.'

She looked at the river running beyond the maize-fields and laughed.

'Wilt thou have some chocolate or a biscuit?' I said.

'I have eaten; do thou eat.'

A man in a coat all patches, his knees showing through the rents in his trousers, came over the road.

'The water you are drinking,' he said, 'will have got warm.' Then, to the girl, 'Run, fetch her some cold water!'

'It does not matter.' I had not the presence of mind, or perhaps the courage, to say I was afraid of typhoid. 'It is not very warm.'

'Bah,' he said. 'Run, fetch her some cold water, quick!'

'I do not want to give you trouble,' I stuttered, 'what I have is cold enough.' But already the girl had taken the bottle, and helplessly

I watched her pour its contents on the ground. A minute later she came back with it; I could only hope she had filled it at a spring. 'Is it not better?' she asked; 'is it not colder?'

Resolutely I drank. 'Much colder,' I said.

A woman in black had been sitting some little way off. Now she came to join us: a handsome old woman with delicate straight nose and ivory skin drawn tightly across high cheek-bones; and together with the girl she began to question me in the accepted way. Was life dear in England, was there poverty? How much a week did I earn? How much had my shoes cost? I was wearing the tennis shoes I prefer for walking. 'Sixty thousand drachmae,' I said incautiously, translating fifteen shillings into what at that time was its Greek equivalent. They pointed ironically to their own feet shod in flat pieces of leather tied with rope over the instep. Ours cost nothing, they said, we make them ourselves.

'What do you say,' asked the man, 'will there be war again?'

'I do not believe it.'

'But everyone talks of war.'

'I do not believe there will be war.'

'If there is war again what will become of us?'

'Art thou certain,' the old woman begged, 'there will not be war?'

'Where is thy village?' I asked her. 'I do not see it.'

'Up there' (pointing to the heights above the valley). 'Up there I stay. But not in my own house. In a stranger's house I stay!'

'What happened to thine own house?'

The andartes, she said, had burned it (the fashionable word 'symmorites' had not, I fancy, reached this remote district). 'My son would not go with them, he did not want to fight with them, so they burned our house, in '48 they burned it. I had nowhere to live, to Athens I went. Two years ago I came back to our village, but we have no house. In strangers' houses we stay, in strangers' houses!'

'The andartes turned me out,' said the man. 'I escaped and went to Naupaktos. I had ten goats, the andartes took them. You can see' (pointing to his rags) 'the state I am in now.'

'In strangers' houses,' repeated the old woman, 'in strangers' houses!' And again she implored: 'Art thou certain there will not be war?'

But the girl had other preoccupations. Waiting alone with me for the bus to pass, 'How old art thou?' she said softly; then: 'Wast thou older than I when thou wast married?'

As the bus began its long swing south-westward through wooded gorges to Naupaktos and the sea I could hear two passengers speculating about me. 'She is a foreigner,' said one. 'But she speaks Greek,' said the conductor. I was grateful when a woman (a lawyer's wife, she told me) offered some friendly advice about hotels and restaurants at the journey's end; Naupaktos is not too modest to provide some choice. The town has another name. From its anchorage two centuries ago a Turkish admiral set out to meet the Christian fleet commanded by Don John of Austria, and was beaten in the battle called, after the harbour, Lepanto. Today it is a cheerful little place with Venetian walls and a graceful circular harbour, with a tower watched from across the Gulf by a mountain; a town not quite solitary, for we approached it through villages where the bus picked up new passengers. One pair, entering with a downtrodden mongrel, mistook my exploratory gesture for fright. 'He is a hunting dog,' they assured me, 'he does not bite.'

Taking the advice I had been given, 'Hotel Rex,' I said when I got out, 'I want the Hotel Rex,' and I set off with my rucksack as I was directed. The streets and the square were beginning to fill with evening crowds, well dressed in the summer manner of a provincial seaside town; among them a smooth-faced man in sharply tailored white linen who came up to me with civil enquiry. 'Did I want a hotel?' 'The Hotel Rex', I repeated. 'It is mine,' he said.

I was tired, dirty and dishevelled; I looked like a tramp. The Hotel Rex was new and clean, with a certain smartness; only the delicate courtesy of the Greeks to foreigners could have made me feel that I was not merely a welcome but a distinguished guest. A boy of about twelve took me to my room, explained proudly the operation of the electric lights, and made up my bed; one of the industrious, well-mannered and capable little boys who all over Greece are to be found mastering a trade. The Rex had gone to the extravagance of installing a shower, and when I came downstairs to ask about next morning's bus I had bathed and put on a cotton dress which though crumpled was clean. Night had drifted down on Naupaktos with glimmering lights, the hum of voices, the squeal of a distant radio. The little boy was sitting on the steps under the lighted porch, murmuring in his child's voice with a woman servant. Walking up and down outside, an elegant ghost in the darkness, the proprietor was waiting for me.

'Why did you not come sooner?' he said reproachfully. 'I wanted to show you round, I wanted to take you to see the town, but you stayed in your room.' I asked to be taken to the bus-station, and as he guided me through back streets we played the question game. Why was I alone? Where was my husband? He addressed me, I noticed, with the familiar 'thou', and gripped my elbow to emphasize a point of talk. Had I any children? Then, sharply, 'Why not?' For some days I had been planning a reply to this inevitable question. 'God is to blame,' I said, 'not I.' 'Ah,' said my companion darkly, 'That One . . .'

I dined alone at the Ethnikon restaurant. The lamb cutlets were delicately grilled, the beer was iced, and I sat in a haze of scent from some night-flowering creeper. Afterwards I walked through the town – looked at the war memorial, drank a glass of beer at a café, met again my kind adviser on hotels, passed a cinema where, at the end of the summer season, an English film, 'a masterpiece', was being shown: 'Night and the City', with a star whose name, written in Greek as Gkoutzi Gouiders, I deciphered as Googie Withers. At the hotel I asked the woman servant to call me at five to catch the first bus of the day; I was just flopping thankfully into bed when there was a knock. With a blouse over my night-dress and holding a skirt round me (for a dressing-gown is not among the necessities to be carried walking over miles of Greek roads) I went to the door. It was the conscientious proprietor again.

'Why dost thou wish to be called so early? There is no connection at Antirrhion until nine o'clock. Thou wilt sit, two hours thou wilt wait. Take the second bus, there is a connection. Why so early? Why?'

'Whatever thou sayest,' I answered faintly. I shut the door and, too tired to force myself to write the day's encounters in my diary, got back into bed. But before, stunned with air and sun, I fell asleep, I fancied voices complaining. 'God does not wish us to live,' they said; and 'In strangers' houses!'; and 'Will there be war? Art thou sure there will not be war?'

VII

In the café opposite the bus station a radio was playing 'Turkey in the Straw'; at eight in the morning Naupaktos twittered with life. 'She is a foreigner': the travellers were holding the usual conversation. 'But she speaks Greek', said the conductor, and smiled at me. In buses travelling long distances in Greece the passenger buys his ticket in advance and is given a numbered seat; first come, best served. By some confusion I had taken the place reserved by another traveller; when I apologized we fell to talking. He came, he said, from a village on the other side of the Gulf, near Patras; now he was studying medicine in Athens. Did I find Greece much changed? True, he said, at last the country had peace and a chance to improve the conditions of the people, but for how long? Did people in England think there would be war? Would there, would there be war?

He was on his way to Athens, he would cross the Gulf at Antirrhion. There the long slit of sea which cuts Greece almost through from west to east narrows; the promontories of Antirrhion on the north, Rhion on the south, make the passage no more than two kilometres wide. Traffic between Athens and Jannina (which was now my destination) is ferried across the Little Dardanelles, as the channel is called; a steamer would take my neighbour southwards to Rhion and the road eastward to the capital. 'In a quarter of an hour,' he said, 'you will have a bus; you will not have to wait long.' His own ferry was drawing in to the quayside as, after our forty-minute journey, we arrived. With last words of advice, with handshakes and friendly wishes, we said goodbye, and I settled down at a rusty iron table outside a cafeneion to wait.

Antirrhion has a ruined Venetian fort and a scatter of houses, no more. A point of arrival and departure, it lives life in spurts. But the fever of politics and the quick Greek curiosity possess even this desultory place. The boy who brought my coffee opened conversation. A young man sitting on the doorstep in patched clothes and cap joined in; one or two passers stopped to listen; in a few minutes a circle had formed.

'Are you American?'

'No, no, English.'

'English, eh? Tell me, is England richer than America?'

'Indeed no, America is a rich country, much richer than we are; since the war we are poorer still.'

There was a stir of amusement. 'Like us,' said one of the questioners.

'Let me speak the truth,' I said. 'We are not poor as Greece is poor. But we are no longer a rich country.'

'But they give you money to travel? How much does it cost to go to England by airplane? . . . Ah, but it is dear. To Germany it is cheaper; somebody told me how much. Is it cheap living in England, is it cheap?'

'Much dearer than here. In Greece it seems to me that living is cheaper than a few years ago. Are you satisfied, is it a good Government you have now?'

'Good, it is good. The last Government, all thieves they were, everything they ate. But these' (reflectively) 'I do not *think* they steal.'

The doorstep-sitter began to talk of currency exchange and foreign loans, subjects which my vocabulary could not compass.

'I remember,' I said, diverting the conversation, 'when I first came to Greece many years ago, when Pangalos was Prime Minister, they took the notes and cut them, so that a hundred-drachmae note became worth let us say sixty-six drachmae.'

'You remember? And before Pangalos, there was Protopapadakis who tried to get a foreign loan, but he could not, so he made a forced internal loan.'

I looked at the economist in his patched workman's trousers and collarless shirt. He was beginning an argument with the rest of the circle, an argument too quick and I daresay too well-informed for me to follow. I was relieved when at half-past nine the ferry came throbbing and clanking in to rescue me from a conversation I knew I could not sustain, when the bus rolled ashore and I could join the travellers who already that morning had made the long trip from Athens.

My company to Agrinion, the next stage of the journey, would make, I could see, smaller intellectual demands. For the second time that day mistaking my place, I had taken a seat next a window, but I was at once turned out, imperiously, by an old peasant woman, wrinkled, sallow, carrying a cloth bundle.

'I must have the window,' she said.

'Is it thy place? I have made a mistake.'

'I must have the window,' she repeated, 'the car catches me.'

'Oh,' I said vaguely, 'I am sorry.' For the moment I did not understand her phrase. She rested her head against the window, and as the bus began to climb I could hear her sighing and clucking.

'It catches me,' she said again. 'Does it not catch thee?'

'No,' I said, still at a loss. 'No.'

'Ugh, it catches me,' she said. The bus climbed higher, and the worn old face turned a shade yellower.

'Art thou not giddy?' she asked, and now I remembered that to a Greek countrywoman a trip in a mountain bus is like a sea crossing – or rather a journey by air; the conductor keeps a pile of paper bags for emergencies.

'No,' I answered, thankfully. 'I am not giddy.' (The Greek word for the traveller's nausea is most apt.) 'How far art thou going?'

'To Agrinion,' she said, crossing herself. Clearly she found the journey as dangerous as it was uncomfortable. Presently we were in the plain again, and rattling past some hamlet. She roused. 'They say we shall go through Missolonghi,' she remarked. 'I have never been to Missolonghi.'

'Nor I.'

'Was it not at Missolonghi that Byron died, the lord?'

'Yes indeed.'

'I should like to see Missolonghi.' At the next village she crossed herself again. 'Is this Missolonghi?'

'Not yet.'

'Thou wilt tell me when we come to Missolonghi?'

'Certainly.'

'He was a brave one, that Byron, they say.'

'They speak truly.'

Then again, crossing herself, 'Is this Missolonghi?'

'Not yet.'

At last we came to the Aetolian coast, flat, swampy, once fever-haunted, to the town of Missolonghi with its new stucco houses and the long horizontal lines of its lagoon.

'This is Missolonghi.'

The old woman considered. 'They say there is a statue of Byron, the lord; I should like to see it.' She rearranged her cloth bundle, put her hands on her knees, and pushed herself to her feet. Then she said, querulously, 'I have never been to Missolonghi.' And she got out of the bus. There was a halt of five or ten minutes. The passengers stretched themselves, strolled, returned; the driver climbed back into his place. But the old woman did not reappear, and I moved to the seat by the window to look out for her. 'She will come back, the old woman?' I asked a grizzled peasant sitting behind me.

'How should I know? Thou hast her place, so never mind.'

And we sped north across the marshy plain with its reeds and maize-fields without her. One of the travellers asked me if I was German. The heat of my denial must have stirred him, for at Agrinion he put himself out to show me the way to the start for Jannina. I found the bus office in turmoil and the waiting bus surrounded by a shouting crowd. It was midday and, though we all stood in the shadow of the street, faces glistened with heat. Who should be left behind? There was not room for everybody. Haversacks were hoisted to the roof, and tossed back. A policeman remonstrated excitedly with two soldiers. A man in a black homburg stood hopefully balancing a bicycle above his head. Amidst the uproar an old peasant sat unmoved on an upturned basket. He wore, on this dying summer day, a thick knitted vest, a shirt, a pullover, a woollen waistcoat and a jacket. I looked at the box in his hands. It bore a coloured picture of a gun-dog holding the bloody carcass of a bird under his paw; in English I read: SPECIAL CARTRIDGES.

I had a moment's alarm lest I should not find a place, but I need not have fretted. A foreigner, I was led without ado to the front and most favoured seat; the last gesticulating traveller was somehow accommodated; and off we went on the final five-hour stage of the journey. Agrinion, a fair-sized town, is the centre of a rich tobacco-growing district; we drove northwards through tobacco-fields bordered with reeds. In a village on the shore of a lake a panegyris, a festival, was in progress. The square was lined with stalls: pots and pans, glasses, stockings, bales of vivid cottons, ikons, hung, swung, trailed in the sunlight; under the trees on the outskirts crowds sat drinking and singing, their horses tethered in ring after ring. They began yesterday, said my neighbour, a long-faced man with a prim fair moustache, it will go on for several days. What feast is it? I asked. With deliberation he took from his pocket a little paper-covered book and searched the pages. Over his shoulder I could read the title: 'I am the Lamb of God.' But there was no answer; at least he gave me none.

Well-being coloured the landscape for the rest of the afternoon. At Arta, a prosperous-looking town on the river Arakhtos and once a Byzantine city, we made our last halt, the travellers tumbled out, and I was left to my luncheon of biscuits and fruit in the company of a tall, sad-faced man in a cap who, with a respectful gratitude which disturbed me, accepted a packet of biscuits, but instead of eating pocketed them. Then we went north across a plain rich with tobacco, maize and groves of oranges and figs, and into a plane-shaded valley. A friend in Athens, discussing the recovery of Greece after the Occupation and the war with the Communist guerillas, had spoken of hydro-electric schemes which would transform the life of villages in the north, and now at an elbow of the river-gorge we came on the work in progress, the building of a barrage. I took out my map. A passenger borrowed it; yes, we agreed, this was the barrage of the river Louros. It was one of the projects of which I had been told. Here was Greece doing something more than recovering its old life; it was not only Athens which was changing. 'God does not want us to live' – thinking of the poverty by the river Mornos where I had passed twenty-four hours earlier I knew I must not regret the alteration – or the shadow of alteration, for the very flesh of the Greek countryside tenaciously resists the invasion of the contemporary. Into so Greek a frame of mind did I persuade myself that when, after crossing a pass and coming in splendid sight of the lake of Jannina, we were stopped just outside the town at a police control-point, I was half-indignant at being asked to identify myself. Jannina is garrisoned, and its position near the Albanian frontier has made it a strategic centre. But I brushed that aside. I am English, I said, as if that ought to be enough.

'But have you no papers at all?'

'I have a passport,' I said sulkily, and handed the policeman my string bag, which served as hand-bag, to hold while I rummaged in my rucksack. The civility with which he waited till I found my passport, and, bowing, handed it back put me to shame for days.

Rich landscape, busy towns, the solid or the self-contained look of my fellow-passengers – I might have thought the day's journey without shadow. But there is the story still to be told of the man from the islands.

VIII

As we drove along the coast of the Gulf of Arta we had passed in the distance a village of new houses. Behind me in the bus there were sardonic comments: 'My new house!' 'They think a tent is good enough for us . . .'; and during the halt at Arta I realized that the melancholy man whose thankfulness for a few biscuits disquieted me had been one of the speakers. 'You are from Agrinion?' I asked. 'No, I have come from Zakynthos.'

Now I understood the stricken face. This was the first week of October in the year 1953: less than two months since the earthquake which had wrecked three of the Ionian Islands, Levkas, Ithaca and, most murderously, Zakynthos or Zante.

'From Zakynthos? Then' (hesitantly) 'you were there in the earthquake?'

'I was there, indeed I was there.'

'You were not hurt? You suffered nothing?'

'I lost everything I had, my house, clothes, everything was burned . . . ruin, ruin!'

'But you yourself, your family, you were all saved? You were not in your house when it happened?'

'I was by the shore, I was working; you see, I am a longshoreman. Suddenly I hear it, like the end of the world; I look, a great cloud of dust, fire; I run, like a madman I run to my house; the walls, the roof, everything has fallen, my wife and three of my children are buried. I dig, with my hands I dig, I find them, I pull them out; a little longer and they would die, everything is burning, everywhere fire, fire. My wife's mother is still buried; I dig, I dig; I run to find help, the police have nobody, I ask the English, the sailors, they come to my house, for hours we dig, till one in the morning we dig. But there is nothing, nothing.'

'Nothing? You never found her?'

'We found a little bone, charred, nothing else; a bone' (he took hold of his left fist) 'like this, the bone of a hand.' His sad peasant's face under the cap drooped in vertical lines of horror. 'Nothing but a piece of charred bone, nothing.'

Half-ashamed to speak of sympathy with an experience so huge, I could do no more than continue, in the Greek manner, with my questions.

'Without your house, with everything lost, how do you live, you and your family?'

'In tents, they gave us tents. Now that it is still summer we can live. But they have put the tents outside the town in the fields where the ground is soft. When the rains come it is not like here' (waving towards the plain of Arta) 'where you have snow, perhaps, and afterwards nothing; in Zakynthos it may rain for a month without stopping. Then I do not know how we shall live. We are many in a tent, you will see eighteen people sleeping in one small tent. We have no clothes, I have only what I am wearing now; I have only this' (touching a khaki pullover) 'which the English gave me. Already the children are ill, when the winter comes I do not know how we shall live.'

It is the common practice of the poor in Greece when talking to foreigners to speak slightingly of their own people. The British Mediterranean Fleet had indeed come to the rescue of the Ionian Islands. But I was aware also of the resourcefulness of the Greek authorities themselves, overburdened though they already were by the inheritance of war. How great was the effort of self-help I should presently discover. Yet it was not for me to reprove the man from Zakynthos if in his poverty and wretchedness he felt, wrong-headedly, that he was forgotten by his own people.

'You are going to Jannina? You have work there?' I asked.

'I have a child there, a boy, six years old. When the earthquake came, when our house was destroyed, in the first days they took

some of the children to be looked after, some to Athens, others to
various places. The child I speak of they took to Jannina, he is in the
Children's City there. His mother cries, she wants him back, I am
going to fetch him.'

Children's City: I had heard the phrase before without knowing
what it meant. For the moment I passed it over without enquiry.

'Your other children are with you in Zakynthos?'

'Not all. I have a little girl, five years old, they took her to Athens.
I wanted to bring her back too, I thought I would go to Athens, but
I am afraid of not finding her.'

'If they took her to look after her, did they not tell you where
she was?'

'They told me, they wrote, but I am afraid they have moved her.
Sometimes they move the children from Athens, sometimes they
send them to Rhodes, to Macedonia. I said I would fetch the boy
from Jannina, I worked, for two weeks I saved money to pay for the
bus; see, I brought only this to eat on the road' (bringing out a single
rosy apple), 'but now if I go to Athens it is a long journey, I must
have more money, and if I do not find my little girl . . .'

'Surely if they moved her they would let you know?'

'They said they would tell me. Here is the letter; you see, they say
they will write, but I have heard nothing. I am anxious, terribly
anxious.'

I took the letter: typed, official, but reassuring. The address, in a
suburb of Athens, was Paidopolis: the Children's City; and once
again I forebore to ask what it meant.

'The letter says your little girl is well and you need not worry.'

'But that is a month ago, I have heard nothing more. My wife
cries, I don't know what to do.' He took out an identity card. The
photographs showed all his family: himself, his wife, seven children.
'You see,' (the blunt, blackened finger pointed to a child, plump,
indistinct, with fair hair dragged up into a bow), 'the little girl.'

'She is pretty,' I said; then, remembering the necessary ritual
phrase, 'May she live!'

'I am anxious, terribly anxious,' he repeated despairingly. 'My wife wants to have her child back, I don't know what to do. People say the children are not happy; how can I be sure? Perhaps they have taken my little girl away and I shall not be able to find her. How do I know, perhaps they have killed her . . .' His blue eyes filled with tears, and miserably, with the heartrending candour of the poor, he wiped them.

'But no, no,' I said hastily, 'you are mistaken, why do you say such a thing? You have no reason. The letter says your little girl is safe, now you are going to see your little boy; you will find all well.'

At Jannina I watched him get out of the bus and stand, dejected and uncertain, in the empty square. 'You will find all well,' I said again. 'You are going to take your little boy tonight?'

'Yes, if they will let me. The bus leaves early tomorrow.'

'Where will you sleep? You will find a bed?'

'For us it does not matter. We shall find somewhere on the ground.'

'No, that you must not do. Take this, it is not much, for the boy at any rate. When you have found him, come to my hotel and ask for me, so that I shall know all is well. You will come?'

'I will come.' He took my hand and kissed it in the peasant's thanks.

'One thing,' I said, 'I do not understand. You say that in Zakynthos you have no houses, no clothes, you sleep in tents, the rains will come, there will be illness in the winter. Then why do you want to take your children back?'

'If we must die,' said the man from Zakynthos, 'let us die together.'

IX

JANNINA, CAPITAL OF EPIRUS, is as I have said a garrison town. Twenty miles to the north in the direction of the Albanian frontier the country becomes a military area, and since I wanted to penetrate this territory I had been provided by the Press Department with letters of introduction. I went at once to the office of the Nomarch, the Prefect of the Nome or province. But he was out, and I must telephone later. I spent the dusking hour before dinner loitering through the town – past cafés and shops, in public gardens, through the old Turkish quarter which slopes to the lake, and down the long street of the silversmiths. The place is too large to have kept either the curiosity or the friendliness of the market towns, and when I sat down to dine in the Hellas restaurant I felt solitary and out of joint with myself. I had not been able to plan for the morning, I was not sure whether I had chosen rightly in coming to Jannina. At the table on my right was a party of five, men and women, eating and drinking with a more festive and a flashier air than is usual in a Greek provincial restaurant. As I ordered my dinner they looked at me, but reflecting that a foreigner, and a woman dining alone at that, should not stare resentfully back, I occupied myself between courses in writing my day's notes, and tried not to listen to the voices and the laughter. I had finished eating when the waiter came to stand gravely at my side.

'The gentleman,' he said, 'offers you a drink.'

'A drink?' I said, frowning; 'What gentleman?'

'The gentleman at that table.' I turned round; one of the cheerful party was beaming at me.

'I hear you are speaking a little Greek,' he said in English. 'You are American?'

'English,' I said. 'You are from America?'

'Yeah, I come from Massachusetts. This here is my home town, I come to see my family, my friends, then I go back. You let me offer you a little cognac?'

'Thank you very much,' I said, 'that is very kind of you.'

'It's nothing.' His party looked on smiling, delighted by their companion's citizenship of a foreign world, anxious also to show their own goodwill. While I drank my cognac the visitor from Massachusetts told me his story: leaving his native country, working in America, establishing a business and a family; I responded with the directness one learns in Greece; we exchanged names and addresses. When I stood up to leave we shook hands, and with an engaging mixture of American and Greek warmth of manner: 'I am glad to know you, Miss Powell,' he said, 'you are a fine lady.'

At the Acropolis Palace Hotel the man at the desk had messages. The Nomarch had telephoned, and someone was waiting to see me. I looked into the corner of the hall which served as drawing-room. There stood the man from Zakynthos, carrying his cap in his hand. The little boy who hung on the other hand was clean and neat in what I took for some kind of school dress; he looked well cared for, and sad. There were two other people in the room: an elderly man in a lounge suit and a youngish woman wearing uniform of the type which women designed for themselves when they began to take a hand in public life: her official shirt-blouse was heavy with medals. Both were addressing themselves to the man from Zakynthos. Why, they cried, did he not leave the little boy where he would be looked after instead of taking him back to the cold and the rain and the sickness of a winter in tents? The woman's voice rose in sharp educated tones; deferential, stubborn, standing with a peasant's composed stillness, the father answered in his low, murmuring, halting voice; while beside him, holding his hand without moving, the child listened gravely. As I waited the woman was called to the telephone; furiously the elderly man carried on the argument. What lies were these, he shouted, about the children being unhappy? And being killed? Lies, lies, he yelled, standing up and waving his arms. Melancholy, obstinate, the father interposed his apologies and his defence.

At last the argument ended, and I went to greet the man from Zakynthos. The child, at a sign from his father, seized my hand and silently pressed it to his cool soft lips. 'So thou hast found the boy,' I said, 'and I see that he is well. You are going back in the morning?'

'We are going back.'

'And thy little girl in Athens? She is well, thou wilt see, as the boy was well. Is it not better to leave her where she is?'

'I do not know; I do not know what to do.'

'In a few days I shall be in Athens. If thou wishest I will try to find out if she is still there.' I took from his hand the typed, reassuring letter; once again the imploring blue eyes filled with tears. 'I will write; do not worry. I will find her, I will write.'

I watched the two figures going hand-in-hand through the hotel door into the night, the tall father in his peasant's clothes and the little boy in his neat child's uniform. Then I turned with polite sympathy to the man who had been upbraiding.

'You have difficulties,' I said in Greek.

'Difficulties?' He rounded on me, savagely, in English. 'This stupid fool talking about his children being killed! All he wants to do is to take them back to die in a tent. And people who don't know any-anything . . .' He looked at me and snorted.

'But,' I said, still pacifically, 'he is a very simple man.'

'He is not simple at all, he is a fool. Because his wife cries he takes his little boy back where they will have no house, no fire, they will be ill. A fool, a wicked fool,' he shouted. 'All those lies about the children being unhappy . . . And then people who know nothing about it coming here . . .'

Struggling to keep my temper, I went to my room. It was still early, and I knew that I could not sleep yet. For a few minutes I walked up and down by the bed, silently trouncing my opponent in argument. Then I reflected that by my withdrawal it was myself I was defeating; after all I wanted to learn what was to be learned. I stiffened myself and went downstairs again. The uniformed woman had finished her telephoning, and I addressed her inoffensively in English. She was, I presently discovered, a worker for the Queen's Fund, an organization set up by the Queen of Greece during the guerilla war; its main object at that time was to care for children made homeless by the fighting or in danger from the Communist raids in which thousands of boys and girls were being carried off beyond the frontiers of Greece. It was to this end that the Children's Cities of which I had heard were set up: centres where boys and girls were housed, fed, clothed and taught; and it was to this service that the uniformed woman, like many other cultivated Athenians, was dedicated.

For the moment her dedication was getting the better of her; she felt, I fancy, as Florence Nightingale felt when the Irish Catholic nuns got in her way in the Crimea.

'So you know a little Greek, do you?' she said sardonically in excellent English.

A little, I said, sullenly aware that the language I could stammer had been picked up in villages and country taverns and was risible in the ears of an educated woman.

'Indeed. Do you know anything about Greece?' The voice was rapid and aggressive, and I was foolish enough to be exasperated into answering that I knew a great deal about Greece.

'I see; you know a great deal about Greece. Then no doubt you know that this man who was here, this man who took his little boy away, was breaking his word. They all, you know, all the parents, signed a paper agreeing to let their children be looked after for eight months; and now, because his wife cries, he comes and takes the boy away after a few weeks. Selfishness, nothing but selfishness!'

I thought of the agonized blue eyes, the journey without food, the grave, silent child holding his father's hand, and said nothing.

The voice still hectored. 'Do you know anything about the Queen's Fund?'

'No.' For a moment I fought with myself. 'I should like to know,' I said. 'I am interested in the work being done.'

Next day, if I wished, she said, I might visit the Children's City in Jannina. There was, her look added, little hope that it would do me much good. With frosty politeness we parted for the night. They were right, I told myself as, still bristling, I got into bed; she and her companion belonged to the unsentimental servants of Greece who brought practical help instead of the foreigner's romantic notions. Still I could not forget the words of the man from Zakynthos. 'If we must die, let us die together': wrong-headed, credulous, obstinate – and yet, it seemed to me, if the day comes when the peasant and the working man no longer speak in such terms the antique virtues will have gone out of Greece.

I had to read the *Guide Bleu* until two in the morning before I could compose myself to sleep.

X

Aᴜᴛᴜᴍɴ ᴛʜʀᴇᴀᴛᴇɴᴇᴅ ᴇᴀʀʟʏ that year, and I was awakened at half-past seven next morning by cold and rain spitting through the open window. But when I set off once more for the Nomarch's office the streets were hot. The Nomarch received me with informal kindness and the desire to give practical help which is so often a characteristic of the authorities in Greece. 'Where did I want to go in Epirus?' 'Northwards towards the frontier', I said; 'I should like to see something of the devastation of war, something of the rebuilding; but since I had never been in Epirus before I should like his advice.' An interpreter was brought. But I battled on in Greek, only to be paid out for my conceit by the arrival of a group of high officials of the Queen's Fund – one of them, I believe, was the President – who formed a waiting audience. Among them I recognized with mortification my opponent of the night before; I was the more shamed since she joined her companions in listening with an encouragement which was civil as well as friendly. My rout was complete when I had to admit that I was spending no more than a single day in visiting Epirus, a province roughly half the size of Wales and given by its sufferings in the war against the Communists and its situation on the Albanian frontier a unique place in Greek feeling.

A route was planned for my derisory day. I should go north, as near the frontier as possible, to a village called Ktismata; on my way back I should see Asprangheli, one of the rebuilt villages. The Nomarch's personal assistant, sent to help me in getting a military and diplomatic pass and finding a suitable taxi-driver, urged his willingness to come with me and interpret. 'No,' I said, 'I would rather go alone, question, however inadequately, for myself, and see with my own eyes.' A little before midday off we drove, north over the plain of Jannina.

'We will eat on the way,' I said to the driver. His name was Pericles. 'We shall find a restaurant somewhere?'

'At Kalpaki.' Kalpaki: the name is famous in Greece. Ancient Epirus included the southern part of what is now Albania, and since the Balkan Wars, when the district of Jannina was brought within their border and Albania became a state, the Greeks have laid claim to what they call Northern Epirus. At Kalpaki the road divides. Ahead are the two routes from Albania into Greece; the fork is a strategic point. In 1940 the army held its ground here against Italy and presently drove the invaders back. And in 1947 when Markos and the Communists failed to take Konitsa they turned south to Jannina; at Kalpaki they met a Government force moving north and were routed. A little before we came to Kalpaki my driver pointed to the right of the road. There is the hill where the army stood in the autumn of 1940, and a little farther on the hill from which they attacked; with the national sense of gesture the Greeks have marked out on a slope a huge white ὄχι, their word for No! It is their No to Mussolini, the No with which on October 28 Metaxas answered the Italian ultimatum; it is their *Ils ne passeront pas*. But the Greeks still wait for their lost province. At the fork, where we turned left towards Ktismata and the frontier, I saw a roughly painted notice, bitter reminder of disappointed hopes: 'To Free Epirus', and a backward-pointing arrow; an arrow pointing forward, 'To Epirus which waits for freedom'.

The tavern was amiable, dirty, fly-bitten and crowded with police, or rather gendarmerie, for in Greece, as in France, the town and country police are distinct from one another. I told Pericles to choose his lunch and asked for an omelette and cheese for myself. 'Will you have an ouzo?' I said. It was an idle formality. He was already ordering drinks not only for himself and for me but for a friend among the local police, and when those were done he called, without further reference to me, for another round. This masculine authority was reflected in the talk which went on over my head.

'Who is she?' someone would ask as he passed our table.

'She is a foreigner,' Pericles would answer, 'a journalist from England. She knows a little Greek but' (with a disparaging look) 'not much.'

At last amidst rough, benevolent cries from the company we went back to the car. 'To Ktismata,' I said. Kalpaki is about twenty miles north-west of Jannina, Ktismata lies perhaps ten miles on to the west. The road, a wild stony track, serpents through bleak hills; the soil is sullen with the memory of battle; not a living creature except a few soldiers at border posts and a sentry to whom I showed my military pass. Ktismata is one of the last villages before the frontier. The hills beyond it are Albania, the valley into which it peers is Albanian. Of the original village nothing remains. War has washed it all away: war with Italy, when the enemy came in from Albania, war with the symmorites, the Communists. Yet people have crept back, striking shallow roots.

The village is a thin circle on the rim of a hill. In the centre there is a large, flat open space; driving across this, we came to a little white-washed house. When it was decided that I should visit Ktismata my acquaintance of the Queen's Fund gave me a letter of introduction; I was to take it to the Children's House. 'What is the Children's House?' I asked. 'Another branch', I was told, 'of the work of the Queen's Fund.' In villages where the people had suffered to the limits of endurance and the children had been deprived of common education, centres had been established to teach and help. The white-washed cottage I saw now was the Children's House, and on the doorstep, brought out by the commotion of our arrival, stood the girl in charge.

On the afternoon I found her Miss K. had company, for the doctor who goes the round of the district, staying two days in each village, was on a visit to Ktismata. The rest of the days and weeks she was isolated, a gentle, sensitive, educated girl of perhaps twenty-five among peasants whose whole energies were spent on surviving. Attachment to social service may produce nothing more than condescension. But devotion is always touching, and Miss K.'s devotion was complete. We sat talking in the Children's House, a cheerful little village building, its whitewashed walls hung with simple picture-lessons and texts. A group of children, boys and girls, perched together on a bench. They looked thin but cared for, shy but ready to smile. 'What do you do here in the Children's House?' I asked when we were alone. 'We make a beginning,' said Miss K.

'For the older people there is often little we can do. Their sufferings have taken the heart out of some of them, brutalized others. But we can try to save the children, look after their health, teach them the elements, give them an idea of duty and honour.'

In the open ground at the centre of the village a party of boys were digging. As we walked by, Miss K. called to them, and they greeted us in chorus.

'They had,' she said, 'to be taught even their "good day".'

'What are they doing?'

'They are making a garden to grow vegetables; I have seed for them to plant. I have bought them rabbits to breed from too, so that they will have meat sometimes.'

We crossed the plateau to the quarters of the older boys and girls. In the girls' house there was sewing and weaving – 'And I teach them,' she said, 'to make jams and preserves.' The boys' house was busy with carpentry. 'They are making window-frames for the houses; to buy these would cost 100,000 drachmae' – that is, twenty-five shillings.

'But tell me, if the village was quite destroyed, how has it been rebuilt?'

'With money borrowed from the Government. Many of the loans have not been repaid yet. As you can see, there is scarcely any work to be found here. A few families earn a little by lime-burning, but only a few; it is the bottom of poverty. The people live on maize, onions, bread, perhaps twice a year they eat meat. And they are always afraid.'

'Afraid?'

'You see those houses over there on the ridge? That is a village which stands exactly on the frontier. But nobody lives there now.

All the inhabitants have been carried off to Albania. Here in Ktismata the men go out every night with their rifles, they keep watch for raiders from across the border. There is no peace, no safety. Any night the raiders may come.'

Miss K. looked at me with soft, dark-fringed eyes. 'Would you like to go into some of the houses? . . . Then if I may make a suggestion, perhaps it would be better for you to visit not the best, where they have a little comfort, but the worst houses where they have nothing, so that you can get an idea . . .'

We turned our backs on the promise of the children and walked over the rim of the hill.

'This first house,' she said, 'is a good house, that is to say there is a grandmother who does what she can. May we come in?' she asked the child at the door. From the pale October afternoon we went into darkness: a single-roomed house, naked, smelling of hunger. An old woman sat on a bench of splintering board; on her knees she held a bundle with eyes.

'Is the baby better?' said Miss K.

The grandmother greeted us with dignity. 'She is the same,' she said, 'I do not know what to do.' Beyond her something moved in the dark: a cluster of children, a boy of about seven and two little knuckle-biters in skirts.

'Has she any fever?' said Miss K., and she laid her hand on the baby's forehead. Then to the boy: 'Thou hast a good grandmother.'

'Yes indeed,' said the boy, smiling. He stood at the door and saluted us with gravity as we left. 'Here at least,' said Miss K., 'the children have their grandmother. But usually it is like everywhere else in the country in Greece, the women not only do all the work of the house, they work in the fields as well; there is nobody to look after the children.'

In the next house the mother was at home. 'How is the baby?' said Miss K. again.

'I am afraid,' said the woman, 'I am afraid he will die.' In the middle of the room on a piece of sacking stood a little wooden box. She uncovered it and disclosed the child in his cradle. 'I am afraid,' she repeated; 'have you' (looking at me) 'no medicine you can give me?' The child was the colour of lard, and sweating; he was swaddled. 'He is a year and a half,' said Miss K. to me, 'but he can hardly walk.'

'Have you no medicine?' said the mother again. 'I am afraid, I am afraid, he will not live, he will die.'

'We have refugees too in Ktismata,' said Miss K. as we walked away. 'They are Greeks from across the border, from Northern Epirus. In the house you will see now there is an old couple who fled after the war with the symmorites.'

The house had two rooms. In a corner of one sat an old man with the stillness of long years. Greeting us, his voice mourned on a high note. His wife was mixing flour and water to make the kind of pie called *pitta*. The room was stifling, full of smoke from a fire of sticks.

'I have brought a visitor,' said Miss K., 'a journalist from England.' The old woman wiped her hands on her skirt and welcomed us cheerfully. She was tall, hawk-faced, brown-skinned, even in her squalid and dreadful rags a human being full of spirit. 'Eh,' she said, shouting, 'thou hast come far, far thou hast come.'

'Very far,' I said. 'And thou, thou hast come across the border, from Albania?'

I could not fully understand her answers, but Miss K. translated into Greek within my reach. 'They come from a village' (she waved towards the hills) 'over there, it is a few miles away, you could almost see it. There is no communication, nothing. Yet it is only a few miles.'

In a corner of the hot, buzzing, smoky room something rattled. I looked round, but I could see nothing, only a little box. It rattled again, and the old woman bent to take off the cover. A baby lay inside, thrashing restlessly with its arms. 'It is her grandchild,' said Miss K.

'Has she any relations in Albania?'

Again the incomprehensible story was shouted, and again Miss K. translated. 'She left some of her family behind, but she has no news, she doesn't know whether they are alive or dead. Yet it is only a few miles.'

I looked at the old, self-reliant, vital face, and saw with pain that tears were beginning to shine in its dark wrinkles.

'I do not understand why we must suffer so much, sometimes I begin to lose faith. Perhaps,' said the old woman, dropping her voice as if she might be overheard, 'perhaps God has forgotten us.'

'But no,' said Miss K. 'Thou must not say that. God does not forget, none of us does He forget. Thou art a good woman, well thou workest, well thou carest for thy family. God knows it, He will not forget thee.'

'I do not know,' said the old woman, wiping her cheeks with bony knuckles, 'how do I know?'

As I went out into the clean afternoon, 'Why did she come?' I could hear her asking, 'Why?'

On the way back to the car I was bewildered by the addresses of a grizzled brown man who stood in the path, streaming complaints and requests. 'I do not understand'; I turned helplessly to Miss K. 'Why,' she said, 'do you ask this lady? She knows nothing about it.' The brown man looked at me. 'But are you not,' he said, naming the official of the Queen's Fund, my attacker of the night before, 'are you not Mrs A.?'

Glad to escape, still pierced by the eyes of poverty, I summoned Pericles, who was playing cards and came unwillingly, and we turned for home. We had company; the cook from the Children's House needed to see a doctor in Jannina and I had promised to take her there; and presently we had more, for at a turn in the road Pericles, beside whom for conversation's sake I was sitting, suddenly pulled up, yelled to a couple of gendarmes who with slung rifles were climbing down from the hillside, and invited them into the back of the car. It is common for the driver of a hired car in the country in Greece to give a lift to his friends, and normally it would be surly to protest. But remembering that this was not the first time Pericles had made free with my hospitality I interrupted him as he shouted over his shoulder to ask where the newcomers wanted to go. I was sorry at once. The gendarmes, who clearly had taken me for the driver's mate, apologized with graceful good manners and would have backed out had I not myself urgently invited them; we drove on in embarrassed silence.

It was nearly six o'clock when we set them down. Sunset was drawing the shades over the crests and, looking at a landscape grown chill, I wondered if I had heart for another sad village. At this moment Pericles suddenly swung off the main road and along a track climbing into the darkening hills. 'Where art thou going?' 'To Asprangheli, of course.' 'But I did not tell thee to go to Asprangheli; dost thou never wait to be told?' It was unreasonable of me, for he must have been instructed by the Nomarch's office, and in any case it had been my purpose to see as much as I could. On reflection, then, I said we would go on. We climbed towards the melancholy heights.

Ravaged Epirus has, where the battle passed, villages of three kinds: those formerly destroyed by the Germans and the Italians; those wrecked by the symmorites; and there are entirely new villages built for the refugees from Northern Epirus since the end of the war with the Communists. Asprangheli, as I could see when we drove up, is an old village rebuilt. It was the evening hour, the hour of charcoal scent and small lights in doorways, and children were playing under the huge plane tree which shadows the plateia. Grinding up by car, and at dusk, to a village with no through road, I could hardly pretend to be a casual traveller stopping for a drink. 'Stop here,' I said, 'and wait for me.' My arrival had been hamperingly conspicuous, and I was unsure of my next step as I got out and walked across the square.

With relief I saw a light glimmering under the sign of a cafeneion, and a man coming out to the iron tables and chairs to serve. I asked for coffee. But almost before I had sat down a figure was hurrying towards me with signs of greeting. It was the proedhros, the village president, who felt it his business to welcome a stranger.

A countryman of warm good manners and easy conversation, he proudly summoned for my benefit two villagers who had lived in

America. It is often easier to struggle on in Greek than to follow the English of a man who learned it in, say, Detroit thirty years ago and has scarcely spoken it since. But it would have been unkind to undermine their reputation as linguists. I questioned in English, and their prowess in response was admired by a group now grown to four or five.

'Your village,' I said, 'what happened to it? Was it destroyed in the war?'

'They burn our village,' said one of them, 'Germans burn it.'

'Nineteen forty-three,' the other supplied, 'ten year ago, burn everything, houses, everything.'

'But you have new houses. Did you build them yourselves?'

'We build; the Government give us some material, not all; we build.'

'So you have a new village. Are you satisfied? Are you,' I repeated in Greek, 'satisfied with your new village?'

'Yes,' said the proedhros, 'but the houses are for necessity.' (In English I suppose we should say they were utility.) 'They are not like our old houses. All the same the Government helped us, we have built a new village. We are satisfied.'

While we talked, men were strolling in twos and threes across the plateia, and several paused at the cafeneion to shake hands with the visitor. As usual the conversation turned to politics: the Government, measures of reconstruction, the personalities of the Cabinet. I had the impression of a village turning its back on the disasters of the past and stirring with hope and energy; I was sorry to say goodbye.

'How much for the coffee?' I asked. The proedhros waved me aside. 'That is for us,' he said. As I left the village, animals were being herded homewards: goats and a few cattle. Asprangheli was fortunate in having its barns stocked. But I could not forget Ktismata, spread-eagled on the rim of danger, stubbornly suffering, fighting to breathe. Probably my lugubrious thoughts showed in my face. At any rate Pericles, who in the pleasure of homegoing was singing to himself, broke off with a reminder of my earlier rebukes.

'Perhaps,' he said in an injured voice, 'perhaps you don't want me to sing either?'

'No, no,' I said. 'Sing, please sing; I like it.'

And so it was to the tune of some Epirot love-song that we rattled back to the lights of Jannina.

XI

I<small>N HIS LAST</small> year or two Humfry had often talked of walking over the Pindus range. The Pindus, running southward from Albania, cuts northern Greece in two; plains stand on either side. Humfry wanted to start from the Albanian coast, strike into Greece, and cross the range to the plain of Thessaly on its eastern side. We never made the expedition, and I had not thought of doing it alone. In any case since the war there had been little chance of going for a walk in Communist Albania. But when the idea of visiting Epirus had seized me I remembered. I could not begin at the coast, and I had no hope of struggling as far as Thessaly, for I should have no more than a single day for walking. But I might undertake part of the journey. Jannina and its lake lie in one of the plains which flank the Pindus on the west; the foothills are within a few miles. And Metsovo in the heart of the Pindus is only sixty kilometres away by road – less than forty miles: Metsovo which holds the key to Greece, since it commands three vital passes, to Epirus, to Thessaly and to Macedonia. The Italians in 1940 made a drive through Albania towards Metsovo but were held. In 1941 the Germans reached it and were irresistible. The name had for me a dark, mountain-echoing sound. I planned, then, to turn eastward from Jannina, cross the Pindus via Metsovo, and so circle back again to Athens.

There were, I learned, buses from Jannina to Metsovo. But I wanted to walk, to talk to people on the road, to take my time and feel in my feet and lungs the mountains which to my imagination had seemed so romantic. On the other hand I did not aspire to walking forty miles, and light as my rucksack was I did not want to carry it. In the evening after my return from Ktismata I went to the bus station to see what could be done.

The ticket-clerk, a ginger, collarless man with a face like a bristly plum, was working behind a table in the corner of a cafeneion. At my approach he stood up civilly and showed anxiety to help. Was there I asked, a bus to Metsovo early in the morning?

'Certainly, at seven. Do you want a ticket?'

'Let me think,' I said. 'Did the bus make a stop somewhere about ten or fifteen kilometres from Jannina, at the edge of the plain perhaps?'

A little mystified, 'At the fifteenth kilometre,' he said.

I reflected. If I got down at the fifteenth kilometre I should be forty-five kilometres from Metsovo: about twenty-seven miles, a possible walk but not one to which I cared to be irrevocably committed.

'Are there other buses?'

'There are three buses a day, in the morning, at midday and at four in the afternoon. Do you prefer to go by one of the later buses?'

'No, by the early one. But wait a minute. Let us say that I get down at the fifteenth kilometre and walk a little way along the road. When the midday bus comes, shall I be able, if I want it, to get a place on it?'

'Yes indeed, I will tell the driver.'

'But I am not certain. Perhaps when the midday bus passes I shall not want to take it. Shall I find a place on the afternoon bus too?'

Three or four of the customers in the cafeneion had left their tables and now stood in a circle round us, listening. The ticket-clerk looked at them in a savage appeal for sympathy.

'I will tell the driver of the afternoon bus too,.I will tell all the drivers.'

'One other thing. Can one send luggage, a bag perhaps, by the bus?'

'Of course, you can take whatever you wish.'

'But if I am not travelling myself? I mean, can I leave my luggage on the bus and call for it at Metsovo?'

'Certainly, you will find it at the office at Metsovo. Then you do not want a place on the bus?'

Fascinated, the listeners pressed in, and others came to look over their shoulders. 'Yes, yes,' I said, 'but only to the fifteenth kilometre. There I shall get down, but I want to leave my luggage to go without me to Metsovo. Perhaps when the midday bus passes I shall take it, perhaps the afternoon one; I do not know; it depends. But when I get to Metsovo I shall find my luggage waiting? You are sure?'

'I am sure.' He took a long breath. 'Then you want a ticket to the fifteenth kilometre?'

As I paid I preened myself on conveying a complicated project. I had, I felt, done pretty well, and I hoped somebody would agree with me. 'It is difficult,' I said, falsely modest, 'for me to explain all this. You must forgive my bad Greek.'

Silence. Then 'Eh,' said one of the listeners, 'thou didst not learn it well.'

XII

Aftea such a parley it was with a nervous tightness in the chest
that I began the day. When I was called the sky was slate. But it was
only five o'clock, and as I walked an hour or so later through the
hollow streets I thought the light was quickening. I watched my
rucksack being lashed with the other luggage under a tarpaulin on
top of the bus. I had crammed into it everything I had except my
string bag, in which I carried a plastic mackintosh, a packet of biscuits,
some chocolate, cigarettes and two ring-shaped rolls which I bought
from a hawker at the bus-stop. Although the season was late the
weather I had so far enjoyed encouraged me to expect that the sun
would soon break through. In a cotton dress, tennis shoes and socks
I was equipped for a hot day.

The bus swung off through the outskirts of Jannina and round the
lake, and began to zigzag up the mountain-side. At the fifteenth
kilometre it halted, and I got out. One or two houses overlooked the
road. A group of passengers who had come to their journey's end
waited for their luggage to be untied, then disappeared into their
homes. The bus drove on, and I began to walk. Startled faces looked
back at me from its windows, and several people ran out from the
houses to gape. But in a few moments I was out of their sight round
a bend, trudging with my string bag.

The road ran along wild slopes tumbled with dark scree and
cracked at the elbows with water-courses. Rivulets leaped secretly
in their chimneys and hissed down to the valley. I could not see the
tops of the hills; the early light had cheated me, and now the sky
scowled. The view was all black and grey: black mountains, grey
clouds, grey rocks, and presently, splashed down the slope above me,

a herd of black goats. After I had gone two or three miles I saw the dust on the road dented with light rain. I put on my mackintosh, and I was wearing it when an old shepherd with a crook came climbing up to the road.

'What material is that?' he said, pinching the plastic as we passed the time of day. 'Does it cost much? The rain does not come through?'

I gave him three cigarettes, was much thanked, and went on in the chilly morning. The road plunged downwards, swerving round the mountain curves. A lorry came grinding behind me and pulled up.

'Where are you going? Do you want to get in?'

'Thank you,' I said, 'I prefer to walk a little.'

Half an hour later it was a man and a girl in a Red Cross van who stopped to offer me a lift.

'Thank you, I am all right. Perhaps I shall take the bus when it passes, but I want to see a little of the country first.' And persuaded at last that there was nothing to be done with a mind so deranged they drove on.

At about ten o'clock I came to the twenty-fifth kilometre and the bottom of the descent, to a few houses, a river and a bridge. I sat for a few minutes in the cafeneion, drinking an ouzo, eating my rolls and looking at the muddy, hurrying river. Then I went on, counting the kilometres. It was raining steadily. But for once I had escaped the despair which usually seizes me in the first miles of a long walk and urges me to give up then and there. The cool soaking air made walking easy, and when another lorry overtook me I was not tempted to accept a lift.

'But where are you going?' said the astonished driver.

'To Metsovo,' I said, and went through my recital about the bus.

'Alone you are going?'

'As you see I am all right, I like it.'

'But it is raining, you will get wet.'

'Never mind, I have my mackintosh, the rain doesn't come through.'

'We are going to Volos,' urged the driver. Volos is far on the opposite side of Greece, one of the eastern harbours. It was as if someone a few miles east of Manchester had encountered a stranger tramping to Buxton and had offered a lift to Skegness.

'Thank you, you are very kind, thank you very much, but I must walk a little and see the country.'

'As you wish,' said the driver at last, shrugging his shoulders. 'Then goodbye and a good journey!' And he clashed into gear and rattled on.

It was about midday when I came to my next pause, a few houses and a shop at the thirty-eighth kilometre. There was a cafeneion. I went in, took out my biscuits and chocolate and asked for an ouzo. In the interior gloom I could see figures sitting at a table by the wall, silent; beyond them, the open door and the road-ruts filling with ochre mud; the air had the smell of rain seeping through thick peasant cloaks. The strangers watched me with painful curiosity, and to end their torment I gave them the chance of opening conversation by offering round my chocolate. Where have you come from? Where are you going? On foot and in the rain? Yes indeed, in England we have much rain, at this season and in the summer too. 'Much rain and no ouzo,' I added; and flighted no doubt with my modest drink I decided to walk on through the afternoon.

'The midday bus from Jannina will stop here?' I said to the boy who served me. 'Thou wilt see the driver? He may expect to find me here, for I told them in Jannina to ask him to look out for me on the road. Wilt thou tell him that the Englishwoman who came by the morning bus has gone on, walking? I will take the last bus instead, in the afternoon. How much for the ouzo?' I added.

One of the cloaked strangers interrupted. 'We offer you the ouzo,' he said.

'But no, that is not right; this is a cafeneion.'

'Never mind, since it is your first visit here we offer it you.'

'Thank you, I shall remember. Some day I hope I shall come back.'

I had not gone a mile along the flat of the valley where the road now led when I heard hooves trotting smartly behind me, and a minute or two later a man riding a mule pulled up at my side. He was wearing a cap too large for him, pulled down so as almost to cover the back of his head. Black hair curled round his nape, and the wide jutting peak of the cap shadowed a young, dark, triangular face with high cheekbones, a neat moustache, a round chin smooth-shaven, brilliant teeth and an expression sharper than is common among country Greeks. The teeth flashed.

'You are going to Metsovo?'

'Yes. And you?'

'I too am going to Metsovo. If you wish we can go together, you can ride the mule.'

'Thank you, I do not want to ride.'

'Why not? It is a long way to Metsovo, you will be tired. It is a good mule.'

'Thank you, I like walking.'

'Never mind, I will keep you company. Give me your bag, I will carry it.' And he began trotting beside me.

It was indeed a good mule, and I wondered how long I could keep up the spanking pace. The midday bus overtook us and splashed into the distance. 'Eeeeh!' cried my companion in the muleteer's ascend-ing scale, cheering his animal on; 'Soo, Soo!' My pride would not let me fall behind.

'Thou goest well,' said my companion, dropping into the familiar address, 'well thou goest.' But at the end of the valley he jumped down. 'Now thou must ride.' I was reluctant, for walking kept me warm in the grey rain, but he insisted, and for half a mile I jogged along, listening to the creak of the pack-saddle and smelling the wet animal smell of the mule; the rain, sliding under the hood of my mackintosh, oozed down my neck. My companion, separated from his mount, was diminished. I saw him now as a small man; his coat, ragged and, like his cap, too big for him, dragged round his ankles; the dark, eager face bent towards the road, he trudged behind me with the countryman's short, steady, unresilient step.

'Why dost thou go to Metsovo?' he asked, bending back his head to look up and blinking in the rain.

'It is my job; I am a journalist.'

'A journalist, eh?' The sharp eyes turned in the smiling face. 'But why dost thou go on foot?'

'I must see the country. I must see how things are going in Greece.'

He broke into a run to catch up with the mule. 'Once I met two men who were looking at the country to make a map. They were concerned with geography. Art thou perhaps the same?'

I was thankful for a suggestion which so persuasively explained my irrational journey. 'The same,' I said.

I was miserably cold. My feet, as I sat sideways on the pack-saddle, had no cover from the rain, which soaked steadily through my socks and canvas shoes, and the mackintosh felt like iced treacle against my cotton dress. 'I must get down,' I said, 'do thou ride.'

'Later, perhaps; now we will walk together.'

The road climbed through a landscape softer than I had seen that day, with deciduous trees turning and trembling in the wind.

'At the village up there I have a cousin.'

'What is thy name?'

'Baos, Manoli,' he said, in Greek fashion giving his surname first. 'And thine?' He walked with a dogged stride, leading the mule and leaning against the rain and the slope of the road. I should have liked to make a better pace, for by now some obstinacy had made me decide to let the afternoon bus go when it overtook me and walk all the way to Metsovo. But I was committed to my company. Slowly we beat our way uphill.

The village, when we came to it, turned out to be a house or two and a cafeneion. We stopped to drink coffee, for which Manoli refused to let me pay. I was the less able to insist since his talk with the man who served us was in a language I could not understand; I caught only one single word which I took to mean Englishwoman.

'What language is that you are speaking?'

'It is Vlach. I am not Greek, I am a Vlach, and my cousin the same.'

We walked up the road to a house where a woman with flat-cheeked, smiling face was waiting on the steps: 'My cousin.' Struggling with my impatience to be away, I shook hands with the cousin, her husband, a friend, and a boy of about ten. 'Would I like to see her house?' 'Yes indeed: gladly.' A striped rug was spread on the wooden floor, four cushions were ranged against the wall. 'Here we sleep, all the family,' she said, laughing. In the corner stood a cradle. I should, as at Ktismata, have said a box, a bundle of cloth, but there was the baby, its head and body completely covered from air and light. A few weeks earlier Roxane Sedgwick had taught me a ritual to be observed with babies – for simply to admire a child is to invite misfortune, perhaps even to cast a spell. 'May he not suffer the evil eye,' I said, and spat. I was gratified to find that the gesture was received without surprise.

'How many languages do you speak?' said the boy when we came out.

A little startled, I reflected. 'Let us say three,' I answered. 'I speak French and a little Greek, and of course English; and,' I added vaingloriously, 'I used to know a little German, but I have forgotten it.'

'That is four languages,' said the boy. 'Languages are good. We,' he went on, as one not wishing to boast, 'we have two languages.'

'At home,' I asked Manoli as we walked on, 'do you speak Greek?'

'No, we speak Vlach. Greek I learned at school.'

'From where dost thou come, from what place?'

'From Metsovo. We are many, we Vlachs, in these parts.'

'Art thou married? What is thy work there?'

'Bah, I am still young. I live with my family, my father is a blacksmith. But I do not like the work. I am a musician.'

'A musician?'

'Yes, I play the fiddle. I have it with me.' He waved towards a package bumping against the mule's flank. 'I go round with two or three others, we play at weddings and feasts. Yesterday there was a wedding at the village above the place on the road where I met you, that is why I am travelling. My father does not like me to go away and play the fiddle, he wants me to work with him as a blacksmith. But I want to be a musician.'

'With that work canst thou live?'

'There are many weddings and feasts, but not enough. I want to go to Athens, I could play in a taverna perhaps, one can make much money. But my father will not let me.' The triangular face flashed its gipsy smile.

The brief sweetness was gone from the landscape now. The road wound along black melancholy hills; on our right the valley was drowned in the rain. I was half-drowned too. We moved at a crawl, and to distract myself from discomfort and fatigue I encouraged Manoli to talk.

'Thou art not afraid, then, travelling alone? Tell me, kyria Nteelees, how didst thou know when I first spoke that I was not a thief, that I was not going to rob thee?'

I refrained from pointing out that we were on a main road frequented by buses and lorries, and that after my explanation at Jannina and along the route there was probably not a living soul within miles who was unaware of my transit. 'I know,' I said. 'From the face of a man, I know.'

'That is true, well thou sayest. With the eyes' (he used a phrase strange to me) 'with the eyes one cuts a man.' I saw him frown as he thought. 'But those are fine words. Supposing a shepherd attacked thee? There are rascals everywhere. I tell thee, once my sister was in Kalambaka, she went to find an acquaintance, she asked at a house, and some rascal, he said he would show her the way, instead he took her far off to a ravine, a desert it was, with difficulty she escaped . . .'

We plodded on. Once my companion's delicacy urged him to bid me go on ahead. I loitered, shivering, beyond the next bend. At last Manoli followed with his mule, holding the reins in a fist pressed against the small of his back. Bent forward, zigzagging, with his giant cap pulled low and the wind wrapping his long, ragged coat tightly round him, he looked like the poor wayfarer in some dreadful fairy-tale. But when he caught me up his protuberant eyes shone with interest.

'Thou hast no children? None at all? Eh, perhaps thou dost well, with children there is nothing but trouble, one must feed them, clothe them.' For several minutes we walked in silence. Suddenly: 'To have one child or perhaps two is good. When a man dies he is gone, he is forgotten. But if he has children his name does not die with him. For that reason it is good to have children, so say I.

'Yes, brothers I have as well as sisters. One of my brothers was killed by the andartes, another was taken but he escaped. Me they did not catch, I was a soldier, I was in the army when we fought against the andartes, the Communists. Here at Metsovo there was a battle, the andartes were on one side of the valley, the army was on the other side, a long time it lasted. At night the andartes came down to the village to get food. But us soldiers, they brought us food by airplane. Thou wilt see the place where we lay out on the mountain.

'In the army I learned to smoke, but not then, long before, in '41, when I was a prisoner. The Germans had us all together, Greeks, Serbs, I don't know who. They put barbed wire round us, there were towers with guards; it was at Salonika, I was there for six months. We were hungry, people used to throw bread over the barbed wire for us. Some of the Serbians were good, they shared their bread with me, and there it was I learned to smoke.'

The afternoon bus went past us with a soft spattering of wheels in gravel; the light turned from pale to dark grey. The road still climbed, swinging right and left in monotonous bends. Inside the folds of the mountain there was cover from the north. But as we turned the outside elbows the wind sprang at us with bared teeth. We heeled over under its weight, then staggered on with faces contorted by the cold. Manoli turned his cap like a shield against the knives of rain. Under it his eyes, opened so wide that pupils and whites were visible in profile, glittered with fantasy. The stories, half-heard, half-blown away down the streaming slopes, grew more grandiose.

'. . . A German, an officer,' I caught as it blew. 'He says to me: Thou art a Communist, he says. No, say I. Lies, says he, certainly thou art a Communist. No, say I, no, I am not a dirty Communist. And for that they beat me with a stick' (letting go the reins in his enthusiasm and holding his fists together) 'as thick as this.

'But I was never afraid of men, never. Only one thing did I fear: mines. Always I was afraid of mines. But men, never.

'At the end of the war, I mean the war with the andartes, we all wanted to go on. All the boys were ready. On into Albania! we shouted. But they did not let us, I don't know why.

'Liberty or death, that was my saying. Liberty or death!'

For a mile or so – perhaps it was less than a mile; by then I was incapable of judging – I was deprived of the distraction of talk. 'This way,' said Manoli, 'it is nearer'; and we left the road for a track which, instead of zigzagging upwards, was cut round the shoulder of a hill. The path in the rain was a purgatorial mixture of sharp stones and mud; it was often too narrow for more than single file; slithering, trembling with cold, I went ahead. I had no idea how much farther we had to go, for I had long since lost count of distances. Anyhow it was useless to try to hurry Manoli, stumbling fifty yards behind with his beast. Reason told me that we were on one of the mule-tracks, older than any metalled road, which shorten the last approaches to almost every village in the mountains. But it was past six o'clock and almost dark, and I was beginning to doubt at last if I should ever see Metsovo.

'There, it appears,' called Manoli. It was only then, staring down-hill in the dusk at a grey huddle of houses like dark wet feathers lining a nest, that I remembered Metsovo would not be a cheerful modern town with bright streets and hot baths.

But at least it would have walls and roofs against the wind and the rain. At the entrance to the village (for it is scarcely more) Manoli and I parted, he to lead his snorting mule down a sodden hillside to his home, I to drive myself the last hundred yards to a hotel. With rat-tail hair dripping under the hood of my mackintosh I must have given a passable impersonation of a witch, and thinking back I am not surprised that two children, catching sight of my socks coated with yellow mud, my cotton skirt sticking to bare legs purple with cold, should have pointed and burst into screams of laughter. At the moment I was too wretched to see the joke. Had I been Elisha I should certainly, like the prophet when rudely addressed as a bald-head, have summoned a couple of bears to teach the young a lesson. As it was I could only turn on the mockers with angry rebukes, incorrectly framed in an accent which merely sharpened their enjoyment. Scowling and muttering, I went on. And once again I was to feel ashamed of my ill-temper when a village policeman first showed me the way to the cafeneion which was the bus station, and then when my rucksack, object of so much planning, was found safe and waiting, carried it for me across the plateia to the inn.

I was made ashamed, too, of my doubts of Metsovo itself. 'From Jannina you have come, from Jannina? You have walked?' cried the woman in the inn. 'But why did you not take the bus? You are wet to the bones!' There was a hospitable bustle which had an echo of eighteenth-century travel: hot water fetched, an extra towel to rub my feet, a pair of slippers lent me. I tore off my cold glutinous clothes. But my teeth were still chattering when, in a dry dress and sweater, I went to ask for food. The woman was cooking in a kitchen which, in the Greek taverna manner, opened out of the restaurant with its stained table-clothes on bare, splintered wooden tables.

'Come and warm yourself by the fire, see, I will bring you a chair. I am glad you have come. There is a foreigner, a Frenchman, staying here, who does not talk Greek. He speaks only with his chauffeur, a Greek who understands a little French; I cannot say a word to him, it worries me, I am sorry for him. But you will be able to talk to him, it will be company. What will you eat? I have rissoles, I have soup made with wheat and cheese, it is good for the cold, it will warm you.'

'First,' I said, 'I will have an ouzo.' And I summoned Manoli, who had reappeared and whom I could see sitting alone with an air of modest expectation, for a drink. The hot spirit did not thaw me. When the foreigner, a silent, wedge-shaped man, appeared, I stirred myself: invited him to sit with me, bought him a drink under the pretext that Manoli offered it. He bowed solidly and settled his isosceles form opposite me. Yes, he said, he was doing work connected with a hydro-electric scheme, he was collecting and despatching wooden supports for the barrage on the river Louros which I had passed two days earlier. He spoke French with a thick accent which I found difficult to understand; perhaps he was not a Frenchman. I did not enquire; with Manoli in the party the triangular conversation was difficult enough as it was; and when the stranger withdrew to a table shared in complete silence with his chauffeur I was glad to be quiet myself. The wheat and cheese soup warmed me a little, but it was all I could eat. I sat stupefied, envying the appetite with which Manoli despatched the plate of rissoles I had ordered for him. At last I drank a glass of the local red wine, which I found excellent, and dragged myself to bed. My head was stuffed with hot cotton-wool and buckshot, my feet were ice-cold, and I still intermittently shivered. What a place, I said to myself furiously, what a place to get pneumonia in; and fell asleep.

XIII

A LEMONY SUN woke me at half-past six. I had never felt better. There were only three days left of my stay in Greece, and if I was to do what I planned I must be back in Athens by night. That meant catching the early bus which crosses the high Pindus passes to Kalabaka and Trikkala in the Thessalian plain, and hoping to find a connection by train or bus at midday. I got up and dressed. My clothes were crinkle-dry. My shoes were still sodden, but I had nothing else. As I dragged the squeaking things on, Manoli tapped at the bedroom door.

'I am coming with thee to Trikkala, I shall be company.'

'All right,' I said, 'if thou wishest' – supposing that he had some work in prospect; and I rammed my possessions into the rucksack and hurried out.

I did not like to stop for breakfast until I had bought my ticket for the bus. With some vague sense of indebtedness to my companion of yesterday I found myself buying one for Manoli too. It was a cloudy-bright morning, but cold, and custom made me think it a folly to set off on a long journey without so much as a piece of bread. I fancy there is no more than custom in the idea, unless convention comes in too. The more one travels in Greece the less one finds it necessary to observe the rules in which an English stomach is brought up. Climate changes us, no doubt. In England long-sleeping, gourmand, late-rising, I find myself in the dry Mediterranean air waking easily with the sun, capable of walking all day with little sleep and less food. Habits of mind too alter with the scene. In London I can barely endure to travel from Piccadilly to Oxford Circus without something to read, in Greece I face with equanimity a whole day empty-handed in a bus. But this morning in any case custom had to be ignored.

It is true that as we stood in the plateia Manoli remembered breakfast.

'Dost thou want a cafedhaki?' – that is to say, a coffeekin; the word is commonly used for the small cup of Turkish coffee served everywhere in Greece. But characteristically he thought of it too late, and at half-past seven off we went, empty.

'Look,' he said as the bus climbed the steep ascent, 'there it was the plane dropped supplies for us when we were fighting outside Metsovo.' It was salutary, after the childish discomforts of the walk from Jannina, to be reminded of the proportions of hardship. Every mile, every cruel hillside spoke of the tenacity of men. It was to reach and command this road that Mussolini in 1940 sent his Alpine division from Albania along the Pindus; they had nearly reached Metsovo when they were held and trapped in the mountains. For years the Pindus gorges into which the triumphant Greeks had looked from the crests down on the outwitted, outmanœuvred enemy had been a phrase to me, a shadowy cleft in a page of newsprint. I could guess now what it meant to lie out in these hills, and in November. In winter the road is sometimes impassable; snow and fog lay their hands on its shoulders. There is no other way, or none to speak of, between the two plains, no other linking of Epirus with Thessaly and Macedonia. Any invader, Italian, German or Communist, must make for the Metsovo road.

Even here one could see Greece coming back to life. On a hillside timber, lying like spilt matches, was ready to be taken down to the Louros barrage; it was, I supposed, the business of the engineer I had met the evening before. And my companions in the bus were not thinking about the severities of war.

'Thou rememberest,' said Manoli as we grumbled higher and higher, 'yesterday I told thee about the girl from a bordel – excuse my using the word – who was in a car when it was caught in the snow at night? There was a landslide, the car could not go on. Here it was, see, here at this very spot.' Cloud hung across our way; it was as if we were driving through cold, wet smoke.

'Play something for us,' said the man in the opposite seat, 'play something to pass the time.'

'Yes, yes, play something,' cried half a dozen voices.

'What shall I play?' said Manoli, opening the case and taking out his fiddle. Somebody shouted the name of a song of the region. Manoli scratched out a tune, then rested fiddle and bow on his knee; head held stiffly up, eyeballs fixed in a stare, he sang in a loud, metallic voice, forcing out sustained notes and trills from a straining throat. It was a love-song with a lively rhythm; the company sang the refrain with him. The tune was strange to me, nor had I heard the next song. But when I chose a song familiar enough farther south nobody in the bus knew it, and Manoli sang alone.

The road ran through pine woods, cold and dripping with cloud and rain. I was thankful, when at about a quarter to nine we stopped at a cafeneion in a clearing, for a cup of Turkish coffee and a piece of dry bread. There was no ignoring Manoli's expectant look, and I treated him to the same frugal breakfast. I was making a mistake, I knew. In any case my error was soon pointed out. The bus was empty when I went back to my place. But I was joined by a bearded old man in a grey peasant smock and a little black cap like a shallow fez, who sat behind me, hesitated, then leaned forward politely.

'Excuse me, I should like to know if you and the musician are travelling together?'

His intonation of the word 'together' made it clear that he found my relation with my gipsy-faced companion puzzling.

'No, no,' I said, 'we met by chance. He is going to Trikkala, and so am I. But I am not staying in Trikkala, I am going much farther – to Athens.'

'Ah,' said the old man, 'to Athens!' – as if that explained every-thing. And he leaned back, satisfied.

I was already anxious about the second part of my trip and I talked to nobody for the rest of the bus journey. The day had turned grey. When we went over the pass into Thessaly it was like crossing a bridge in the clouds, and the plain ahead of us was colourless under a worsted sky. Landscape and soil looked softer and richer than on the western side of the Pindus: a greener vegetation, clumps of brambles on the hills; there were parties of men working on the road; and when we reached the plain and halted in Kalabaka underneath the mesa-like rocks to whose sides and tops the Meteora monasteries cling there was a feeling of bustle, of rebuilding. But I could not stay to look. The bus set off along the straight flat road to Trikkala, and I was still a passenger. So, of course, was Manoli.

The excellence of the bus service, I was to find, did not extend also to the planning of the time-table. At Trikkala I hurried from the bus and ran to ask about a connection for Athens. It was about midday.

'Yes,' said the clerk, 'the bus for Athens leaves at eight tonight; it arrives at four in the morning.'

'But,' I said, 'tomorrow I have a long journey to make, I have to leave early and make arrangements before I go. Is there nothing earlier?'

'Earlier?' he answered, shocked by my impatience. 'Nothing earlier; the morning bus went half an hour ago.'

'Is there perhaps a train?'

'The trains I don't know; I don't think so.'

'I am going to the railway station,' I said to Manoli, who, reduced in this urban setting, stood humbly holding my rucksack. 'What dost thou want to do?'

'I will come with thee; I shall be company.'

'We must hurry, then.' We bundled into a taxi, and drove to the railway.

'Tonight there is a train.'

'Nothing before tonight?'

'Nothing; the morning train went half an hour ago.'

'Nothing if I took a car to Larissa?'

'Nothing. From Larissa it is the same train.'

I looked at the taxi-driver, who had come to join in. 'Could we overtake the train farther on, say at Lamia?' He shook his head. 'If the weather were good we might catch it, but with the rain the direct road to Lamia is all mud, we should have to go round by Larissa.' 'It has rained for twenty-four hours without stopping,' said the stationmaster.

For a moment I stood in exasperated hesitation. In Greece to hire a car with a driver is cheaper than it is in England, and to take a taxi for a day's outing in the country is not unheard of. All the same to make a ten-hours' journey by hired car was an extravagance I could not afford. Yet with the fanaticism one spends on the trivial I felt my trip was ruined if I were not back in Athens that night. Perhaps at Lamia, seventy miles south of Larissa, I might find some train, some bus unknown to the time-table.

'Can you,' I said to the driver, 'take me to Lamia?'

'Certainly. I must get some petrol; then – wherever you wish.'

'That is settled, then,' I said to Manoli. 'On the way we will put thee down in Trikkala. Thou wilt tell me where thou wishest to get out.'

It was not until later that I saw his point of view. At the time I felt only irritation when, at our parting, he asked sulkily for money: 'for my expenses in Trikkala,' he said. 'For thy expenses? But thou wast the one who asked to come; I did not ask thee.' In my annoyance I forgot my Greek and instead of the word for 'invite' I used one meaning 'ask a question.' I was angrier still when, having for the sake of a friendly parting been given a few shillings, he asked for more. Later on I told my chauffeur why I had been grudging. 'The scoundrel!' he growled. 'I thought you had employed him as your guide.'

But in truth I believe that Manoli felt himself wronged. I had paid for his bus ticket, I had bought him food and drink; not only had I tacitly accepted what he regarded as his help, I had behaved like a rich foreigner. No doubt I had overstepped the bounds of what is right for a woman, even a foreigner. Greece, beneath the austerity of its landscape and the severity of its rustic morals, is a sexual country, of its heat engendering extreme desires; it is also a masculine country in which, except on the most sophisticated level, a woman must not claim a man's right to order, to decide. I have always felt conscious in Greece of being a woman. Yet the conditions of solitary travel force on me the superficies of a man's authority. And though I try not to offend people's sense of what is fitting, with my poor Greek it is easy to misjudge, easy to misfeel a situation. Manoli may well have thought my eccentricities entitled him to make a bit more out of me.

But the true reason for his glum looks came to me long afterwards. With the optimism which sometimes intoxicates the simple, he had seen himself transported much farther than to Trikkala. 'I want to go to Athens, I could play in a taverna': an Englishwoman mad enough to want to walk twenty-seven miles on a wet day along a bus route, yet rich enough to sleep in hotels and hire taxis, would surely not jib at taking him to the capital and recommending him to some restaurant frequented by other wealthy foreigners. He had recognized me as the agent sent by heaven through the rain to help him achieve his ambition; he had not hesitated; 'I am coming with you.' And yet here he was, standing with his fiddle-case at a street-corner, while the instrument of Providence disobligingly prepared to travel alone to Athens. Remembering my last view of the disconsolate figure in the long tattered coat, the sly gipsy look turned sullen, I should not be surprised if he had persuaded himself that I had pressed him to travel with me to Trikkala.

Clouds drooped over the plain when we came out of the town and began the long drive. We were on ground strange to me, but the slaty light reduced every mile to a common melancholy. I could think only of hurrying on, and when, after we had rushed through Larissa, capital of Thessaly, and Pharsala, scene of Pompey's defeat at the hands of Caesar, the driver asked if I minded his turning on the radio, I was glad of the distraction, and we pounded southwards to the accompaniment of Mary Martin singing 'I'm in love with a wonderful guy.'

Since there was no time for lunch I had brought some chocolate and a bunch of grapes. 'Excuse me,' said the driver deferentially, 'do not eat so many grapes, they will be heavy in your stomach'; and indeed they were a chilly meal for the day. It was beginning to rain once more. We stopped in some town or other for yellow cello-phane to cover the headlights and make fog-lamps of them; then we climbed into thick mist on a pass. Once, in the plain, we slowed down for me to see a gravestone beside the road; it was put up, said the driver, by the Germans, a memorial to a British colonel killed in the retreat of 1941. A little farther on, 'Exactly here,' he said, 'the andartes, the symmorites caught me once. I was driving a lorry, we were a party taking supplies to Athens. The andartes had blocked the road. It was dark, they came down on us from the hills, two thousand they were, with rifles. They took everything from us, food, clothing, shoes, everything; they left me nothing but my jacket.'

'When was that?'

'In 1947, in the Communist war. They were everywhere in the mountains round here.'

'And in the Occupation too, were there not andartes in these mountains?'

'Yes indeed. But then there were many true andartes, patriots who fought for their country. Afterwards they changed. They robbed, they killed, nobody was safe.'

At Lamia we stopped to warm ourselves with coffee. The bus had gone, but not long before us; and, counting my drachmae, I took fright.

'Do you think we can overtake it? Let us try; do what you can.' And yet I could hardly believe it when, perhaps an hour later, we saw ahead of us a bus racketing through the puddles, when my resourceful driver hooted till it stopped, ran to bargain with the conductor, persuaded him to take on, and in mid-career, a new passenger. It was already late afternoon, and soon it would be dark. I climbed in, waved to my kind driver, and we were off. I was grateful to have my head surely towards home, and with the sense of effort relaxed I scarcely noticed the hours passing on the long journey southwards: the lighted villages, the fog on the passes, the lorries roaring towards us out of the capital. At last, looking out of a steamy window, I saw a shining new petrol station swim past and, in front of it, a man sitting on a stool with his head bowed in deathless boredom over folded arms. I glanced at my watch. It was past ten o'clock; and there were the streets of Athens polished by the first rains, and all the flittermouse stir of a Mediterranean city.

Already the dark Pindus, the villages of Epirus, seemed months behind me.

XIV

Aﬀter all i was not to miss my visit to Mycenae, and next morning when the automotrice pulled up, Frosso and I got out. It was a lucky time for a visit. During the official junketings in Athens I had met a Greek scholar who was making new finds at Mycenae; I was touched that, although for seventeen years my knowledge of archaeology, always faint, had been dwindling until it vanished altogether, as Humfry's widow I should be invited to see the discoveries. In other ways too this was a looking back. Eight years earlier when the jeep had taken me to the Fair Helen there had been not a bridge, not a railway line left whole. Now we had hummed for three hours along the remembered track and through a landscape which might have stood, transfixed by light, since summers before the war: the golden-brown plain, the bay of Salamis, Megara on its dusty hills, the Corinth Isthmus and the Canal suddenly gaping beneath us, Acrocorinth humped over its temple; and then, looking back across the Gulf, the toy line of houses at Loutraki where the mountain meets the sea, the crested peninsula running westward to the Heraion, and on its forehead the lighthouse.

Outside the station a man in a frayed round straw hat, its wide brim shading his face, stood waiting with a donkey. I looked without recognizing him.

'Kyria Payne,' he said.

I stared again, and in the shadow I knew the face of Kosta, eldest of the brothers who keep the Fair Helen inn. In 1945 he had been absent, and it was seventeen years since I had seen him. We used to say he was like the Duke of Urbino in Piero della Francesca's portrait, and, with his hooked nose and ironic, commanding look, so he was;

but handsome, tall, conscious of a powerful physique. The man I saw now was still handsome, but he was an old man: the teeth broken, the hair grey-bristled, deep ruts in the weathered skin; even the body was smaller, and he walked, not merely with the peasant's economical movements, but with the stubborn short steps of one who has grown stiff in a lifetime of mountains paths.

'Kyrios Papadimitriou sent me,' he said, 'I have the donkey for you to ride, I will take you to the excavations.'

We clopped up the straight road to the village, half an hour away along the avenue of pepper-trees. In 1945 the countryside had been shadowed by war. Now, with the Communist defeat shrinking into the past and the Peloponnese open again to travellers, the family at the inn could be easy, and when Frosso and I stopped at the entrance to the trodden earth terrace women and children ran from the house and flung themselves on us with embraces and hand-kissings.

'You will drink a coffee,' they said, 'later you will come back'; and we went with Kosta up the hill-road with its fringe of oleanders, past the village graveyard and the chapel, past the track which leads to the tomb of Agamemnon, until we came almost to the Lion Gate, entrance to the ancient citadel.

The Cyclopean walls which buttress the citadel on its height enclose, amongst the complex of ruined foundations, the circle of graves sunk shaft-like into the rock where Schliemann, when he dug at Mycenae in the 1870s, found royal treasure. Now both Greek and British archaeologists were making fresh discoveries, and Professor Papadimitriou, digging outside the walls, had come on a second Royal Grave Circle. As we approached we could see, close to the roadside, workmen standing in the flying white dust; beside them, a wheelbarrow tilted by a trench, spades and pickaxes, a few planks lying on the stacked earth. In the mending-shed fragments of pottery were stacked on the shelves; a man was working with plaster and glue. The new graves were close to the tomb called Clytemnestra's, which when I last saw it had been in ruins; now it had been restored, its beehive roof rebuilt with the blocks lying on the site. Some Athenian friends also were visitors, and together we stood under the dome and looked out at the sunlight. Then we went past slopes waving with tall creamy spikes of marine squill to the hotel which the Tourismos, the tourist bureau, has built on the hill above the village. For safety Professor Papadimitriou kept the valuable finds locked here in his bedroom: the necklaces, the gold diadems, the bronze pins with heads of carved rock crystal, the patterned gold-leaf, paper-thin, which once adorned a dress. Box after cardboard box was opened to show forms of extraordinary elegance. As we stared astonished at the littered table he put in my hands a little bowl of rock crystal. It was carved in the shape of a duck, the head turning back to make a handle. The grave had not fretted it, and the cool skin of stone was smooth as water to the touch.

We ate in a party at the Tourismos Hotel. The building, well secreted, does not offend when discovered, and the view from its forecourt is splendid. The food was good, and supplemented by fresh figs from my friend's garden in Athens; the service was urbane without losing the country flavour of Greece; I almost stifled a feeling of infidelity at sitting, for the first time in all my visits to Mycenae, at a table other than the Fair Helen's. When we came out, work was beginning again at the excavations. One of the richest of the newly discovered graves was being finally cleared, and with a hospitality all Greek Papadimitriou invited Frosso and me to watch.

The shaft was deep. We climbed down a ladder and sat on a shelf of stones. An autumn wind was gusty on the slopes above. Dust from the dry soil, grit from the sides of the tomb, stung our cheeks and rattled against the walls. The dweller in the grave slept at our feet: naked and white, the bones of a girl lying amidst her royal finery, her necklaces and pins, her diadems, her gold ornaments. The fore-man, a tall young Greek in a torn patched shirt, was using the familiar tools: the knife to scrape away the hard soil which held the trinkets embedded, the soft brush to flick off the powdering earth; when the scattered necklace was freed he lifted the beads with tweezers. Squatting, silent except when Papadimitriou spoke to him, he worked with a craftsman's concentration: digging delicately with the point of the knife, bending now and then to blow away a few grains of dust. Once we heard argument, and looking up from our rectangular pit saw a strange woman's face leaning over us. The foreman worked on. The face was joined by another, and we could hear that the argument was in French. Fragments of earth from the lid of the shaft dripped down. The faces continued to stare. At last Papadimitriou spoke.

'Ce n'est pas permis, Madame,' he said. With haughty exclamations the tourists turned and went.

The afternoon rustled by in the tiny precisions of archaeology. The last patterned, flat strip of gold, dull-gleaming, crumpled with the centuries' weight of earth and stone, was knifed free; frowning and intent, the foreman lifted it. The leaf did not break, and, smiling for the first time, he sat back and let his tensed shoulders drop. We climbed out of the grave. It was nearly twenty years since at the Heraion of Perachora I had watched a man working with knife, brush and anxious hands to redeem the hammered and engraved bowls of bronze, the carved ivory figurines which time had sucked down. Now the springs, the summers on the Perachora headland rushed back into focus; the detail was sharp, the days separated themselves. It was as if, when I clambered down into the uncovered grave, I had indeed returned to the past. In my heart I could see the mountains beyond the Gulf, the lighthouse, the camp in the pine-woods, the store-tent with its flaps open and, in the late sun, the day's finds being packed and labelled.

It was dusk when we came back to the Fair Helen, and the inn was bringing out its lamps.

'Come, sit down,' said Agamemnon, lighting us to a table. 'You will drink an ouzo? What do you wish me to prepare for you to eat? Tonight we have meat, if that pleases you, with rice. And to drink shall I bring you rhetsina?'

The household sprang into life: voices calling in the kitchen, the women fetching napkins and plates, and the children hushed into whispers. While we ate and drank the three brothers stood in attendance, talking.

'At midday,' I said, 'we could not eat here, for we were invited by Professor Papadimitriou.'

149

'I know,' said Kosta, 'we understand.' Then, with a meaning in his voice which at first I did not recognize, 'That foreman up there, does he work well?'

I was on the point of answering with enthusiasm when I recollected that the brothers had long experience of excavation. Before the war, walking in the Argolid with Humfry, I had seen how both Kosta and Orestes eyed the ground for a likely site to explore. Both, I knew, had served with foreign archaeologists as well as Greeks, with the British, the Swedes, the Germans.

'Eh,' I said, with a care for professional jealousy, 'it seems to me that he works well enough, but what dost thou say?'

'Bah,' said Kosta briefly.

It was better to talk about the past, old friends, the family.

'Only last year,' said Orestes, 'it was only last year our mother died.'

'I heard; I am sorry. How old was she?'

'Seventy-four; only last year it was we buried her, up there in the graveyard where your husband lies, the late Payne.'

I remembered her as a handsome, tough old woman in lustreless black: black skirt, black bodice, black headscarf. In the twenty years between our first and our last meeting she had seemed to me never to alter. Now, after living through the war, the Occupation, the Communist insurrection, she was gone. But no other face was missing when Frosso and I said goodbye. The three brothers, their wives, their children crowded to the doorway and into the road. Their voices followed us as we set off, and not for the first time I knew that I was inheriting the respect which had been Humfry's. Kosta walked with us half the distance to the station. Then he turned back, waving, and we trudged on, the sound of our footsteps loud in the night. Crickets sang secretly by the roadside, a dog barked and was answered. But my mind was still on a moment in the afternoon.

After the end of the day's digging Frosso and I had walked down the hill towards the village cemetery. In the valley below us a boy was driving home a flock of turkeys. He was singing to himself; his voice, a little roughened between childhood and youth, rang clearly through the evening air. Behind him the enormous wall of the mountain waited for darkness before it closed in on the living and the dead. But already it had edged nearer; only the boy, happily singing his melancholy song, ignored the night. I pushed open the gate in the low wall round the cemetery. Rusty holders for the candles of All Soul's Night leaned in the dry long grass over unvisited mounds of earth. But the path to Humfry's grave was trodden clear, oleanders grew by the headstone, and young iris-blades were piercing the tangle of dead leaves in the enclosure. The wind had dropped, the cypress behind the headstone stood like a statue. Far away, in the plain on whose rim I stood, a train went with caterpillar-crawl on its way to Argos. In the last brightness the landscape wore the look of immortality. Space, solitude, silence; and looking at the grave by my feet, fancying, as the living cannot but fancy, that the dead care where they sleep, I asked myself once again after all the years whether I had been right to choose Mycenae. And once again I thought that one could not have wished for a nobler grave.

XV

AT NIGHTFALL THE storm broke over Athens. Rain came in crowded thick strokes, hissing and boiling on the pavements; thunder banged about in the splitting sky. Yet by morning the sun shone amidst clouds like strands of luminous hair, and the taxi which took me at half-past seven to the bus-office drove through blue-shadowed streets. In the bus for Loutraki I sat next to an elderly Athenian with a wooden leg. We fell into talk: the journey, the weather, the year's crops; finally the Government.

'Ah, madame,' he said, 'governments are good or bad according to the state of affairs in the country. When things go well, if Churchill, let us say, is Prime Minister people will say Churchill is good, if Attlee is Prime Minister Attlee is good; you know it yourself. This year in Greece we have a heavy crop of olives; so we have a good government.'

Once again the familiar route I had followed by rail on the journey to Mycenae: Eleusis, with Salamis looking at us from the sea, Megara, the Skironian cliffs. Then at the Isthmus we turned our backs on the Canal bridge, Corinth and the Peloponnese, and the bus drove northwards the few miles to Loutraki. We were there soon after ten o'clock. I was to dine in Athens that night and, binding myself as best I could to be there in time, I took a ticket for the five o'clock bus back. Then I bought some grapes and, at the kiosk in the square, a bar of chocolate and a packet of biscuits, and set off out of the little town: past the thermal springs and the row of hotels by the shore, and along the road which from the Corinthian Gulf can be seen driving its zig-zag gash up the mountain-side towards Perachora village. But

152

I was not going to the village; not yet. I would come back that way. First I was going to the lighthouse.

I had seen the site of the Heraion excavations only once since Humfry died. In 1936, a month before his death, we had gone there together for the day, walking along the shore from Loutraki; a year later, I had tramped down from the village and wandered alone among the temple-foundations and the empty trenches. That was my last visit. Though between 1937 and the outbreak of war I had twice been in Greece I had not tried then to make the excursion. Why, I cannot now understand. Perachora is the heart of my Greece. Again and again, travelling in the country, I have come in sight of the long, humped promontory: from the slopes of Parnassoss above Delphi, from the top of Arcadian Kyllene, sailing along the Gulf from Patras, going southwards through Corinth to the Argolid. And the summers of our encampment: the north-wester driving all day through the pine-woods without taking breath, the lighthouse on its headland riding the striated peacock sea, workmen calling to one another in the valley by the harbour, the thrum of a benzina at night beating round the headland into the other Gulf, the Halcyonic – here is the essence of my feeling for Greece. Into those weeks imprisoned by waves, rocks, wind, sun, trees, weeks when the repetitive days and nights multiplied and re-multiplied every sensation, every image on the retina, a long experience was concentrated; knowledge burned into me with the salt in the air. And yet after the first solitary return to the village and the Heraion, though every time I went to Mycenae I saw as I passed through Corinth the lighthouse on the headland I never set myself to reach it. I did not even go back again to Perachora village. An enforced separation was needed to remind me of my attachment. During the war my anxieties fastened on my Perachoran friends; more and more, cut off from news, I recalled their faces, tried to imagine their lives. The very fact of their poverty, their isolation, made them represent for me the stubborn endurance of the Greek peasantry. When I went back in 1945 the place I most longed to seek out was Perachora. The village I saw. Only the light-house was out of reach.

Now after sixteen years I was going not only to the village but to the Heraion, to the lighthouse. I know it, I said to myself, like the back of my hand; I was as excited as an exile coming home. I resolved to take the route we had always taken. The Heraion, Perachora village and Loutraki are the points of a broad, shallow triangle; the village being the apex on the north, the Heraion lying on the left hand, to the west, Loutraki on the right at the extreme eastern end of the Corinthian Gulf where the shore curves into the Isthmus. The path by the shore between Loutraki and the Heraion is the base of the figure, the shortest distance between the two points. Nevertheless during the excavations we had found it quickest, when walking from Loutraki to the lighthouse on our journeys to camp, instead of following this straight line from its beginning to start up the road towards the village, then, turning left, to drop down through scrub until we came to the path in the olives. But there seemed to be new buildings on the outskirts of Loutraki. The turning-point had always been difficult to find, and confident though I was I doubted whether in this I could trust my memory.

'Where,' I asked an old man sitting on the box of an ancient victoria, 'shall I turn off for the path to the lighthouse?'

'To the lighthouse? But it is a long way, my child, thou wilt be tired.'

'No, no, I have walked there many times, but long ago, before the war. I know the path, only where I must leave the road I do not remember well.'

I climbed up the hill. But I could not identify the spot where, according to him, I should fork left. I stopped, turned, irresolutely walked back, turned again. It would take, I reflected, about three hours to walk to the lighthouse. I must allow another hour and a half for doubling back to the village, and I must be there in time to catch the bus which, I was told, left for Loutraki at half-past three. Already I had wasted some of the minutes of the day. But I knew that the familiar path must lie somewhere below me in the pines and the olives. I gave up the search and began to scramble through pincushions of scrub towards the Gulf.

Presently I could hear voices. A family group, men, women and children, were gathering olives, shaking the purpling fruit from twisted trees; a mule, tethered in the shade, struck hollow restless notes from the ground with its stamping.

'Down there,' said the woman, 'the path is down there, it is near.'

I plunged on; behind me their silence told me that they were watching. At the bottom of the slope, in the burned grass and the faded cistus plants, a faint track ran westward. Now I knew my way, and, turning my face in the direction of the lighthouse, I walked with the Gulf on my left and the spine of the promontory hidden among the trees on my right.

The path rambles by the sea, sometimes along the beach itself, and in a few minutes I could see the water restlessly glittering at the foot of the sloping shore. On the other side of the Gulf a black extinguisher of cloud hung on the peak of Kyllene; occasionally an experimental roar of thunder puffed out, and a pale theatrical light flickered under the cold dark hood. But ahead of me to the west, where the arms of land opened wider, the sky was clear, and the Perachora promontory lay in light. The tiny path twisted through sapling pines no higher than my shoulder; yellowed thistles and the low, flat, thorny shrubs of the wilderness caught at my ankles as I passed. Insects whispered and beat their wings. Grasshoppers the colour of dust whirred creaking from patch to naked patch of dust. The earth, the sun-sucked vegetation sang the tune of solitude, and in the humming, vibrating stillness I could feel my heart beating with expectation.

Indeed I remembered. The path climbed between boulders to a cliff. It was seventeen years since I had last gone warily this way along the ledge, but as I looked at the swell pouring over the rocks below I knew the place as if I had passed yesterday. Often, in a landscape recreated by memory and filled with figures long since vanished for ever, I had imagined myself wandering over a field where corn grew among the olives and a dry watercourse came from encircling, pine-covered slopes down to the stony beach. Now I came to the place in reality. The corn was bleached stubble, the soil grey as a dead bone, but the curve of the field was the same, and I knew where to cross the watercourse. The landscape was uninhabited. Yet as I went through it, slipping a little as I had always slipped on the loose pebbles which marked the track, the past walked by my side. The mountains beyond the Gulf, the headland stretching away towards the lighthouse rock, the empty sea – I could never forget a stone of it; and nowhere, I thought, nowhere in the world is the scent of the pines as drowsy.

It was not yet midday when I reached the shed which serves as a chapel by the spring, but since there was water I stopped for my meal of grapes, biscuits and chocolate. The place is sacred to the Little Virgin. Its name had been friendly in the days of the Heraion excavations, for the lighthouse has no fresh water and we sent for supplies every day; two men sailed, or if there was no favourable wind rowed, a journey of an hour and a half along the coast, and filled their load of empty petrol-tins at the Little Virgin's; there is no nearer spring. Pines shade the source, and wasps and flies were hovering and crawling drunkenly round the sweet water. I drove them away, drank from my hands, and went on in the sunshine, thinking about the routine of life at the Heraion twenty years earlier.

By now, I reckoned, I was more than half-way to the lighthouse. The landmarks had been as I imagined them. Soon I should come to the lake of brackish water which, connected with the Gulf by a man-made channel a few feet wide, lies behind the coast-line where it dips before rising to the last savage crests. After that I had only to follow the track round the far end of the lake and up through the woods to the plateau where we used to make our camp: a clear, wide track, I remembered, with here and there in the rock the marks of a road cut, centuries ago, for ancient wheels. I felt I was almost within sight of the lighthouse, which all morning as I walked had been shut off from me by the huge mass of the promontory's head. It was rather as a matter of form than from any uncertainty that when I reached another landmark, a fisherman's hut on the shore, I shouted to ask if I was on the right path.

'Straight on by the shore, straight on!'

I went on past the boat drawn up on the beach and the rickety wooden jetty. This part of the walk was over even ground. Here the coast-line flattens out and the precipitous spine of crags recedes inland. On my right there were level fields. Ahead, a low rim of rocks rose from the sea; behind it the lake must lie. But the way surely did not lead up to the rim. I ought, I felt certain, to skirt the boulders and tramp along a beach of shingle ground small by a million storms. But there was no vestige of a path. The rocks met the sea; there was no encouragement to edge round them. Once more I hesitated, turned, walked back a short way lest I should somewhere have missed the track. No: so far there was no mistake. Again I looked at the tumble of rocks, made to clamber round it and faint-heartedly drew back. Perhaps memory was false. Perhaps after all the path climbed to the rim above; from there at any rate the lake should be visible. No more time must be wasted if I was to reach the Heraion. I scrambled upwards.

It is easy in such goat-country to mistake a trickle of pebbles on a hillside for a path, and for a minute or two I thought I had found the track again; another few yards, and I should stand on the seaward edge of the cup which holds the lake. The sun had slid behind clouds, and in the dull light it seemed suddenly important to hurry. I heaved myself to the top.

Ahead there was a flat expanse, a plateau with straggly olives and rough terrace-walls separating the fields. Of the lake, not a sign.

I must not say that I was lost. I knew on which side the Gulf of Corinth lay, in which direction the Heraion and the lighthouse. I could go back and find the track from which I had strayed. And since the plateau in front of me was cultivated land there must be a way out of it. In crossing it – and I knew it could not extend far – I did not risk putting myself in a worse case. But I had lost the way. In that terrain where every rock, so I once fancied, had a shape I could never drive out of my mind, I had misread the landmarks.

Once more fear of wasting time urged me not to turn back, and I set off, half-running, across the terraced fields. The black cloud-mass on Kyllene was shifting and dissolving, and the storm was striding over the Gulf towards the headland; a benzina, sails furled, a boat in

tow slapping the waves after it, went tut-tutting towards the Canal
and the shelter of the Isthmus. But in a moment I was out of view of
the sea. The sound of the engine grew faint, then died altogether,
and in a silence no longer fretted by the obstinate voices of flies and
grasshoppers I stumbled over the clods of baked earth. Any minute,
I told myself, I must see the lake. From the direction I had taken I
should come to it at the far end, the end nearest the Heraion. It would
be no distance then to the path through the woods.

Yet when at last I saw the lake below me in its bowl of pines I could
not tell at which end I stood, The steely water, the heavy green trees
pressing down to its margin, the reproving solitude: not a murmur,
not a stir – the landscape looked quite changed from the sparkling
place I thought I knew. I stumbled down the slope. A few cyclamens
lurked among the rocks and the thorns; once more there was the
smell of pines. At the water's edge, still no path. But to the right the
reeds and the dried mud were trampled, and though I knew that I
ought to be making my way to the left I turned to circle the lake in
the opposite direction.

In Athens I had been told that the Heraion was known, now,
for a day's expedition into the country: a drive, a picnic, bathing
from the harbour. Remembering the loneliness of the headland, the
rough walk down from the village and the still longer one from
Loutraki, I had asked what route the picnic parties took.

'Oh, they've made a road from the village. You can drive nearly
all the way to the Heraion.'

At the time I had shrunk from the thought of the wilderness tamed;
afterwards I had dismissed it as incredible. But now I searched eagerly
for the road: in the Greek phrase, the carriage road; at least it would
give me my bearings. There was nothing in sight but the opaque
water, the steep wooded shores opposite and the dried marshland at
my feet. I looked at my watch. It was twenty minutes past one. And
now I realized that not only had I forgotten the way, I had forgotten
the distance. Certainly I had wasted time by losing the path. But even
had I not lost it I should have found that I had miscalculated. There
had never been time to walk to the lighthouse. I must renounce yet

again the dream of seeing the Heraion, and turn towards Perachora village. And unless I found a way out soon from my circuit I should not reach the village either.

It was at this moment that I struck a clear path, and thankfully recognized the mule-track between the Heraion and the village. If I turned left, westward, it would take me past the lake and along the ancient chariot-road through the woods towards the lighthouse. To the right it led up a valley towards the village. With longing I looked to the west. Now I saw the landscape as I knew it: the low shelf of rock between the lake and the Corinthian Gulf from which I had just come; the pinnacled cliffs, tufted with pines, where the promontory rises to its dragon-head. Defeated I turned away into the valley.

XVI

Perachora lies in a small upland plain. The spur of Geraneia
which is Loutraki's mountain cuts the village off from sight of the sea,
and the fields are surrounded by foothills besides. Even now, I
reflected, beginning to hurry through the olives at the wide flat
entrance to the valley, even now I had no time to waste; just as I
had misjudged the distance to the lighthouse, no doubt I was wrong
about the journey to the village as well. I might still have a walk of an
hour and a half before me, and more if I lost my way again. Luckily
the track was broad, much broader than I remembered: a level,
stony way, with ruts in the dust. There could be no more than one
route between the village and the lighthouse. Then where was the
famous carriage-road? The wheel-marks answered me. The pebble-
track I walked on was the carriage-road. The old mule-path had been
hospitably levelled, and the swarms of visitors to the Heraion I had
been told of must come bouncing this way down from the village.

Today there was no sign of them. The track climbed the mountain-
side, then dropped again to sparse olive groves. There are no houses
between the lighthouse and the village. Still, one might expect to
meet a passer-by or two, a girl with a donkey, perhaps, carrying
fodder. I saw nobody. Once I stopped to listen. No sound: not a
bird, not a lizard rasping over the rock. Once from the lip of the
valley I looked back; and now at last, beyond the lake and the pinnacles of rock, I could see the lighthouse. Then the hills closed in
behind me. Hurrying on, I found with dismay that the track forked.
My memory insisted that I ought to bear right. But the right fork
was a mere path. The carriage-road curved left. In the end the carriage-
road could not fail to reach the village. I turned left.

This blindness and deceit in the memory, these repeated hesitations are, I know, trivial matters. Even within my own plans they were negligible. Nothing in the course of life would have been altered had I given up the journey to the village; had I gone back to Loutraki too late to catch the bus my hosts in Athens that night would have suffered no more than exasperation. Yet I had too often imagined the return to Perachora to accept the failure of my day. To fall short in a romantic excursion, in any excursion at all, is teasing. This excursion was the echo, perhaps the last echo, of ten years of my life. And some note in the solitude urged me on. I felt as if I were surrounded, and could move only forward. The track curved farther and farther to the left, away from the point towards which I was sure I should be making; forgetting the sweat which had started to trickle down through my hair, I followed it. For two or three hundred yards I assured myself that I could not be mistaken. Then I stopped. Once more the path forked. Now both forks were of equal width. And at that moment the storm-cloud which, ever since I turned my back on the Gulf, had been shadowing me stooped to breathe on my neck. It began to pour with rain.

The long leviathan of the Perachora peninsula, raising its hump between the Gulf of Corinth and the Halcyonic Gulf, narrows at its head, and the lighthouse stands on little more than a knife-edge. But behind the lake the promontory broadens and at its base, between the Corinth Isthmus on the south and the shore of the Halcyonic Gulf on the north, it offers a wide expanse of savage rocky country. If at the point where I stood I took the wrong path I risked not simply a mistake of half-an-hour or so. I might struggle on for miles, only to find myself at one of the remote villages on the far side of the peninsula where it looks on the Halcyonic Gulf. Again I stood listening, hoping for some human sound, however distant: a man working in the olives, perhaps, or leading his mule. Silence. I looked at the hills, thinking that I might remember a shape or a contour. In their green fur of pines they all looked the same. And now I was truly lost: in the country which I had boasted I knew like the back of my hand completely, absurdly lost.

XVII

'I MISSED THE PATH,' I told them at Perachora later, 'so I did not go
to the Heraion. I got as far as the lake, then I looked at my watch and
saw I had no time to reach the lighthouse. So I turned round and came
to Perachora.' But I never told them that I was uncertain of the path
to the village too, nor did I confess to the fright I was in when I
fancied myself lost. Indeed by the time I came in sight of Perachora
it seemed impossible that I should ever have faltered. Within a
hundred yards of the fork a track which had appeared to be leading
away from my course looped back towards the east, and with the
Loutraki mountain, storm-capped, before me as signpost I climbed
through woods to the Perachora plain. The rain hesitated, then
stopped altogether, and thankfully I took off my plastic mackintosh
and walked in sun hot enough to dry my cotton blouse, drenched
with sweat. Soon I came to the shoulder of the hill. At the far end of
the arid little plain there was a mound of powdery houses. It was
Perachora village.

To the English the word village draws a picture of country
orderliness: the church tower, cricket on the green, cottage gardens
looking over their walls at the well-kept road and the two genial
pubs. Perachora is all muddle to the eye. No hierarchy of houses
discloses itself because there is none. The road which comes up from
Loutraki has worn itself out by the time it reaches the outskirts and
the rectangle of unpaved earth which serves as plateia. Within the
village there is no road worth the name. Coming from the Heraion,
the visitor enters by an unmade track; enquiring further, he bruises
his toes on the rocky goat-steps which wind between the cottages.
The village is built on a slope. In summer, when dryness devours the

earth and casts the débris of drought over everything living and dead, the houses with their broken tiled roofs, with the mud-bricks exposed where the pale-washed stucco has fallen away, make from a distance the impression of a greyish-yellow rubbish-heap.

Even after the rain the desert was not washed out of the air, and I walked towards a shell of dust. Midway across the first field I passed a woman riding a mule.

'Good day,' I said, and 'Good day,' she answered. When she had gone by she called out, and I looked back.

'Dost thou not remember me?' she cried in the high trombone voice which carries from hill to hill.

'But certainly,' I said, lying, 'how art thou?' She laughed, recognizing the lie, shouted something which I did not understand, and kicked her mule on. I walked towards the village, wondering how many people, after eight years, I should indeed remember. A few yards from the first house a group of little boys were playing by a terraced wall. In a surge of sentiment which made me long to include every Perachoran in a theatrical gesture of reunion, I smiled at the children.

'This village,' I said fatuously, 'is Perachora, isn't it?' I felt as if such overflowing goodwill must be recognized, as if something in my face must proclaim the homecoming exile. The boys stared. Then one of them answered in a clear, polite, childish voice.

'Yes, here is Perachora.'

'And where is the plateia?'

'Here' (pointing ahead) 'is the plateia.'

'Thank you,' I said, gazing at the blank space where eight years earlier my jeep had pulled up amidst a welcoming crowd. My watch told me that it was a little before three o'clock. There was time to see the Perachorans before the bus took me back to Loutraki. But I had to find them first. I walked across the plateia, searching for someone to tell me the way.

On my left a terrace of trodden earth was shaded by a thatch, a stork's nest of reeds supported on spindly poles. In front of the house a young man in a cap was sitting astride a wooden chair, his arms across the back, his head on his arms, yawning. As I passed he lifted his head and watched me.

'Good day,' I said, 'I am looking for the house of Niko, the light-houseman.'

The young man stood up. 'The house of Niko? It is up there.' He pointed up the hill. 'Are you not kyria Payne?'

'So thou rememberest me?'

'Certainly I remember you. At once as you came into the village I knew you. Sit down! Where have you come from?'

'From Loutraki; that is to say I tried to walk to the lighthouse, I got as far as the lake, but it was late and I turned back and came to Perachora.'

'On foot? Ah, you are tired.'

'Bah, I am used to it. Dost thou not remember how we used to walk when we were digging at the Heraion?'

'At the Heraion, yes, indeed I remember. At once as you came into the village I knew you, I said to myself: It is kyria Payne.'

'It is a long time ago.'

The young man looked at me in civil appraisal. 'You have grown old,' he said, 'your hair has turned white.'

'It is a long time ago,' I repeated. 'Twenty years.'

'I remember. You were like a bird then, hopping here and there. I remember you dancing at the party for the workmen and their wives. We used to say you were not like a married woman, the wife of the Director.'

Wryly I reflected that in the eyes of a Greek peasant, accustomed to wives who trenched the vines and tramped behind the mules their husbands rode, I had looked like Dora Copperfield. 'But thou,' I said, 'thou must have been a little boy. Didst thou come down to the Heraion?'

'Of course. I used to help when they were measuring the stones, in the temple, in the cisterns. Don't you remember?'

'Welcome,' a voice said. A man was standing by my chair, holding out his hand. He was a little older than my first host: fair-bristled, round-headed, a broad, easy-tempered face turned a little sulky with too much brooding over the ouzo: a face like Vasili's at the light-house. But it was not Vasili. Just in time I recognized Spiro, Vasili's brother and Yanni's; a handsome little boy in our Heraion days, the ex-soldier who had been of the party at my visit in 1945. Already the rumour of a foreigner's arrival had blown round the village.

'I will take you to Yanni,' said Spiro. 'You know that Yanni has the cafeneion now?'

'I know; he had it when I came to Perachora after the war. And Vasili, how is Vasili?'

'He is well, well he is. Today he is at the lighthouse; he is captain now.'

'So I shall not see him; I am sorry. I tried to get to the lighthouse, but I had not enough time. And thou: here in the village dost thou work?'

'Eh,' said Spiro, turning away from a distasteful subject, 'you see I cannot work, with my hand. Ten days I have not been able to work.' And indeed his left hand was thickly bandaged.

'What didst thou suffer, with thy hand?'

'A thorn, I don't know what; dirt got in, all my hand was poisoned.'

'Poh, poh, what an ugly thing. But it is better?'

'Better, better!' Spiro shouted, his voice suddenly rising in a peasant's impatience with feminine solicitude.

The cafeneion, which is also the village restaurant, is on the right hand of the track which, climbing through Perachora, serves as a main street. The wooden floor is raised a little from the sloping, bumpy ground; there is the impression of a verandah. Inside, the long, bare room has a few tables and chairs and at one end a counter behind which the store of bottles is kept; the cooking is done in some back corner, and the family quarters, I suppose, are beyond.

I could not recognize in it the place where, eight years earlier, we had argued about EAM and drunk a toast to democracy. Then we sat in some other room; but of that reunion I remember not the walls, not the ceiling and the door, but the faces and the words. Today I walked into a cafeneion which had forgotten the war, or at least had learned to put it out of mind. The thick coffee-cups on the iron tables, the men in patched working clothes and caps sitting in the lethargy of the afternoon – it was every cafeneion in every village in Greece; the pose might have been held for twenty years. Only the figure which came to greet me was a little altered. Like Spiro, Yanni had felt time crawling by.

'Welcome,' he said. 'It is many years since we saw you.'

There were the dark, romantic eyes with their gleam of irony, the mouth shaped, under the small moustache, like a passionate girl's. But the black hair was turning grey, the teeth were gapped; and I saw that handsome Yanni carried the sign of his calling, a round belly under his apron.

'Sit down, sit down,' he said. 'What can we offer you? Would you like some eggs? We have cheese, we have yiaourti, what will you have?'

'Nothing, I thank thee; I ate at midday; nothing.'

'But something thou must have,' said his wife. 'Perhaps thou wilt drink an ouzo, or a little rhetsina? Something thou must have.'

'A coffee,' I said, 'but I have eaten; nothing else. I came not to eat and drink, but to see you all.'

'Where have you come from?' said Yanni. 'Last time you came from Mycenae, in '45, wasn't it? Where have you come from?'

'From Loutraki,' I said again. 'I wanted to walk first to the light-house, but I missed the path. I come to the lake, I look at my watch, it is one-twenty; so I turn round and come straight to Perachora. It is necessary,' I explained, 'that I catch the bus back to Loutraki. It goes, they tell me, at half-past three.'

'No, no, half-past four, I think. Eh,' (calling across the room to a man with grizzled, cropped hair, sitting with a newspaper), 'tell me, the bus for Loutraki, what time does it leave?'

'Half-past four.'

'Half-past four,' Yanni repeated. 'That is the driver, he will not go without you, you have time. But why must you leave so soon? It is eight years since we saw you.'

'I must be in Athens tonight. On Sunday I leave for London by airplane, I have my ticket.'

'By airplane? How many hours to go to London?' said Spiro.

'By airplane, a day; by train, three days.'

'But it costs a lot, eh?'

'A lot; you have to be rich to come by plane. As for me, I had work to do in Athens, so they gave me my ticket.'

'How many pounds does it cost?' Yanni asked.

'A hundred pounds.'

'Gold pounds?' For a moment Yanni's mind went back to the war, when the guerillas were financed by the British and there were gold sovereigns in village houses.

'No, not gold; paper.'

'Ah, paper.' The disclosure lowered the prestige of air travel, and interest cooled.

'But tell me, how are you all in the village? Every time a friend visits Greece, when he comes back I ask him: What news of Perachora? But nobody knows anything.'

'Well, we are well; the same we are.'

'In the war with the symmorites, you suffered nothing? You had no trouble in the village?'

'With the andartes?' said Yanni, using the historic instead of the injurious word. 'Here, nothing.' His face, suddenly shuttered, banged the door on the subject. Only his wife, in a woman's long-contained impatience with disturbers of peace for good or ill, muttered: 'Eh, the andartes . . .', and gave a long, complaining sigh.

'So everything is well with you? And the crops? They tell me you have good olives this year.'

'Good, good,' said Yanni, with the intonation of a man not given to enthusiasm.

'And work? Is there work for the village?'

'There is' (inclining his head in modified assent). 'And there is poverty too. Always there is poverty.'

'I remember how before the war thou wouldst speak of the poverty in Perachora. But are things not better? Tell me, is your Government now a good one?'

'Good,' said Yanni, 'I don't know. It does not seem to me that things are better. Do you know how much bread is?'

So many drachmae for an oke – a weight of roughly two pounds and three-quarters – I should have known without being told. The bases of life in the country are bread and oil, and a man measures his economy by their cost. 'It is very much,' I said mechanically.

'Do you think they will come to dig again at the Heraion?'

'I fancy not. I think they would not find anything more.'

'Who knows? There may be antiquities still in the earth. You have seen the road we have made from the village?'

'I have seen it: the carriage road,' I said, trying to keep irony out of my voice.

'A good road, is it not? Now it would be easier for the excavations; a car can go by the road.'

'Do people often go down from the village to the Heraion by car?'

'Of course, of course! There are many visitors.'

I was remembering the cloudy solitude of my walk from the lake when I became aware that someone had come quietly to stand behind my chair. One of Yanni's family, I thought, or a customer; for in a village it is natural and accepted that anybody shall join in a conversation with a foreigner. The newcomer did not speak, and I felt rather than heard that he was there, listening silently, almost secretly. At first I did not look round. But after a little it seemed to me that the voiceless presence standing patiently there had something to say to me. I turned in my chair. A man with thin, greying hair, a broad, bony skull and a little moustache was waiting, looking at me with reproachful urgency. The body was shrunken, and the jacket hung loosely. The face had shrunk too, had fallen in at the lips; it was the face of an old man. I stared at him, and he gazed back at me, his head a little drooped. He looked like an old dog who is no longer certain of a welcome. It was two or three seconds before I recognized Niko of the lighthouse. Time, as I took in the face which had once been all fire and gaiety, grated in my bones.

'Welcome!'

'Well have I found thee!'

'It is long since we had news of you.'

'It is the first time I have been in Greece for eight years. I have only a few days, but I could not go back to England without visiting Perachora.'

'So you have not forgotten us. But why did you not write? How am I to know what has happened to you, whether you are alive or dead?'

'Ah, for me to write in Greek, thou knowest . . . But I never forget you all, never do I forget Perachora. Tell me, how are you all, thy wife, thy daughters? And thou, dost thou not still work at the lighthouse?'

'I have finished, I work no more.' He drank off his coffee. It had been laced, I noticed, with spirit, cognac perhaps; Yanni had brought the bottle without a word, as if in deference to the habits of a regular customer and the foibles of an old man. 'Shall we go to my house, shall we go?'

As we went I saw that a trickle of water from the spring still ran down the middle of the main street. High on the hillside a stony bypath led to Niko's home. The house was built with an outside staircase leading to the living quarters; on the ground-level beneath them was the animals' stable, with a mule snorting in the straw. At the top of the stairs Niko's wife, a plump, smiling woman, now middle-aged, with a wall eye, folded me in her arms.

'How dost thou? How hast thou been? What a time, what a time, since we saw thee!' she repeated, clucking. 'Come in, sit down, rest thyself!'

Two girls came hurrying. Unlike their mother, who wore the traditional bodice, full skirt and head-scarf, they were bare-headed and dressed in the city fashion: cotton summer dresses, heeled shoes. They both embraced me.

'Dost thou remember Theodora?' asked the mother.

I looked at the taller of the two: a young woman of about twenty-eight, confident, laughing, with dark, bubbling hair. 'Theodora? Was it thou, that time we went down to the lighthouse?' When, the year after Humfry's death, I had walked from the village on my last visit to the Heraion, Yanni had refused to let me go alone; a donkey had been saddled and a little girl had been sent with me. 'Was it thou?'

'Yes, do you not remember?'

'I remember. I asked thee what thou wouldst be when thou wert grown up. Thou saidst – a dressmaker!'

Theodora laughed uproariously. 'And I am a dressmaker! I became one!'

'And thy sister?'

'She too is a dressmaker!'

'Where do you work?'

'But here, here in our village!'

I remembered the room from my visit sixteen years before: the bed with the white bedspread, the white cloth on the table, the yellowing family photographs on the walls. We sat in a circle: Niko, myself, his wife, the two daughters, and a pale girl in black who, like a poor relation, sat in shadow without speaking to the end of my visit. I never discovered who she was.

'What can we offer thee? We have cheese, we have eggs. Dost thou wish me to boil some eggs?' said Niko's wife.

'No, I have eaten; nothing; I thank thee.'

'At least you will have some grapes,' said Niko. The dish was put before me. 'Eat, take some!'

'It is a long time,' I said once more, searching to break the embarrassed, formal silence.

'And you did not get to the Heraion?' said Niko.

'No, only to the lake.' I told my tale again.

'To the lake – what a pity! She got to the lake, she looked at her watch, but she was too late . . .' Theodora repeated my story to her mother and sister.

'Do you remember that time you came to the lighthouse with your husband, with the kyrios Payne? When Vasili and I called to the benzina as it was passing and it took you back to Loutraki?' said Niko.

'How should I forget? It was the last time we came to the Heraion together. Dost thou remember, we had to climb down the rocks where it was steep? I was frightened, and thou and Vasili, you took me by the hands . . .'

Niko's voice began to come to life. 'We had a towel, we signalled to the benzina, "Stop! Stop!" we shouted.'

'What things have happened since then, what things? In 1945 I last saw thee. How has life been in the village since the war?'

'Eh,' said Niko, bringing out the words with a ring, 'we die.'

'What sayest thou: you die?'

'Well, shall we not all die?'

'Not yet, let us hope! But tell me, those whom I used to know, are they well?'

'The doctor is well, but his wife, poh, poh, she has aged.' Niko's wife used words meaning: she is a wreck.

'And Aspasia, the old woman?'

'Aspasia is dead, last year she died,' said Niko.

'Old Michael, her husband, is dead too,' said his wife.

'But eat!' Niko cried suddenly, pushing the dish of grapes at me; 'Eat, take them!' His daughters smiled at one another, then – the sophisticated younger generation blushing for its unpolished elders – glanced reprovingly at their father. 'Eat, take them!' he shouted again. His voice crackled in mock ferocity. For a moment the impudent jester of the lighthouse revived. I remembered a time when, if he spoke, the women in the house were silent. Now the note of command was short of breath. There was a protesting murmur from Theodora. No longer sure of his authority, Niko looked furtively from face to face. The moment was over, and under the smothering indignities of age he fell silent.

To keep him in countenance I went on eating. 'I see you have made a road down to the lake,' I said to him.

'A good road, is it not? Will they come and dig again at the Heraion, will they come?'

'To dig, no; I think not. But do many archaeologists go to visit the place?'

'Many; all the summer, and in winter too; many come. A pity they don't dig. Where are they digging now?'

'In Turkey,' I said vaguely, 'and in Mycenae.'

'They should come to our village,' said Niko decisively.

When at last I moved to go he turned and began to search under the bed. 'Bring some paper,' he muttered to his wife. He dragged out a cardboard box. From it he filled with fresh almonds the brown paper bag she brought. 'We have nothing to offer you,' he said, 'but at least when you go back to England you will have something from Perachora.'

'What a pity that you must go,' cried Theodora. 'Next year you must come again, you must stay for two or three days, we will make excursions together, we will go to the lighthouse, we will go to Corinth, we will celebrate!'

As I said goodbye the mother took my left hand and looked at the two wedding rings. 'Thou hast married again,' she said solicitously. 'Is he good, good is he?'

'Next year!' I called back to the group standing on the steps outside the little whitewashed house. 'Next year!' Theodora echoed. Niko walked with me to the cafeneion and the bus. 'This time you will write. You have my address. If you do not write how are we to know what has happened to you?'

'I will write,' I said as I shook hands with Yanni. At the door of the bus I looked at my watch. 'What time is it?' the driver asked. 'Half-past four.' 'Half-past four? Shall we go, then?'

XVIII

In an afternoon still edged with gold we swung down the road to Loutraki and the Athens bus. So in one village at least, I thought, the war is over. Nobody speaks of it any more. The Perachorans survived it, as they survived the guerilla struggle, and now they go back to their old ways, now they concern themselves with today and to-morrow. They grow old, they die, but they are the same. And I reflected with astonishment – for in imagination it is always oneself who is stable in an inconstant world – that I was the feather in the wind. Grief, like love, makes vain. Seventeen years earlier I had flattered myself that I could forget nothing.

But now I had forgotten the way to the lighthouse.

Ever After

I

Back in England in the autumn of 1953, I felt that my Philhellenism had outlived both romanticism and the deflation which sometimes follows it. At any rate I tried to look at Greece as a living country and not the reflection of an egoistic feeling.

I had some correspondence. At Christmas I was touched to receive from a Main Street somewhere in Massachusetts a card signed with the name of the American-Greek I had met in the restaurant in Jannina. And there was a letter from the man from Zakynthos. Before I left Athens Frosso had come to help me to find his little daughter. Carrying the official letter he had entrusted to me we had driven to the Children's City, a large, institutional building on the way to Piraeus, where we were admitted to see a shouting, working company of girls in uniform: elder girls learning crafts, younger girls crowding round a teacher; and there, detached by the matron from a cluster of dark eyes, was the child from Zakynthos, shy but composed. Since I can write only nursery Greek, on my behalf Frosso sent a letter to the father: his little girl was well and cared for, he need not be anxious. But it was too much to expect that he would leave the child in safety.

'As for my little girl', he wrote, 'about whom you had the kindness to write to me, unfortunately at the insistence of her mother I was obliged to bring her to be with us, and now that unhappy one shares our misfortunes; we are crowded all together in Zakynthos. The bad thing is that we live in tents, and thus to our poverty and our nakedness the damp and the cold are added, dangers which frighten me more than the earthquake, for my wife and two of my children are consumptive, and the greater part of the winter they

M   *177*

are in bed. What will happen to us? If God is good all is well. But the earthquakes continue daily. May God protect us.'

Someone else must have composed the letter, for my friend, I fancy, could scarcely write; at Jannina when I asked for his address he called on the hotel clerk to put it down. 'The grateful virginal kisses of my children' – the phrase with which he ended was certainly borrowed. The sadness and the resignation were his own. A year later I was to hear from him again: sickness, need, the troubles as hopeless as ever to relieve. At a distance I could understand better the despair of those who had tried without sentimentality to help him.

Whatever my sympathies, I settled down to separation from Greece. I had work in London with limited holidays which I could not spend, and did not wish to spend, to please myself alone; I saw no chance for a long time of another visit.

No doubt it is common to find experience repeating itself. A region of feeling and being and doing, a landscape with figures long left behind floats into view again. One thinks one has changed trains in life, but there at the windows are the same stations on the same line. After Humfry's death I had withdrawn, at first unconsciously and then deliberately, from the world of classical learning. I had always been a foreigner there, a resident by marriage only; I could not pose now as a native. I kept a formal connection with a few archaeological institutions. But I had no true link, and when I met an archaeologist I was embarrassed by the assumption that I should still understand what he was talking about. It was a language I had forgotten, a country I should not frequent again.

Suddenly I was invited to re-enter it.

The British School at Athens, of which Humfry had been Director during the Perachora excavations, was digging now in the island of Chios. The site, with remains ranging from the early Bronze Age in the third millennium B.C. to the early Christian era, was at Emporio, a tiny place on the shore where it looks south-east towards Turkey. The narrow channel between Chios and Asia Minor must have been one of the main sea-routes of antiquity, and the suggestion was made that here was the place to search the sea-bed for ancient wrecks, not only in the harbour and in the neighbourhood of Emporio, but up and down the east coast of the whole island.

The invention of the aqualung, which allows a diver to move as freely as a fish under water, made the project feasible. Underwater exploration was just then becoming the fashionable sport; and with Cousteau, great pioneer of submarine archaeology, busy ladling up amphorai, ancient wine-jars, from a third-century wreck at Marseilles, there was encouragement to put the invention to scholarly use. The Emporio dig gave an opportunity, the first, of carrying out under-water reconnaissance in conjunction with excavation on land. All that was needed was the equipment and a party of divers willing to put themselves under archaeological direction. The divers came forward: students of the School, enthusiasts from outside headed by David Garnett's son Richard. The *Sunday Times* made the School a gift of the equipment, and offered me the chance of going to Chios to report the results.

I hesitated. I wanted to go to Greece. But I should not be able to travel where I liked. I should have an awkward piece of work to do. Above all, I did not know my company.

To join an archaeological expedition in Greece, at any rate in a place as remote and isolated as Emporio, is to be shut up with strangers in an open-air box. The walls which keep out silence and solitude and the delights of speaking to nobody are impassable. Breakfast is eaten in a circle which may break up only to cry good-night. There is no escape, nowhere to go. And this time the party, the land archaeologists and especially the divers, would consist for the most part of young men and women half my age. With shrinking I pictured myself panting in the wake of a school of human porpoises. After all the comfortable years of choosing one's own company, after the long freedom from feeling obliged to do things one is afraid of doing, it would, I felt, be rather like going back to school.

But, of course, I said yes.

II

NOT UNTIL ITALY was left behind did summer come to meet us. At London Airport there was cold rain in the morning air; at Rome a hot, vicious wind blew, the sky was sulky and the tarmac was wet; south Italy was marbled with cloud-shadows. But the Ionian Sea glittered, and when the airplane landed at Hellenikon, airport of Athens, heat pressed in on the travellers, the earth exhaled heat. It was the Athens I knew best, Athens before the months of summer have leeched and faded it. At midday the sun turned everything white, houses, walls, shops, and the Athenians, as if putting on protective colouring, walked in white suits through white streets. At night the chairs outside the cafés were all taken, and under the electric lights rows of eyes watched the strollers on the pavements; through open doors in dark streets the radio sang; the city whispered amorously with voices and sauntering footsteps. That evening I dined with friends. We sat in the courtyard of a taverna in the old quarter of the city over the food and drink I think of as Athenian: ouzo with black olives and taramosalata, roe beaten into a paste with oil; rhetsina with baby lamb cutlets; cherries heaped in a bowl of ice. The shadows of leaves climbed on the whitewashed walls, the trickle of talk was cool. In Athens, I thought, a summer evening does not cheat you by slipping away unspent.

But I had no time to loiter. Twenty-four hours, and I was at Piraeus, boarding the steamer for Chios. There were no single cabins, and clinging as long as I could to my own company I had asked for a double cabin to myself. SUPER LUX, the ticket called it: a double bed, a lamp, a basin with running water, the whole thing shut away by itself in coolness on the first-class deck – contrasting it with the berths I had slept in when I first travelled in Greece, I was ready to agree. The porter waited for his tip and I counted the pieces of luggage.

'How much?'

'Whatever you like.'

I had not travelled in an island steamer since the war, and Frosso had told me that the porters nowadays had a fixed tariff which they were obliged to show.

'But the tariff? What is the tariff?'

'Whatever you like,' he said again, beaming.

Once more I tried. 'But you have a tariff, haven't you?'

'Eh, tariff, tariff,' he repeated, crackling with delight, 'whatever you like you will give me.'

Defeated, I paid him off – but no longer in extravagant figures. After the war inflation had brought Greece to a point at which money was reckoned in thousands of drachmae, and if the taxi-driver at the end of the journey said: Ten, he meant: Ten thousand. Now the old paper money, I found, was being replaced by new notes counted by the single drachma instead of by the thousand. Little by little the traces of war were being effaced.

The local steamers, small cargo and passenger ships which make the round of one or another group of the islands, usually leave Piraeus in the evening at six or seven o'clock. If they are bound for the Aegean Sea and the Archipelago, for the Cyclades or the Sporades or the Dodecanese, they sail south-east between Attica and the island of Aegina until they round Poseidon's temple on Cape Sounion. The sun was still shining as we thrummed out of port, past the coalers and the big cargo-boats from the Americas and the caïques with their forest of masts. But already the clear sky was shading behind the mountains in the west, and soon I looked back to see Piraeus flushed with sunset. I took a deck-chair from the stack and settled by the rail, looking towards Attica. The coastline darkened. The air blew fresh off the water, and my skin was sticky and chill as I sat hugged in a sweater, watching the rolling, scaly, purple-black sea. A party of dolphins paced us: one giant superbly bounding beside us, a smaller pair following, their lustrous arched bodies leaping and diving, switchbacking in perfect unison between air and waves. The moon appeared above Aegina; her luminous track slid on the water at our side, coldly pursuing us. From the land a lighthouse swung its lariat. As we crept southwards the wind took body; it was no longer the force which on land strikes and draws back, but a solid thing, pushing with all its weight, incessantly. Under its attack the passengers round me retreated. The man in the overcoat and the dark hat called his little boy and led him by the hand into the saloon; the young wife going home after visiting her mother in Athens, the woman from Detroit determined to see the village in Chios where she was born, one by one they gathered themselves and went in. The water, flecked with bubbles, raced by. The ship was steady. But the lonely predicament of the voyager by night suddenly frightened me. I was glad to join my companions.

In Greek seas the cost of a ticket does not include the cost of meals; the passenger orders his own dinner and pays for what he eats. I chose synagridha, a Mediterranean fish which so far as I am aware has no common English name; drank with it a glass of rhetsina, and for a while sat eating cherries, benignly watched by the stewards in a dining-saloon three-quarters empty. Their company made me forget the insecurity of the sea, and at ease I finished my coffee and went to bed. It was no more than ten o'clock. I feared I should not sleep. But I had scarcely put out the light and pulled up the rough-textured sheet, or so I fancied, when a change of noise brought me to myself. It was morning; the ship's engines no longer pounded, but beat gently amidst a general silence. Then running feet, shouts, the rattle of a chain as the anchor was dropped; and peeping from behind the curtain of my deck cabin I saw the harbour buildings of Chios town, nacreous in the six o'clock sun.

III

CHIOS LIES CLOSE to Asia Minor, at its closest no more than five miles from the Turkish shore. It is a fertile island, and has been rich: rich in fruit and vines, rich in mastic, a resin used to make varnish and to flavour sweets and the drink called in Greece masticha. The wine of Chios was a celebrated export in the ancient world; Virgil praised it. Today it is still a favourite; and as for fruit, there are still great orchards in the plain south of the capital. But the island bled in the War of Independence, when the Turks landed a punitive army and slaughtered tens of thousands of the inhabitants; and the earthquake of 1881 brought disaster again. Chios was not reunited with Greece until the Balkan War of 1912. In the Second World War, when it was occupied by the Germans, it was an island for escapers; hundreds of Greeks sailed secretly across the straits to Turkey.

The island faces towards Asia Minor. There are ancient sites up and down the east shore, and the capital itself, also called Chios, stands on an eastward harbour. Emporio, for which I was bound, lies in the mountains of the coast south-east of the capital – in the mastic-growing region, among the Masticha-villages as they are called. But when I arrived the district was strange to me. At the end of August 1939, scurrying back from an Aegean holiday at the news of the Russo-German pact, I had spent a few hours in Chios. I remembered a hot walk to a dusty repository of bones and skulls, relics of the massacre of 1822. I remembered dusk as we waited for the steamer to Athens, girls and young men in separate groups strolling past the cafés, the harbour buzzing with apprehensions of war. That was all; and now, on a June morning of 1954, I could not recall a single land-mark as amidst the crowd of passengers and porters, the luggage and the cargo, I looked for a taxi to drive me to Emporio.

The car, with a dark, brooding man driving and the owner sitting beside him, rattled southwards out of Chios town, across the Cambos, the fruit-growing plain, past estates with walled gardens.

'How far to Emporio?'

'An hour, an hour and a quarter.'

We left the orchards behind; now the hillsides were dotted with dense-leaved shrubs.

'Those trees, what are they?'

'But masticha,' said the driver, surprised by my ignorance.

We passed a village or two, skirted dry slopes. At about eight o'clock a large village was ahead of us on the road.

'What is that place?'

'Pyrghi; here we turn for Emporio.'

We swung left off the road and down a winding track covered with angular stones which lay where, without benefit of steam-roller, they had been thrown. The car bounced and shook; beneath it the stones rasped and ground together. After four or five miles the valley opened, and between mountains the sea came into view. The track ran past a house or two; ahead, arms of rock embraced a harbour. The water blinked in the sun.

'Emporio,' said the driver.

The track ended at the shore. The car pulled up and I got out: a few forlorn houses, a deserted taverna, a beach deep in seawrack. It was still only quarter-past eight, and I had not warned anybody of the day I should turn up. The driver dragged my luggage out and put it on the sandy shingle; one or two figures appeared from houses and hurried towards us. The first-comer was an old man in an apron.

'Kyrios Hood is here?' I said, naming the Director of the excavations.

'Kyrios Hood is not here.'

'Not here? Where is he then?'

'He has gone to the town, to Chios,' said one of the group which had collected, 'he went this morning.'

'When will he come back?'

'Tomorrow he will come back; with the motor-car he went.'

'Never mind,' I said. 'Where are the English, where are they digging?'

'Over there,' said somebody, 'by the shore.'

'No, no,' said another voice, 'up there on the mountain.'

In the confusion the old man shouldered my suitcase and began to make off shakily towards the hills.

'Stop, stop!'

'No, this way!'

At last there was decision. 'To the house she must go, to the house.' A young man took my luggage and set off barefoot along the shore; screwing up my eyes against the naked sun, I followed a hundred yards to a house with a verandah looking on to the harbour. It was the excavation headquarters: the office, the studio, the dig-house.

For a visitor to an expedition in Greece to turn up at breakfast-time is not unusual. My sudden appearance was received with hospitable indifference, and I was thankful for it. Only two or three people were about. Most of the archaeologists had long since gone off to their work in pits and trenches, and the divers were not expected until the next day; I was their forerunner. A young woman introduced herself politely; she was the wife of the assistant director. Should I like something to eat? Coffee, a boiled egg, bread, margarine, honey; I sat in the shade of the verandah eating an English breakfast and struggling to disentangle my company. Michael Ventris and his wife were both working as surveyors on the expedition: not until afterwards did I realize that Ventris was the young architect who had astonished scholars by his work in deciphering the mysterious Minoan script. (Tragically, he was to be killed in an accident a few years later.) The friendly dark-haired girl was a student having an idle morning because work on the Bronze Age Pit was broken off for a day. Where then, I asked her, was everybody working? At the temple on the hill, she said, or at the house-foundations; she waved towards the mountains across the harbour. Already heat recoiled from the rocks. What should I like to do, see the temple? Certainly, I said with the newcomer's anxiety to appear a good sort, ready for anything. We set off briskly up the hillside.

Emporio has a long history long forgotten. To the patch of level shore and the low promontory south of the harbour came, over four thousand years ago, the people of the Bronze Age, setting up their rubble houses, shaping without a wheel their cups and dishes and pots for storage. In late Roman times, about 600 A.D., the promontory was fortified, and Christians set up a baptistery in the plain beneath the Roman fortress and behind the site of the Bronze Age settlement. Between the two eras the Greeks settled. In the seventh and sixth centuries before Christ they built a city on the slopes to the north overlooking the harbour and the plain; and, on a saddle of the mountain above the city, a temple.

The mountain, the highest of the district, serves as a landmark; on its summit there is a chapel named, as chapels on Greek heights are commonly named, after the Prophet Elijah. The bottom slopes rise curtly from the harbour. There is an ancient road up to the temple, but it winds leisurely round the flanks of Mount Prophet Elijah. 'I *think* this must be right,' said my guide as we left the path and took to the scrub. To an arrival from sedentary London life the slope seemed barely negotiable, and from all fours 'I suppose we haven't missed the way?' I faintly repeated. For twenty minutes we climbed. At last, hallooing, we heard answering shouts, and dragged ourselves over the rim of a tiny plateau. There before us was the sanctuary: an altar-stone and the foundations of a temple of the sixth century before Christ, the wall-blocks lying in order where an earthquake had tumbled them. Eastwards across the straits a faint shape of land was Turkey. Far below us the sea slept cool under its summer haze. But on the mountain the sun was brutal, and the sweating workmen were muffled in white cowls, headscarves tied under the chin and quilted to make a stiffened brim over the eyes. Every morning they carried their heavy gear, their spades and pick-axes, up the unkind hillside.

'And at midday,' I asked the archaeologist who was directing the excavation of the temple, 'what do you do?' 'We stay here,' he said, 'we bring our food.' Once up and down the hill was enough. Even the men digging out the floors and column bases of the ancient city on the lower slopes preferred to make no more than one journey a day.

The rest of us, as I learned, ate together in the taverna at midday. Breakfast and tea were provided on the verandah of the dig-house by the assistant director's wife and by a member of the archaeological party who combined housekeeping with the work of excavation draughtswoman. For dinner we gathered once more in the taverna. I was lucky to meet my company by degrees, for I am slow to make acquaintance; arriving as I did while they were few I could learn the faces one by one. We were a land party at first (for as I say the divers were still on their way): a group of six or seven archaeologists, students, architects and the visitors who are drawn to watch or practise excavation. There was nothing to distract us from eyeing one another. Emporio is a summer village. Or scarcely a village: a settlement – the taverna with its reed-shaded terrace on the beach; a wine-shop used as cafeneion; and a few houses in the season occupied by urban visitors, by holiday-makers and the sportsmen who come to shoot quail in the plain of Dotia to the south, the rest of the year a home for the spiders and the wind. The families who serve the place leave it in the winter and go back to Pyrghi, the inland village which I had seen on the drive out. Pyrghi is visited daily by bus from Chios town. No bus comes to Emporio, though a lorry or, as I had seen, a taxi will sometimes bounce down the ribbon of stones to the harbour in its horse-shoe of rocks and mountains.

The expedition was variously lodged in tents and the empty houses along the shore, and when I arrived at Emporio I was given the choice of sleeping under canvas or under a roof. I thought with nostalgia of the camp among the pines at Perachora, and chose a tent. It was at the land's edge where the fields dropped a few feet to the beach, with no shelter from the sun, and in the siesta of the first afternoon I sweated and suffocated. Wait, said someone at tea-time, wait until we get a strong wind; you'll go up like a kite. But I persisted. We bathed from a shingly beach over the hill to the south; gathered on the dig-house verandah for ouzo; and straggled across the seawrack to dinner in the taverna. The fare was the same as at midday: a stew of vegetables, chiefly potatoes and onions, baked beans, and the pale sweet cornflour pudding which the Greeks call crema. Too new to find it monotonous, I listened to the complaints of the rest; on the first day at school one reveres the grumbling veterans.

'What on earth are we to do about the divers?' said one, 'I read somewhere that they have to eat four pounds of meat a day.'

'Is it difficult to get meat here?'

'They kill once a week up at Pyrghi, so we have meat once a week, on Sunday; that's tomorrow.'

'The divers will have to do their own fishing, that's all,' said another voice. The divers – there was a faint hostility in the title, as if a set of outsiders had to be accommodated during, let us say, the rebuilding of their own school. I recalled the animosities of life on the Heraion headland, the shuttered stares at visitors and new arrivals, and began to feel more at home. My tent, too, when we dispersed, looked familiar. The shadowy rectangular interior, the camp bed and the chocolate-coloured blanket, the wooden bench for table, standing across the farther tent-pole with my brush and comb, a torch, a pitcher of water, an enamel basin – the camp equipment was, I guessed, the same we had taken year after year to Perachora, and the storm lamp might have been the very one by whose light I used to undress in the tent under the pines.

It was only ten o'clock when I fastened the tent-flap, blew out the lamp and got into bed, an hour when in London I should probably be settling to work, and though the long outdoor day should have tired and composed me I could not sleep. The silence seemed to me to rustle and crackle and hammer. Somewhere a donkey brayed, pumping out its desires and its loneliness in gasping cries which died down into a deflated, snuffling groan. (At the Heraion, too, we used to hear a donkey crying at night from the field where it was tethered.) The evening had been almost still, and the night was hot. But now I could hear the stirring of wind, and the sides of the tent began to flap against the poles, against the wooden bench, against my pillow. I got up, dragged the bed away from the canvas, and tried to steady one or two pegs which had loosened in the shallow soil. The wind still whipped the tent, banging the walls in and out with the noise of someone opening and closing a tin box. I lay in bed remembering how at Perachora the prevailing north-west wind, the maistros, had slept at sunset, only to wake again at dawn.

At last I felt the inability to follow a thought which is the beginning of sleep. At that moment, so it seemed, there was the chink of a foot against a pebble inside the tent. Frightened awake, I turned my head cautiously to look over the edge of the bed. I must have dozed for some time, for it was no longer night-dark. Now indeed I could have believed I was back on the Perachora headland, in the tent where the lighthouse cat, pausing in her nocturnal hunting, would come to drink from the water-jug. There by the pitcher – frozen for a second in the attitude of flight, crouched flat like a lizard on the ground but with one forepaw lifted and curled underneath her – a black cat stood and stared wildly at me. I called to her. But when I took my arm from under the sheet she flashed away, body and tail rippling in one straight line over the invisible scampering feet. A gust of wind rattled the canvas at her as she slid under the flap. And now the confusion of drowsiness came on me in earnest, and with the names of Emporio and Perachora tangled together in my head I wandered, lost myself and slept.

IV

LIKE THE WIND which puffs across the sea suddenly in the night, the arrival of the first diving party stirred Emporio out of its quiet. In the morning, the indolent occupations of Sunday in camp: anybody coming to bathe? Then at midday the Director reappeared, bringing Richard Garnett and a group of others, and all at once the place bustled. Mattresses, blankets must be provided. There was no room inside the taverna for so large a table, and we must eat on the terrace outside. On the beach a little Greek crowd, men, women and a gentle melancholy donkey with poor Neddy's air of drooping at both ends, watched while the equipment for aqualung diving was unpacked from its crate. Forgoing the siesta, a few of the English stood by, bored with the time taken, afraid to leave lest some entrancing thing should happen when they had gone.

With the increase in our numbers and the new kind of exploration now to be undertaken, the party must be rearranged. At the far end of the beach, on the rocky edge of the bay opposite our headquarters, a house stood by a tiny quay. This was to be the divers' house; and since the machine for charging the aqualungs with compressed air was heavy and needed a stable base, the quay must be the place for it to stand. Greek volunteers carried the squat complex of pipes and valves along the beach and set it down. The aqualungs were fetched and laid side by side on the quay. Once, looking back towards the taverna and our headquarters, I saw what seemed a dreadful hollow man, with dangling arms and legs cut off below the knees, advancing over the seawrack. But it was only a bearer bringing the thick rubber suit which Richard Mitchell, one of the experienced divers, used against the cold in deep waters.

Not until the second morning was the equipment in its place. Then the divers began the struggle, continued on and off throughout the expedition, to keep the machine working. An aqualung contains enough compressed air for a man to stay under water for, say, half-an-hour: less or more according to the depth. After that it must be re-filled; and if there is no compressor there can be no diving. In the taverna, in our headquarters, in our tents we listened for the engine. From dawn the divers wooed it; and sometimes across the bay we heard morning and afternoon the tut-tut-tut of its stroke. Then there would be a wheezing sigh and the clatter would stop. There was a leak; a valve was ill-tempered, a screw out of sorts; in the comprehensive Greek phrase for mechanical disorders, it had broken. And hour after hour the divers, their naked backs blotched and peeling in the sun, squatted on the quay, tinkering, winding, cursing; or if a car from the village was going into Chios town, taking back, perhaps, some visitor to the excavations, one of them would ask for a lift and tramp round the streets behind the harbour, searching for a mechanic.

But on the first day the cylinders were ready filled, and the divers could hardly wait to use them. There was a volunteer, too, from the archaeologists; a party of four fish-men waded into the harbour and, leaving the sparkling afternoon, disappeared under the water. The rest of us ran for our bathing-dresses. I came back bringing as well flippers, mask and schnorkel, equipment much envied by the land-party, for though by 1954 swimming with frog-feet and breathing-tube was a commonplace in France, among English bathers it was still unusual. As I put the things on I assumed a confidence quite false. Instructed by Richard Garnett, I had made a few gingerly essays to use them in London swimming-baths. But I still felt uneasy in the rubber flipper-feet, no matter how much they helped one along in the water, and breathing through a metal tube in my mouth, with the rubber rim of the glass-fronted mask pinching my nostrils shut, I was downright wretched. Nor had I up to then really seen the point of the impedimenta. I recognized that they enabled one to swim or float lying flat on one's face without turning over for air, and that through the mask one could see as clearly in water as in air.

But in a swimming bath these are poor benefits. And so far even at Emporio when we bathed from the beach over the hill there had been nothing to look at through my glass panel except greenish water and greyish sand.

Lifting webbed feet with the duck's gait which they force on their wearer, I waddled into the verge, then swam flapping towards the point where the divers had vanished. They had plunged not far from the beach, for there had been talk of submerged masonry in the harbour, and from a boat you could distinguish what looked like a fragment of a column. At first I saw only the brown hair of weeds undulating over the sea-boulders where it grew. Then, as if lying on a roof of pneumatic glass, I was looking down on the divers. The water was no more, I dare say, than twelve feet deep, and any diver could have eeled to the bottom without aqualung or any other help. But the four half-naked figures on the floor seemed to be not creatures from the air at all. They belonged to the sea and its weeds. They moved with submarine deliberation, hovering in the water as if there were no such force as gravity, no such property as weight or buoyancy; their very colour – a faint, drowned, greenish shade infecting the pink or brown of flesh as well as the blacks, the greens and blues and greys of bathing-trunks and equipment – was of water. And now, as I thrashed awkwardly over the face of the harbour, I began to see into that other world. Under so thin a ceiling of sea, and so neighbourly to land, its traffic was of small, inconspicuous lives. But with delight my eyes recognized beings whose colours were for underwater. Fish sharply striped and barred hung in mid-depth or slid in hasty little shoals over the scarved and beribboned rocks; the luminous patterns of their bodies were clear in the clear water. A sea-slug, a dark wriggler like a spiky-furred caterpillar, moved furtively across a patch of sand. The black sea-urchins clustered on the sides of boulders were bristled with light; as I swam farther towards the mouth of the harbour I saw once or twice a less irascible cousin, a pink and green dome with blunt, white-pointed spines. All was clean, radiant, polished; and in this aqueous room into which I looked through the skylight of my mask, every rounded block of stone, every draping of weed, every living, creeping, darting, gliding thing was focused and auraed with the unreal clarity of a thumb seen through a magnifying-glass.

There were half a dozen swimmers in the bay, and one of them asked to borrow my mask and breathing-tube. I handed the things over, then turned stupidly back to my observation of the shallows. But of course I could see nothing except greenness. I was blind without my skylight, and since I had been paddling about for some time I made to go in. Once or twice I put my hand as I swam on what seemed to be thicker water. Once I felt in my arm a tiny shock, a pricking ache which did not leave me for an hour or two. I had blundered into one of the jellyfish which in their scores, as I could see when I wore my mask, were drifting towards the beach, and this time the thing had stung me. Perachora, I said to myself, I remember days at Perachora when nobody would venture into the sea, so dense it was with jellyfish.

The diving of the first afternoon was scarcely more than a trial of equipment and terrain, if the sea-bed may be called terrain. After that, when the whims of the compressor allowed it, there was work in earnest. The harbour, to begin with, had to be explored. The shore-level of the Eastern Mediterranean has sunk since the antique world built its ports and cities there, and it was possible that the foundations of some building might lie under shallow water where once was land. Outside the harbour, where sabre-toothed rocks fringe the entrance, there might be wrecks, evidence of trade in the ancient past, in particular of the Chian wine trade. Off the beaches and coves to the north with their reefs waiting to rip up a boat flying for shelter the sea must be searched. And far away, both to the north and to the south of the island, there were ancient sites, harbours known to antiquity where the divers hoped to make reconnaissance. But long excursions were to be undertaken later; first, the neighbourhood of Emporio.

A system of exploration had been devised by Richard Garnett. First, a party using flippers, masks and breathing-tubes swam backwards and forwards over a chosen stretch of water. If anything worth investigating was seen on the bottom a man following by rowing-boat left a marker with a float. Then the divers went down. Should they find something of importance – a marble statue, a bronze – they were not free to lift it. They could only plot its position. The romantic think of archaeology as a treasure-hunt from which the searchers come away with golden trophies for the chimney-piece. But even in the richest excavations weeks may be spent, not in finding tombs and temples, but in establishing some minute historical fact, spinning some thread of theory. And here the diving permit given by the Greek Government was for reconnaissance only. At Perachora we had taken pottery, bronze and ivory from the earth and carried it to the museum in Athens. Off Chios everything except an occasional fragment for identification must be left lying under the sea.

The divers, ravished by their submarine forays, were not discouraged. They hoped, of course, as we all hoped, for some stupendous find. But they were ready to be content with anything: a scrap, a sign that their whole undertaking was not baseless. Luckily the exploration of Emporio harbour, where a number of sunken column-fragments and dressed blocks of stone were found, gave them from the start a useful task. To surface with evidence that a few pieces of masonry had not been submerged where they stood but had rolled into the sea – this may not seem much of an achievement. But it is the stuff of archaeology. Watching and listening, the land-party began to respect the work of the fish-party.

V

THE VOLUNTEER OF the first day came up delighted with himself.
Nothing to it, he said at tea. One had the impression that he was
back from an enjoyable stroll. His nonchalance was contagious, and
I heard myself begging to be allowed to try a dive. My first view of
the lively sea-bed had so excited me that I had forgotten my dislike
of mask and breathing-tube. In any case I thought I should know
what the experience was like. After all I was in Chios to describe an
underwater expedition.

I was startled, when I put the apparatus on, to find myself uneasy
in it. An aqualung diver, a free diver as he is called in contrast to the
helmeted man breathing air pumped from the surface, carries on his
back a cylinder of compressed air (or for a long stay two or even
three cylinders): a thing shaped like a bomb without vanes, attached
by straps over his shoulders and a strap between his legs; two tubes,
leading from it on either side of his head, meet in a mouthpiece
through which, his lips forced into a negroid bulge, he breathes. His
glass-panelled mask covers his nose and eyes; on his feet he wears
rubber fins; a meter on his wrist tells him how deep he has gone, a
gauge at his waist how much air he has left. The aqualung is heavy
to lift, though it is a feather compared with a helmet-diver's equipment. All the same it is buoyant, it will float, it will support a man.
The diver, then, must put on a belt of lead pieces; if its weight is
nicely calculated he can swim downwards or upwards with little effort.

The aqualung can be released by tugging at a tab. So can the lead
belt; 'Here', said Richard Mitchell encouragingly when I tottered
under the weight of the whole caboodle, 'is the fastener to pull if you
are in trouble.' I was already in trouble, for to breathe at all seemed

to me difficult. But perhaps it would be easier in the water. Making, I noticed, melancholy snoring noises, I duck-footed it through the rock-pools by the quay to fling myself trustingly face down in the harbour.

The water was shallow and sunlit; as I drove myself laboriously forward with my flippers the long-haired rocks beneath were as brilliant as the flowers in a glass paper-weight. Swarms of little fish, dark-striped, flushed with the colours of a pearl and so delicate that they seemed transparent, flickered past or hung ignoring me with their black-ringed eyes. I had known, of course, that once I put my head under water I should hear no sound, yet the silence surprised and unnerved me. The water deepened; I began to look about for human company. The first divers had gone ahead, the next had not yet followed. Encumbered with apparatus, I felt incapable of break-ing the surface; nothing for it but to blunder on as I was. I could see nothing but rocks, weeds, sand and the crowds of inattentive fish. Suddenly a sense of inescapable and appalling solitude overpowered me. Will nobody come? I thought desperately. But I was walled in water, and nobody came.

Later I was told I had never really left the surface. Like an iceberg two-thirds submerged, I had been swimming just below the skin of the water, with my air-cylinder visible above it. That I have never dived I deny, for when at last, after what seemed to me an endless submarine journey, I saw the pioneers at work below me, one of them came to stretch out a hand, and holding it I was hauled down a few feet. But as soon as I let go up I floated, helpless as a toy balloon. And now to solitude fright was added. I realized that I had not the wind to swim back to shore: not if I was to go on breathing the aqualung air at which I had been dragging with such effort. To jettison my equipment would be absurd; in any case I had forgotten what tabs to pull. I cast frantically about for rescue. At a little distance I saw a rock, under water but rising nearer than most to the surface. Disregarding the beckoning divers I lumbered towards it, reached it, swung my feet on to it. I could balance, I found, with my head above water; I could take out the mouthpiece, I could gasp for ordinary air. I could even hear ordinary sounds. There were bathers in the harbour by now. One or two of them swam towards me, circled curiously. 'Hullo!' they said. Gulping, struggling to compose my features, I returned a faint 'Hullo!' Then, satisfied no doubt that I had come up for the view, they paddled away, leaving me to my private battle for wind. I had not recovered my breath when, minutes later, Richard Mitchell came to ask if I was in difficulty. Relieved of my lead belt, I swam slowly back to the quay, breathing through my schnorkel and pushing the aqualung in front of me; I was still panting. All day until evening I found myself wheezing as if I were mending from bronchitis.

No doubt I should have left it at that. But persuaded that diving might be easier in deeper water, I had another try a week later. A ship, whose intervention I will describe presently, had taken a group of the divers round the point to the north and anchored some little distance from the shore; the fish-party equipped themselves on deck. Richard Garnett went over the side first with his wife, who had until then used an aqualung only in a swimming-bath; without a second's hesitation she bent her head and dived; from the deck we watched the pair flittering away down until they were lost in the opaque sea. My flippers slithering on the ladder, in my turn I crawled to the water, with Richard Mitchell murmuring advice at my elbow. A row of faces watched from the rail above: the humane, encouraging faces of the English, the dark-eyed, non-committal faces of the crew. I inserted the rubber flanges of the mouthpiece correctly between lips and gums and tried to breathe. The tube seemed to me full of water; I spluttered and pulled the thing out.

'Take her hand!' cried somebody from the deck.

I put back the mouthpiece and let myself go. I felt as if I were choking; the desire to breathe overpowered me and I grabbed the ladder again. The voices from above multiplied their suggestions.

'Throw her a rope!'

'Breathe deeply!'

'Try going down by the anchor-chain!'

I bit on the mouthpiece, abandoned myself to the water, and swam along the side of the ship; half-suffocated, I reached the chain and clung to it. At last I nerved myself to trust the breathing-tube once more, put my head in the water and peered down the line of the chain. There was a pale green silence. The hull curved vertiginously beneath me; beyond it the water darkened and thickened with its own weight. On the empty, sandy bottom there was no stir, no life. It was like hanging over nothing, over death; it was like looking into a limitless glass coffin. And suddenly I knew that my struggle was useless. I could not dive. This time I recognized that I was afraid: afraid of the coffin of the sea.

Half-thankful, half-fretful, I resigned myself from that day to being the watcher from the surface. After the claustrophobia of an aqualung the tiny constriction of mask and schnorkel seemed a mere cobweb; I paddled industriously across bays, morning after morning hung entranced at my skylight over the searchers on the sea-bed. Sometimes the work went on almost at our door. I remember a day when, no boat being available, Richard Garnett decided to swim in his aqualung to the mouth of the harbour, moving on the surface and using a schnorkel to breathe ordinary air until he reached the submerging point – for though the cylinders are buoyant enough to support their wearer, he floats low, with his face under water. Igor Melanofidis, a gigantic Swiss-Greek swimming champion, joined him, nonchalantly driving himself and his equipment through the water without flippers; and with a third member of the fish-party I swam out to watch. We hurried to the northern arm of the harbour, scarcely looking as we went at the floor of the sea and the dark clusters of sponges. At the point we waited, climbing tender-footed over the barbed rocks while Richard and Igor prepared to go down.

The wind outside the shelter of land was cold enough to make us shiver. The swell arched its back against the reefs and inlets of the coast; when we lay on the water to watch the divers our floating bodies tossed and swung. Below us, steep submarine cliffs overhung the canyons of the sea. The bed of the salt streams which oozed back and forth between crags and tumbled boulders was, perhaps, twenty-five feet beneath the surface of the water. It seemed twice as far; balancing above the traitorous sea, suspended as it were by invisible cords over a gulf, I had a moment's dizziness, as if the elements might let me fall. The two divers, now directly beneath us, moved with an unreal deliberation, making huge signs to one another, advancing in long half-floating strides. At the depth where they searched all was sea-colour. The peacock water at the shoulder of the cliffs dulled and dimmed at the foot to a dense aqueous green; the rocks were green, the sand was green, the divers were a pair of pale green fish with green antennae; and from their gills there swam up an endless column of bubbles, at first flattish, like mushrooms, then pulling into pear-shapes as in an iridescent fountain they rushed to destroy themselves against the wall between water and air.

Often the divers came back disappointed. On this occasion, I know, they found nothing except a piece of the wooden prow of a modern boat. But the sea bounded our lives; it was our work and our play, our talk, our spy-glass. Even when the compressor failed and nobody could dive there was occupation in the sea. Richard Mitchell had been asked by some learned body to bring back to England specimens of seaweed; wearing a sweater over his sunburn, he waded by the hour among the rocks. Sometimes he had a net in his hand, and later we would see in the shadow of the house on the quay a jam-pot with patterned fishes hanging quite still in the water, nose to the glass. Once the jar held two tiny creatures, transparent as cellophane and decorated with red and orange; scarlet edged the delicate fins, and from the spine rose a square sail fringed with tangerine.

'I think,' said Richard, 'they may be young scorpion-fish. Their sting is poisonous.'

He collected shells too. Beside the aqualungs on the quay big whorled and hinged sea-things lay or crawled expiring: whelks the size of a hand, the harmless sea-urchin, the pinna with shell-wings shaped like a half-closed fan and lined with mother-of-pearl.

And the sea fed us. Far from complicating the catering, the divers made it easier; we all ate the better for their presence. Every morning Igor took his harpoon-gun and went off, sometimes alone, sometimes with another swimmer, to fish. A couple of hours later he came back with the pouch at his belt full. Only octopus he left alone.

'Octopus,' he said in his slow hesitating voice, 'it takes hold of your rifle' (pause); 'it takes hold of your arms' (pause); 'it . . .' (his hands described some ungovernable substance boiling over the rim of his pouch) 'it comes *out*.'

But he brought us the Mediterranean fish for which I know only the Greek names; night and midday the dish was piled with tsipoura or boiled rophós. As many as sixteen of us sat down to dinner together. With sun, sea, food and a glass of Chian wine we all of us, divers and archaeologists, grew easy with one another. Sometimes I could have fancied myself back at Perachora – except that at the Heraion we were of a generation in which surnames were still used in familiar address and Christian names were for intimates only. At Emporio in the current fashion it was Christian names from the start.

I write as if I had stayed there for months instead of ten days. The hot, silent hours out-of-doors, the curve of sand and seawrack over which we tramped from office to taverna, from taverna to quay, the dazzle of the sea – time in this setting moved without hurry, and left deep prints. The movement had a pattern. The two groups, the land-party and the sea-party, began the day at different hours. At six o'clock the archaeologists breakfasted; at half-past the table had been cleared and there was room for the divers. The archaeologists were already on their way: to the Bronze Age pit, not fifty yards behind the dig-house, to the temple on the saddle of Mount Prophet Elijah, to the ancient houses on the slopes. Presently the divers too set off to their hunting-grounds, or, should the compressor be dis-obliging, to the quay to struggle with it. If the morning's work was near at hand we ate at midday with the archaeologists, all except the party working on the mountain, who picnicked where they were. In the steady blaze of early afternoon we slept. But while the air was still heavy with sun the diggers went back to the pits, and from the quay came the tut-tut of the divers' engine.

After tea on the verandah of the dig-house there were the results of the day's work to be set in order; or one could swim or go for a walk. We met again at dusk for a glass of ouzo, then by moonlight or with torches picked our way along the beach to the taverna. Those who after dinner were not faltering with sleep and fatigue strolled a dozen yards to the village shop. Owned by Pandeli, the old man who on my arrival had shouldered my suitcase, and his wife, it was also the village well-house. In the middle of the floor, under the shelves of bottles, a lid covered a well of sweet, cold water. Outside the house a few benches and tables on a verandah served as cafeneion, and there we would order coffee and a loukoumi, a piece of Turkish delight, and sit for a quarter of an hour. The latest of us were on our way to bed by ten o'clock.

I slept only twice in my flapping tent. I had been given as well (for as a visitor I was privileged) a room in an empty house where I could keep my luggage and do my work; but after the second night Sinclair Hood, reflecting no doubt that I could be more compactly accommodated, arranged instead that I should have a little, bare, two-roomed house to myself, and there, with a camp bed, a bench to sit on and a table for my typewriter, I was happily installed for the rest of my visit.

The first night the wind blew fractiously round the whitewashed walls and cobwebbed shutters, and though it was less active than in the tent, where the morning before it had woken me by knocking the lamp with a crash to the ground, its rattling prevented me from sleeping until I had got up and stuffed a handkerchief between door and latch. The house stood alone, high above the beach at the top of a sloping field, now dry and empty. The short, steep path leading to it ran on round the base of Mount Prophet Elijah; shadowed by the flank of the hill, the house looked down on the curve of the harbour and on the fields between the surrounding mountains. The second evening, standing on the terrace of beaten earth in front of the door, I thought how splendid it must be to wake to such a view. There were no mosquitoes; the nights were not cold. I dragged the camp-bed out on to the terrace. That night, and every other night, I slept cool and quiet in the open air, and knew nothing until at the first sun a party of workmen carrying picks and spades went along the path behind me on their way to the high temple.

VI

Until i reached Emporio I had not known whether it would be possible to post a letter. Taking a look round at the scatter of untenanted houses, the rickety taxi which when ordered would jolt down the unmade road from Pyrghi, I felt that it would be possible but in the case of an urgent letter incautious. I could of course go to Chios town and from there telegraph an article to my paper. But I was uneasy about sending a long cable from an island post-office where it was unlikely that anybody understood more than a few words of English. I decided to go back to Athens and send my article from there.

The bus which connects Pyrghi with Chios town goes at cockcrow, and Emporio is five miles from Pyrghi. The boats to Athens, on the other hand, leave in the evening; to save waiting about all day in Chios town, their port of call, it is worth making the journey from Emporio by taxi. I had company on the drive. In the Greek fashion the proedhros, the president of Pyrghi, who was on a visit to the excavations, crowded with three companions into the car for a lift as far as the main road. And Igor was to come to Chios town; the compressor had broken down completely, and he was despatched to ask for help at a garage. It was half-past four in the afternoon when we drove off. The siesta was over, and the divers were using their time as best they could; the harbour was full of diligent swimmers with schnorkels.

I had a few things to do when we reached the town and, as I thought, time to do them before the boat sailed at half-past seven. I bought my ticket for the journey, left my suitcase in the offices of the steamship company, and asked my porter the way to the post office.

'It is for a telegram,' I added.

'I will show you.' We set off along the quayside.

'Is it far?'

'No, no, there where you see that house, the big one, there we turn; it is not far.'

We arrived, climbed some dark stairs, and found a friendly clerk at a *guichet*. I began in my nursery Greek hand to spell out a message to an Athens hotel. 'I arrive,' I wrote, laboriously printing, 'tomorrow morning.' Somehow it did not look right. I took another form and began again; with an air of helpless solicitude the porter looked on. Still dissatisfied, I was reading through my telegram when a stranger came to wait beside me. He looked over my elbow and grinned.

'Do you want me to write it for you?' he said.

With his help two telegrams were sent. As I went out I turned once more to my porter.

'I want,' I said, 'a laundry.' At Emporio, furnished with an enamel basin and a clay water-jar, I had not aspired to launder more than my underclothes. And to have a dress washed in a Greek village is to hand it over to be beaten in cold water with a piece of wood; it comes back clean but ribby. In Chios town, perhaps, I might do better. At any rate I thought I would leave a cotton dress, worn and bleached by the sun, to be dealt with while I was in Athens. 'Canst thou,' I said again, 'tell me where I can find a laundry?' Before we parted I had asked Igor for the Greek word, and I knew I had it right; I spoke it with confidence.

'A laundry?' the porter repeated. 'Certainly; I will take you there.'

'It will be open at this hour?'

'Open, it will be open.' We moved away from the harbour and began to walk through the streets behind the quayside.

When we had gone a hundred yards, 'What time is it?' he said.

'A quarter to seven.'

'A quarter to seven,' he repeated. We hurried on.

'And your boat, what time does it leave?'

'Half-past seven.'

'Half-past seven.' We crossed streets, turned right and left along

narrow alleys of shops where the evening light cast copper shadows
on tiers of vegetables and fruit. 'Half-past seven,' he repeated again
'I think we shall have time.'

'But is it far?'

'No, no, it is not far; I think we shall have time.'

Chios is a small town, and unless the laundry were in the surrounding hills I did not see how we could fail to have time. But my
companion's hesitation alarmed me.

'Thou art sure we have time?'

'Three-quarters of an hour – we have time.'

All the same I was glad when we came out from the back alleys
into a square with trees.

'There,' said my companion, 'we have arrived. There it is.'

He pointed to a long one-storey building with a public face and
the look of cement. I had expected a shop with a couple of men's
shirts and a child's frock dangling in the window.

'That is it?'

'Yes, yes, that is it.'

There was something written over the front, and I tried to make
it out while we crossed the road. But the last of the sun was in my
eyes. We went up to the entrance. There were steps, and two women,
one on each side of the door; dressed in thick white overalls, they
stood at the ready with the no-nonsense air of attendants in a lunatic
asylum. My porter addressed them civilly.

'The lady,' he said, 'wants – ' . . . I could not quite hear what he
said.

'Certainly,' said one of the women, heartily, 'at once!' And she
and her companion made to lead me in.

Dimly I began to resist. 'I want,' I said, 'to leave my dress . . .'

'Yes, yes,' said the woman, 'this way!'

We were standing inside the door. To the right I looked down a
long corridor; it smelt of steam.

'A dress,' I repeated, 'I am going to Athens, I want to leave it . . .'

'Gladly,' the other woman interrupted, beaming and pointing
down the corridor, 'the bath is this way.'

'A bath!' I cried, squeaking. 'No, no!'

'Yes,' the first woman repeated enthusiastically, 'certainly, a good bath!'

'A shower,' urged the other, 'you would prefer a shower?'

It was several minutes before I detached myself from their good intentions and, leaving my dress to be washed as a pledge of friendship, broke out of what I now realized were the public baths of Chios town.

'A dress?' cried my porter. 'Ah, if I had known I could have asked my wife to do it for you.'

VII

Next morning in Athens the problems of laundry still pursued me. I had been right, I found when I reached the hotel, to doubt the telegraph service; my telegram had not arrived yet. However, after breakfast I was given a room, and I settled down to work. But first I rang for the chambermaid.

'This dress I am wearing,' I said, explaining carefully, 'if I take it off, dost thou think it can be washed by this afternoon? At five o'clock I must leave to catch the boat back to Chios. Is there time for the dress to be washed and ironed?'

In good Athenian hotels the servants are obligingly ready to get such things done quickly. A skirt to be cleaned, a blouse to be laundered – somehow the visitor's impatience will be indulged. But there is a ritual to be gone through first. The chambermaid put on a pessimistic look.

'Ah, by five o'clock,' she said dolefully, 'they will not do it. The evening before, in the evening one must give it to the laundry in order to have it the next day.'

'But what shall I do, since this evening I must leave? In Chios it is difficult to get a dress washed.'

She reflected. 'For the ironing it is easy. Here in the hotel they do the ironing; only for the washing we send the things out. If you like, I could wash the dress myself; thus you would have it this afternoon.'

The formalities had been observed, we had come to the expected arrangement. Gratefully I tore the dress off. 'And now,' I said, 'when I was in the hotel a week ago I left some clothes here. Wilt thou bring them for me? As thou seest I have nothing to wear, and at mid-day I must go out.'

Working indoors in the Athenian heat of mid-June, to be half-naked is a relief, and I forgot about my clothes. Ten o'clock came, and eleven; my piece was nearly done, and I telephoned to Michael Manning, Athens correspondent of the *Sunday Times*, who had undertaken to send it off for me: I would meet him in the hall at half-past twelve. Outside the shuttered windows the traffic of Constitution Square squealed and brayed; the barred shadows in the stale-breathing room crawled along the wall. At last I pulled the page out of my typewriter and looked at my watch. It was quarter-past twelve, and I had no dress to put on.

I took the sheet from the bed, wrapped it round myself, and rang the bell. The bootboy appeared at the door.

'Where is the chambermaid?'

Amusement showed through his respect. 'She has gone to find your clothes.'

At twenty-five minutes past twelve I rang the bell again. This time nobody came, not even the bootboy.

At half-past twelve I telephoned to the hall porter. 'I am expecting a Mr Manning,' I said; 'when he arrives, please ask him to speak to me on the telephone.'

'He is here, I will call him.'

'Mr Manning,' I said, 'my article is ready, but I am afraid I can't come down to give it to you. I have sent my dress to be washed, I am waiting for the clothes I left in the hotel to be brought; would you mind coming up to my room? I mean,' I went on lamely, 'will you forgive me if I receive you wearing a sheet?'

Five minutes later, while the two of us, he in a razor-crease summer suit, I in my toga sheet, were sitting side by side over the typescript, there was a knock at the door, and the chambermaid came in. She was bringing my clothes on hangers, carrying them high with the air of a chorister bearing a banner in a church procession. I could see her struggling, as she looked at what I was wearing, to keep a straight face. But when later in the afternoon, conventionally dressed, I passed her in the corridor, the voice in which she greeted me had a new note. It was, I like to think, the note of familiar friendship.

VIII

ALL MY URGENCY proved unnecessary. The evening boat to Chios was cancelled. Now I had twenty-four hours to wait until the next sailing, and since there was little I could do in Athens I decided to spend the night in Mycenae. I called at Ghiolmans, the Greek travel agency; my friend Thalia rushed to the telephone; there was a place left on the 5.30 bus, the place was mine. Through streets still drowsy, past shops still blind with the siesta, a taxi drove me to the bus station.

'You are American?' While we waited in our seats for the bus to start the interrogation began.

'No, English.'

'I might have lived in America,' said the girl who had spoken to me. She was wearing the bright patterned cotton dress and high heels of the city, but her face under the uncovered hair was a peasant's face. 'When I was a baby an American lady wanted to take me back with her, but my mother would not give me up.'

'She was right, your mother, surely,' I said.

'No, I do not think she was right. Here in Greece I have not had a good life; in America it would have been better. Here it is all poverty and hard work.'

'All the same, is it not better to stay in one's own country?'

'I do not know. All I know is, I work hard and I am poor.'

'In England,' said the girl next to her, 'do the women work in the fields?'

'In the fields, no. But they work: in offices, in factories, they work.'

'The same everywhere it is,' said the second girl, and the first echoed her: 'The same everywhere. Wherever you go you will find hard work, you will find poverty.'

The bus bowled through the last of Athens and out to Daphni and Eleusis, then swung westward beside the railway along the shore of the Saronic Gulf with the mountains on the right, the sea and Salamis on the left. The sun, wheeling down towards the Corinthian Canal, burned in our windows and fringed with light the curtains which passengers drew against its glare; it still shone, but coolly, when we pulled up in New Corinth. There was a wait of ten minutes. Most of the travellers climbed down, stretching. The rest of us bought bags of pistachio-nuts from a hawker and handed them amicably round. Then we rolled on, over the pass at Nemea and into the Argolid.

It was about half-past eight when I got out with my rucksack at Phychtia; dusk muted my footsteps as I walked up to the village. A young man, overtaking me, asked where I came from. 'I have been to England,' he said. 'In the war I was there, when I was a sailor; to Cardiff I have been, I know it well.' At the edge of the village he dropped back and I went on by myself, dusty in an old summer dress and sandals. Dark covered the landscape. I could see only the shapes of trees and the orange gleam of lamp-light in cottage windows; all noise was in a whisper. Just short of the Fair Helen I stopped in the road to look before going in. The terrace outside the inn was quiet, orderly, busy. The lamps whose beam glittered in the leaves of the trees formed a hive of dim light round the two occupied tables; half a dozen visitors sat talking in murmurs which matched the hushed, hot night. From the open door of the house came no sound, only a wedge of brilliance. A girl was serving, moving about on the beaten earth with a faint clack of slippers. By the steps at the entrance children were playing a soft, mysterious game. In the cafeneion on the opposite side of the road men sat at a table; their voices drifted across faintly, as if from a long distance. For a few seconds I hesitated, half-afraid to break into the bubble of quiet. Then I walked towards the terrace entrance.

I had hardly shown myself in the light when I was recognized. 'It is the kyria Payne!' cried a woman. The words were relayed back into the house. 'Kyria Payne!' a man shouted. From the house, from the terrace, from the night the family converged on me. I could see the visitors looking up from their dinner, startled, as well they might be, by the extravagance of welcome to a dishevelled wayfarer. I too was startled; and, as I felt myself folded in the frail web of light and company, flattered, warmed, touched.

The competition of the Tourismos Hotel where the year before Frosso and I had been guests had stirred the Fair Helen; that was clear within five minutes of my arrival. I had scarcely crossed the threshold of the house when Agamemnon was leading me with deferential gestures towards the lavatories.

'Look, kyria Payne,' he said, 'now we have water.' Indeed in place of the primitive system I remembered plumbing had been installed, plumbing with chains which, as he instantly showed me, not only pulled but flushed.

'We have showers too!' Again, as he pulled, the hygienic water flowed.

'Come upstairs, kyria Payne, we have them upstairs as well!' Once more the demonstration: water in the lavatories, showers with real water.

'Wonderful!' I cried. 'How fine you have made the hotel, how fine!'

'Is it not so?' said Agamemnon. 'And you will see, now we have water in the bedrooms.'

Exhausted with admiring, I was led to my room. It was the room I had always slept in: '*Your* room,' said Agamemnon. Still the same two iron bedsteads, the same bare boards; only instead of the enamel jug of well-water there was a basin with a tap.

'How fine!' I cried again, reverently: 'how fine!'

'We are going to put in electric light, but not yet, I don't know when. It costs much money, much money, kyria Payne . . . Bring a towel for the kyria!'

One of the wives obeyed. 'We have everything clean,' she said, patting my shoulder, 'for every visitor we wash the sheets, we wash the towels.'

'Welcome!' said another voice. It was Orestes, come to the bedroom to greet me. In his enthusiasm he made a movement as if to kiss my cheek, then remembered himself and took and kissed my hand instead.

The dust washed from my face and hands, I went down to the terrace.

'Will you eat some soup?' said Agamemnon. 'We have a little meat, good meat,' (flattering) 'not for everybody but for special visitors; afterwards we have cheese.' Soup, meat, salted goat's cheese – I was hungry, I ate everything I was given and finished with the jam omelette which the Fair Helen has served ever since I first went there.

'You will drink,' said Orestes, 'some of our wine, our own which we make for ourselves.' He came to sit with me. Presently one or two others, crossing the road from the cafeneion or appearing unexplained from the darkness, joined us. We talked about the latest excavations at Mycenae, about the day in 1945 when Orestes had come with me to Perachora village; about the family, the children, their education; about common acquaintances. Once I looked round to see the visitors. I recognized them as English, and thought sympathetically of the times when, watching the reception of some friend of the house, my face must have worn the very same look of wooden politeness. The children, squatting and cheeping in the dust, still played on; and their whisperings mingled with our soft talk and the distant exclamations of women working in the kitchen to form a tiny rustling in the silence of the night.

At last the company began to disperse. One by one the men of the village said goodnight, the visitors strode into the house; wondering if I should be able to sleep, I took my candle to go to my room.

'But there is one upstairs too, kyria Payne,' said Agamemnon with proud reproach as I came out of the downstairs lavatory.

'Ah, how fine! I had forgotten.' I climbed the stairs and shut myself in the familiar bedroom. The window looked towards the plain and Argos. I pushed the shutters open and leaned out; there was the scent of thyme, oleanders and cooling earth. A huge, arrogant, white moon hung above me, polishing the sky to the colour of steel; I had the illusion that the light was warm on my skin. A girl laughed and called goodnight, footfalls grated and died, a sheepbell tinkled once and was silent. I listened for the sharp whine of mosquitoes, floating blindly towards the light and my exhaling flesh: nothing. The mountains pressed closer; the night fell still. I blew out my candle, crawled between the rough sheets, and shut my eyes on the moon-lit walls and all the memories of Mycenae.

I opened them again to see the blue light of morning and hear someone rapping on the door to wake me. It was six o'clock.

Once more, sitting alone on the terrace in air cooled by night and sleep, I ate the Fair Helen's breakfast of tea, hard toast and honey; then I set off up the hill. The road was lined with oleanders, an avenue of pink and red and white which stretched all the way from the railway station, through the village, and up to the Lion Gate and the Citadel walls. Though the grass on Humfry's grave was wither-ing and the iris-blades were brown and dry, at the head and foot the oleander bushes were in flower; summer and heat brought their own assurance of life. I went into the cemetery chapel. Humfry's mother had given a painting – her copy of some golden Italian – to hang on the wall; its colours glittered sombrely in the dank twilight of the little cell with the rough stone walls and beaten earth floor. Outside, the sun struck across the plain, dappling with blue and fawn the range beyond. The ferocious mountains which overlook Mycenae were serene, with deep shadows in their folded flanks. And in the beatific morning the village spoke with its domestic tongue: women shout-ing to one another, a girl calling to the brood of turkeys which ran wilfully across the slope of the ravine.

There was still time before my bus to walk a little farther towards the Palace; who can be sure in one life of seeing Mycenae often enough? The road climbed between the oleanders and the smaller flowers of dryness, thistle, stonecrop, thyme. Once or twice I passed in the banks the opening of a tomb, an ancient grave with a passage cut through earth or rock to a burial-chamber; fig-trees had rooted in the walls, spiders had slung their webs across the entrance. It was too early in the day for visitors, and the walls of the Acropolis were deserted. But the gate to the Tomb of Agamemnon was already open. I went in, along the avenue with the stone-faced walls rising higher as they cut into the hillside, and under the huge lintel into the beehive-chamber. All was cool, silent, still; only a few scraps of charred paper showed where someone had made a torch to see the blocks of the dome more than forty feet above. Standing there alone, I expected a weight of solitude, of mortality. But it was the light streaming on the hillside opposite that I felt. Through the doorway of the tomb came the sounds of the world: sheepbells, insects humming; life going on. I felt calmed, I felt steadied as I walked back to the inn; I felt changed. For the first time at Mycenae since Humfry's death I thought only of the future.

IX

THE BOAT TO Chios was crammed. When I got out of my taxi at
Piraeus crowds were pressing round the gangway, cargo was waiting
in piles to be loaded: mattresses, bedsteads, motor-cars, long rolls of
wire netting; by the time we sailed, an hour and a half late, the decks
were loaded with passengers and their luggage, and I had a fight,
making my way past cabins and the fiery-hot mouths of kitchens and
hatchways, to find the party of new recruits for the divers. It was the
boat I had travelled in a week earlier. Once more I had secured the
Super-Lux cabin, and there I slept cool and easy. The English newcomers were not so lucky; the heat in their berths was intolerable. I
too before the war had often suffocated below; better in some of the
old island boats, even if you had paid for a cabin, to sleep on deck
– on a bench, leaning against the bulwarks, in a coil of rope. And the
officers and the stewards were always tolerant of the English;
impecunious students travelling deck, third-class, would often be
allowed, since there was no third-class dining saloon, to order their
meals in the first-class. Some of my new companions, speaking no
Greek, took such favours for granted and, as I learned next day, spent
the night on the seats in the first-class saloon. War and invasion
had not soured the Greek nature, and nobody asked the young
Englishmen to move.

Most of the passengers left the boat at Chios, and we landed in an
uproar: shouts, upbraidings, porters pushing up the gangway past
disembarking women with vast bundles, the crane clattering and
squealing; in the middle of the confusion a brand-new car was
swung proudly to shore and an ecclesiastical party, headed by a
dignitary in purple whom I took to be a bishop, got in and drove

grandly away through the crowds on the quay. I thrust my suitcase, rucksack and typewriter into the first hands which offered themselves and went ashore. But I ought to have suspected that the porterage system was not as easy as it looked. Leaving Chios three days earlier, when making to go on board I had been accosted by a stout, oily stranger.

'Did you pay the man who carried your luggage?'

'Yes, of course. Why?'

'How much did you pay him?'

Cautiously, wondering if I might be harming my laundry-guide by admitting the size of his tip, 'I don't remember,' I said; then, with a sudden idea, 'are you from a trades union?'

The stranger showed his gold teeth. 'A trades union, yes. Each man must give half the money he receives to the union. That is why I ask you what you paid the man.'

'How should I know?' I said, with the air of a harassed tourist. 'I am sorry, I don't remember.' And after an exchange of civil greetings I went up the gangway.

Now, coming to Chios again, I was reminded of the incident when, as I pushed my way across the quay, a man at the barrier asked me for money. I took him for a union representative.

'How much?' I said.

'Whatever you like.'

A little puzzled by this unofficial reckoning, I gave him a tip; then I went over the road to a pavement café to wait for the divers. A hunched old man with sad, red-rimmed eyes brought my luggage and put it down by the table. Was he the porter who had taken it from me on board? I could not remember, but I offered him a few drachmae. To my surprise he refused them. Foolishly thinking to insure him against the rapacity of the union, I insisted; and on that he took the money and shuffled away. I sat down, ordered a coffee, and waited.

A few minutes later a third man came up to my table. 'You have not paid us,' he said.

'For what should I pay you?'

'For the luggage which we carried.'

'You are making a mistake, I have paid.'

'No, those who carry the luggage from the steamer have not been paid.'

'Twice I have paid; three times I will not pay.'

At the tables round me the customers turned to listen; waiter hurried from indoors.

'You must pay us.'

'How many times must one pay here in Chios? I tell you No.'

The sound of the altercation began to draw an audience. Passer stopped, men at adjacent cafés left their coffee; the knot of men thickened into a crowd, gesticulated, argued among themselves shouted. I was still refusing when Sinclair Hood, the director of the excavations, appeared; he had come into Chios town for the day to work in the museum.

'It is impossible,' he said, when I explained what was going on 'absolutely impossible to get off a boat here and pay the right people.'

Encouraged, I sat obstinate. And now the voice of the crowd was changing to a rueful muttering. Among the faces I recognized my friend the laundry-guide. 'What is the matter?' I asked him. 'What are they saying?'

'They say the porters may be fined.'

'But why? I don't understand; I don't want anybody to be fined.'

'Perhaps a fine, perhaps they may be laid off; I don't know.'

It was a relief to see an official in dark blue uniform and peaked cap shouldering towards me. 'Good morning,' he said, saluting; 'will you tell me what is your complaint?'

'I have no complaint,' I said. 'I do not want to make any fuss. But twice I have paid for my luggage to be brought from the ship, and now a man asks me to pay a third time . . . The old man,' I added, 'is not to blame; he did not want to take the money.'

The first official was followed by the harbour-master, and I told my story for the second time. 'I have no complaint,' I said again, 'I do not want to make any fuss; and as for the old man, I am to blame; I made him take the money.'

The harbour-master, a short, slight, spruce young man whose tiny moustache gave the impression of having been carefully weeded, smiled brilliantly.

'And who was it who asked you for money the first time?'

'But I don't know him; someone over there.'

'Very good, very good. I will arrange everything!' He shook hands, saluted, beamed and, before I could reiterate my desire to make no trouble, whisked away. The crowd had dissolved, the porters had gone back to work; the quayside and the café went on with their usual business. I sat down again to compose myself.

I had decided not to return at once with the divers to Emporio, but to go back with Sinclair Hood in the afternoon. There were the finds from other years' excavations to be seen in the museum, and there was Nea Moni to be visited – a monastery in the hills behind the town with, I had heard, fine Byzantine mosaics. I was on my way to the museum when I saw, standing on the pavement outside a building where a naval sentry stood guard, the mournful figure of the old man. I went up to him to say I was sorry if I had made difficulties for him. To my distress I saw that there were tears in his poor red eyes.

'What has happened?' I asked. 'It is not well now?'

'They have laid me off,' he said. 'They have fined me fifty drachmae and laid me off work for ten days.'

'But why? I told the harbour-master I was to blame, not thou.'

'I don't know, I don't know; but they have fined me fifty drachmae and laid me off work for ten days.'

'That I do not understand; it does not seem just to me.'

'I don't know, but thus they have done.'

'If thou wishest, I will go with thee to find the harbour-master and I will tell him again that I was to blame. Let us go; again I will tell him.'

The sentry at the door stopped us. 'What do you want?'

'I want to see the harbour-master; please tell him that the English-woman would like to speak to him again.'

There was a shouted exchange with someone inside. Then we

were led up the dark flight of stairs to the first floor and into an office. The harbour-master, twinkling brightly, was sitting in clean white shirt-sleeves; his gold-braided cap lay on the desk in front of him. He bounded to his feet as I came in.

'Sit down, please, sit down. At your service! You will take a little coffee? At once . . .' (to an assistant): 'two coffees, quick!'

I sat down. The old porter, hanging his head and peering from between his watering red rims, stood in abject patience, and I recognized, standing near him, the man who had asked for money at the barrier.

'Now, please.' The harbour-master clasped his hands before him, leaned over the desk and devoted himself to me. 'What can I do to help you?'

Once more I told my story: my anxiety not to get anybody into trouble, my own errors, the innocence of the old man. 'Now I hear that he is fined and laid off work; and it seems to me that he did nothing wrong.'

'Very good, very good.' The harbour-master turned to the room. 'Go outside for two minutes, leave us!' The two porters shuffled out. 'Now I will tell you why I have fined them. There are three reasons, three things which should not have been done.' He unclasped his hands and, speaking for my benefit with exemplary clarity, ticked off the list on his fingers. 'One. The first man, the man you saw here, should have told you the tariff for luggage – the tariff, so much for each piece, not "whatever you like". That will not do, that "whatever you like". Two. The second man, the old man, should not have taken the money you offered him. Three. They made trouble for an English visitor, a foreigner. For these three mistakes they must pay a fine!'

There was, I could see, nothing more to be done for my protégé. 'I understand,' I said, 'I am grateful for your help and your kindness.' The coffee had arrived on the usual round tray carried swinging like a balance from chains; I took my cup and, with expressions suitable to a guest, drank.

'Let me ask you, so that another time I shall know what to do, so

hat I shall not make a mistake when I come to Chios again: which
orter ought I to have paid?'

'I will tell you.' The harbour-master bent towards me, glittering.
This you should do. You should put your clothes, all the things you
eed, into a light bag. And you should carry your bag off the steamer
ourself, without porters, without anybody. This way you will have
o trouble.'

X

WHEN I MET Sinclair Hood again I told him of the punishmen[t] inflicted on the porters. He was delighted: Serve them right, he said[.] I did not dare to confess that in one case I had tried to defeat justice[.] As we came out of the harbour-master's office and into the stree[t] again I beckoned to the old man: 'Come,' I said, 'come to the corne[r] where nobody can see us.' Altercation and intercession had made m[e] conspicuous, and I did not want to be seen flouting authority. At th[e] end of the street I drew him into a doorway out of sight. 'Tell n[o] one,' I said, 'but I give thee the money for thy fine.' And with [a] gesture borrowed, I fear, from gangster films I slipped into his han[d] as I walked away a fifty-drachmae note.

It was thus with a heart sentimentally lightened that I went to loo[k] for a taxi. In the square a white-haired, grizzled man in shirt-sleeve[s] collarless, unshaven and almost toothless, ran out to hail me. It wa[s] the owner of the car in which I had first driven to Emporio. W[e] shook hands.

'I should have liked,' I said, 'to take your taxi back this afternoon[,] but I am with friends and they may have arranged for another car.'

'Never mind, I understand, never mind.'

'But,' I went on, 'I want to see Nea Moni. They tell me I can hir[e] a donkey for the last hour. Is your driver free to take me as far as th[e] road goes?'

'Free, he is free; at once.'

'Wait then, while I buy something to eat at midday, and I too am[m] ready.'

The driver greeted me with reserve; his melancholy, egg-shape[d] face showed no interest as we drove out of the town and up the roa[d]

which climbs into the hills. This time the boss did not offer to
accompany us and I sat in front.

'It is the first time I have been to Nea Moni. You know the place?'

'Of course.'

'Then tell me, how far is it from the end of the road?'

'Eh, an hour, perhaps a little more.'

'They tell me it is difficult to know the path. Shall I be able to find
a boy with a mule or a donkey to take me?'

'We shall find, we shall find.'

After about five miles we came to a village in the hills, looking
back towards the sea.

'A mule,' he shouted from the window, 'is there a mule to take
the lady to Nea Moni?'

There was no encouraging reply, and we drove on. 'Generally,'
he said, his dark voice brightening, 'the cars stop here, but I will take
you farther. My car is good; it is old but it is good, it will go still
farther along the road.' A boy was coming out of a field with a
donkey. 'Tell me, art thou free to go to Nea Moni? The lady will
pay thee for thy donkey if thou wilt take her.'

'I cannot, I have work; I cannot go.'

I have always found riding a mule or a donkey along Greek
mountain paths uncomfortable; no matter how tired I am I would
rather go on foot. But that morning I was unprepared for rough
walking. I had decided on the spur of the moment to make the expedition, my tennis shoes were in Emporio, and I was wearing
French beach sandals which consisted of perfectly flat leather-and-
rubber soles tied on by a decorative but insecure system of coloured
boot-laces. For once something more than the fear of losing my way
made me anxious to have a mount.

'What do you say, shall we still find a boy with a mule or a
donkey?'

'I do not think we shall find now.'

We had come to the end of the road. A little church with a
precinct wall stood among trees; beyond it, tenantless hills and
valleys.

'Here is a monastery with only one monk; do you want to see the church?'

Respectfully conducted by a monk who, I noted, was wearing an Afrika Corps cap, I admired the icon and lit a candle. Then I came out and looked towards the slopes beyond; I could not bring myself to draw back now.

'I shall go on foot. The path to Nea Moni is that way?'

'Yes; it goes down first, later it climbs.' The driver looked at me and at the landscape; not smiling, but with friendship. 'It is a long time since I have been to Nea Moni, but I know the way; if you wish I will come with you for company.'

Gratefully I accepted, and at a smart pace he set off, first through terraced fields of corn, then along a path which snaked down hillsides covered with prickly scrub and faded cistus plants and struggled up again through pine woods. Slipping on the loose stones, my sandals flapping at every step, I picked my way behind. When we went downhill my toes slid forward beyond the soles; uphill, I bruised my bare heels. I was thankful after half-an-hour to sit on a boulder by the stream at the bottom of the valley and take breath.

'If I had shoes instead of sandals,' I said apologetically, 'I should walk faster.'

'Ah, for walking one must have good shoes.'

'You like walking?'

He took the deep breath of a man who is happy. 'I like walking, I like the country; here is it not beautiful?'

'Beautiful indeed; but usually,' I said, feeling my way, 'the Greeks, it seems to me, do not like walking in the country.'

'When I was a soldier in the war I learned to walk.'

'Where were you in the war?'

'Everywhere – Egypt, Palestine, Cyprus, Italy: I fought at Rimini.'

'At Rimini!' I said admiringly; for it is among the famous battle-honours of the Greeks. 'Tell me, were you here when the Germans and Italians came into Greece?'

'Here, in Chios, but' – at last he smiled, triumphantly – 'I escaped to Turkey. In the beginning the Turks did not treat us with respect. Afterwards they changed.'

We went on; thinking of his story, I was ashamed of making such heavy weather of a country walk. All the same when, at the end of the hour he had promised me, we came in sight of the monastery, its dome, its sanctuary wall framed in cypresses and set on a height in a ravine, I was exhausted. Panting, I dragged myself up the last slope and into the courtyard. I had the illusion, as I flopped down on the stone ledge against the wall, that I was visibly steaming.

Of Nea Moni I remember chiefly a rich, dark, plummy decay. The monastery is of the eleventh century. Time and history and earthquake have shaken it, and the mosaics which glimmer in the church are broken and defaced.

'They are mending the church, the Government give money,' said the old woman, scarved and hooded in black, who showed me round, 'but it costs much, very much.'

I looked up at the empty scaffolding and wondered how a country scorched and split by war as Greece had been from 1940 to 1949 could afford to preserve its monuments. The monuments of two pasts. One thinks of Greece as the white, classical country. But there is also the dark, gold-and-purple Greece which took its colours from Byzantium. Classical archaeologists sometimes resent the intervention of this Christian, ecclesiastical past between themselves and the pagan world; I remember how at Perachora there was nothing but exasperation when a few sherds of Byzantine pottery were found. But the Greeks themselves still look eastward with their Church towards lost Byzantium, towards Constantinople, still recall, as the old woman muttering under the dusty scaffolding recalled, an imperial age.

'The Empress,' I heard her saying, 'gave them a ring as a token; when she was free they were to bring it to her, and she would build a church.' At least I think that is what she said. I only half-understood her stories of miracles: the three men who saw a fire with, in the middle of it, a bush which did not burn; the rescue from storm at sea, and the image of a ship which commemorates it. In the refectory she pointed to a vast table with a face of inlaid stone; underneath, just above the lap-level of a sitting man, a shelf ran all the way round with compartments for, as she put it, the knife and fork of each monk. Whether there are monks at Nea Moni today I am not sure. Outside the precinct wall there was what seemed to be a lay settlement, with women and playing children. The women, I was told, make rag-carpets; we passed a group at the dyeing vats, standing in their own sad black and hanging up to dry long skeins of rag in raw colours of crimson and orange. I saw no man to receive visitors. The old woman it was who, when we arrived, came out to offer the traditional glass of masticha, piece of Turkish delight and tumbler of cold water.

Before we left I was shown a vault, below the level of the courtyard to which it was open. It was, I suppose, the monument described in the *Guide Bleu* as 'a curious water-tank'. At any rate water stood in a pale, glazed, stone-coloured flood under the delicate columns which supported the roof. From above, through some perforations which I could not distinguish, light struck obliquely to fall on the surface in a regular pattern of discs, from each of which a reflected shaft doubled back to the bottom. Though it was still early afternoon, in the dimness of the far end bats were wheeling and screaming. I carried the image of dankness and twilight away with me on the walk back.

I had been heartened by the hospitality of Nea Moni, by the lunch of biscuits and oranges which I had shared with the chauffeur, and by the knowledge that my nose was towards home and the end of walking in beach sandals on stony, spiny mountain paths. But I was glad of a pause at the stream in the valley.

'Eh,' said my companion, encouraging, 'if you had good shoes you would go along like a tough one, we should see.'

'We have not gone far,' I answered, 'but in sandals . . .'

'One thing I learned when I was a soldier: not to drink on the march. Once you drink water, phoo, you are done for.'

'Were you all Greeks together in the war?'

'Of all countries we were: Greeks, Canadians, English, Australians, New Zealanders, even Russians.'

'Russians?'

'Yes, Russians. They were prisoners, afterwards they decided to join with us and fight. We used to talk to them, they learned a little Greek. They were surprised by the freedom we had, it was a marvel to them. "In Russia," they used to say, "you would have your head cut off." That is what they used to say. "You would have your head cut off." '

Painfully trailing twenty or thirty yards behind, I followed him up the slope and through the bristly fields. Now and then he stopped to look back. 'This way!' he cried, pointing out a short cut. At last we passed the little church in the trees and reached the waiting car. He greeted it with jovial affection.

'It is good, the car,' he told me again as we drove off. 'It is old but it is good.'

'How long have you had it?'

'Since before the war; twenty-three years ago I had it first, and even then it was not new.'

'A long time,' I said.

'It is old,' he repeated, 'but it never makes trouble. You saw, it went to the end where the road was bad. The new cars are no good.'

In the square of Chios town I got out, paid him, and shook his hand with gratitude. 'Thank you, thank you very much, it was good of you to come with me to Nea Moni. Without you I should not have found the way.'

'Didst thou think,' he said gently, dropping into the familiar address, 'that I would have let thee go alone?'

XI

WITH THAT QUICK-ROOTING instinct by which human nature manages to look on even the most temporary shelter as home I found myself glad to be back at Emporio. I hurried up the path to my little house, tumbled my clothes out of my suitcase, and hung up the dress which I had fetched from the public baths in Chios. It was clean but, as I noted with wry amusement, unironed and distinctly ribby. Then I dragged my camp-bed into the open, ready. After three days and nights of traipsing about in ships and buses I thought with pleasure of sleeping quietly out-of-doors in the shadow of the Prophet Elijah.

There was news for me. First, of a discovery. Round the point to the north, off the beach called Komi, two surface swimmers with masks had spotted a huddle of pottery among the rocks. The deposit was in shallow water, closely packed, and among the broken amphorai lay some which were almost whole. The swimmers had called the rest of the party. The site had been marked, sketches made, and the archaeologists, looking at these, had judged the vases from their shape to be Attic, possibly of a date as early as the end of the fifth or the beginning of the fourth century B.C. A cargo of wine-jars, coming from Athens empty, perhaps, or going back full: after twenty-three centuries they lay where storm had spilled them, where wind and waves had rolled them, sealed now to the boulders of the sea-bed by the detritus of a million tiny marine lives. The date had still to be confirmed by an authority. But already the diving party felt that their season had not been wasted effort.

The second piece of news was that we were at last to make an excursion outside the neighbourhood of Emporio.

From the beginning, long before any of us had set out from England, it had been recognized that the divers could not hope to explore far without a ship. They could swim to their hunting grounds in the harbour, they could row to the beaches round the point. Farther than that they could not by their own physical efforts move themselves and the heavy equipment they wore. If harbour sites up and down the coast of the island were to be reconnoitred something a great deal larger than a rowing boat, something with an engine was needed. The aqualung expedition might not have been planned at all had not an English yacht-owner, himself attracted to the idea of underwater exploration, offered to put his ship at the disposal of the divers.

The gathering of forces, human and material, had been timed with care. The compressor had to be shipped from England and somehow transported to remote Emporio; this part of the action must begin weeks ahead. The land party would be already on the spot. The yacht would sail from its Cyprus anchorage a day or two before the earliest divers were due to arrive. With luck it should be waiting to carry them as soon as they were ready.

When, a day ahead of the first of the fish-party, I arrived at Emporio, I was half-relieved to see the harbour empty. So far at least nobody's time was being wasted. Next day when the divers appeared and made their first essays in the shallow harbour, there was still no need for the ship. Even on the third morning exploration could go on without its help. But by midday we were beginning to shade our eyes and look towards the mouth of the harbour. 'When,' we asked, 'did they say they were going to start?' On the fourth morning we were full of hope. 'It is bound to come today.' Midday and afternoon went by, and the sun glared on a harbour still blank. Next day at breakfast: 'No yacht?' we said to one another, stating an ugly fact rather than asking a question, since the answer was plain to see, and 'No yacht,' came the resigned response.

Diligently the fish-party coaxed the compressor, swam to and fro in the harbour and rowed to adjacent bays. They made the best of their time. But we were all oppressed by the thought that a day was near when they would have exhausted the possibilities of the sea-bed within their reach. More and more anxiously we looked to sea. Once a masted ship enquired round the point from the south and dropped anchor. 'The yacht!' we cried. Then we saw that it was a caïque with a cargo of cement for road-making in Pyrghi. Once when Igor was in Chios town on one of his compressor-errands the appearance at the quayside of a splendid white craft with a funnel, and for all I know a gun-turret, sent him hurrying off to ask if by chance our benefactors had mistaken their harbour. I forget what millionaire's palace the ship turned out, in the crushing reply, to be. The wind which got up at dawn each day blew in stronger gusts. But the caïques which went up and down the straits between Chios and Turkey were not discouraged. 'Look,' we said, 'the sea is almost calm. What can have happened to the yacht?'

The prospect of fresh divers made the lack of transport still more constricting, and by the time I arrived back from Athens it had been decided that some remedy must be found, even if only a temporary one. To hire a caïque for any length of time would be more than the expedition could afford. But at least, while we still hoped for the yacht, a day's hire could be managed. There were ancient sites which the land-party too might profitably reconnoitre, for a field archaeo-logist is always concerned to find a likely place for excavation. A caïque and its crew, then, were engaged, and a day's trip in which both land-party and sea-party could join was arranged. We were to set off next morning, a Sunday. We were to sail to Kato Phana, a harbour site to the south with, near to the shore, the foundations of an archaic temple. And in spite of some lukewarmness among the student archaeologists, flagging after their week of standing all day in trenches or on mountain-sides in the pitiless sun, it was agreed that we must breakfast at half-past six in readiness for an early start. The evening was enlivened by the anticipation of tomorrow's adventure, and we shouted goodnights as we separated on the beach to go to our tents or our houses. From my terrace I saw light after flickering light extinguished. Then I put out my own hurricane lamp and turned my back on the moon.

Sleep out-of-doors, though it can calm deeply, is not the stupefiant which I at any rate find in sleep indoors, and the sound of my name stirred me awake in an instant. One of the women of the land-party usually called the hour to me as she went down to the beach in the morning; it must be time, I thought, for me to get up.

'Thank you,' I said, 'all right.'

But it was much darker than when I usually woke. The mountains pressed close in the supernatural hour between night and day.

'What time is it?' I asked.

'The yacht!' said the voice in a loud, urgent whisper. 'The yacht has come!'

'The yacht?' I sat up in bed and looked down at the harbour. The water glimmered like black glass. A pearl-coloured moon still hung in a sky turning faint green. And there below, a folded white butterfly, the shining ship floated over her pale reflection.

After all it was not so early. I looked at my watch. Half-past five: Mount Prophet Elijah blocked out the light from the east and made our nights longer. Anyhow the day had begun, and I dressed and went down to the dig-house.

'What happened to the yacht?'

'They were held up by a storm.'

The wind which we had taken for trifling had blown into a fury farther south; and as if a storm were not enough, in Turkish waters the party had run into trouble with over-zealous officials. In the placid arrival by night, in our past week of waiting and our present excitement, there was the flavour of eighteenth-century Mediterranean travel. But now, though for the moment the yacht and her passengers slept, we felt certain of our transport. The divers would have freedom to move.

Meanwhile there were the preparations for our immediate excursion to be made: the food to be got ready, the diving equipment to be carried up the boarding-plank to the deck of the caïque, which had been brought close in to the beach. We breakfasted, of course, far later than half-past six. By the time the engine carried us gently out of harbour it was half-past eight.

A Sunday foray from a dig: the waiting, the remonstrances with stragglers, the late start, the slightly gritty mixture of personalities – in my experience such jaunts are always alike. I might, I said to myself, be back at the Heraion, except that there I was the sheltered amateur, the Director's wife, and now I am the outsider, the professional onlooker from another world. The party, a dozen men and girls equally divided between divers and archaeologists, disposed themselves about the deck, standing to watch the coast go by, sitting, leaning against the mast. Igor lay in his swimming-trunks at the prow, flat on his belly; his body with its powerful shoulders, the line of the torso straight from waist to narrow hips, the lean thighs and long shinbones, had the hard austerity of an archaic statue, a man in limestone. The morning stretched on. Chuffing, clapping into the restless surface of the sea, the caïque rounded point after point. Once or twice we saw flocks of cormorants, sitting on the rocks or flapping into the air as we went by. Nothing else marked the passage of two hours.

At Kato Phana we came to anchor in a large, silent, deserted, horse-shoe bay: no house, no jetty, only encircling hills, rocks, a beach and a shallow valley of dry fields. A plank was laid between deck and shore, but its instability and the look of the razors of rock a few feet below frightened me, and rather than cross the gulf, as I had timorously climbed the improvized gangway to board at Emporio, on all fours, I changed into a bathing dress and jumped into the sea. The divers too were hurriedly changing. In a few minutes the bay was full of swimmers with fins, masks and schnorkels. Backwards and forwards between shore and shore they went, their movement making a pattern of parallel lines. Richard Garnett, paddling slowly, pausing to listen for a cry of discovery, crossed and re-crossed the tracks in a boat. Once or twice he stopped to drop a marker. For a while I joined in the hunt, half-heartedly I fear, for the sea-bed looked to me glum and featureless. But after swimming some distance I tired and went in to dress. The women of the land-party, more useful, had already spread a cloth under a tree, and lunch was being unpacked: tinned tunny, beans, tomatoes, eggs, bread, wine, oranges. I have rarely thought food and drink more delicious.

It was in the afternoon that I was most sharply reminded of expeditions before the war. A few of us strolled a hundred or two yards inland to the temple, along dry paths, between rough terrace walls wedged in which the experts recognized here and there an antique block. A Christian baptistery had been built over the ruins, and the site, though both Greeks and English had dug there, had never been fully explored. Foundations lay half-uncovered in the baked earth. Architectural mouldings leaned against boulders. The valley was scorched by sun, the soil powdered underfoot. In the heat an immense reluctance seized me. I was revisited by the old sense of dragging, aimless as a child taken sightseeing too young, behind preoccupied scholars. When Sinclair Hood, stirred by detecting among the layers of stone a statue-fragment which to other eyes would have seemed just another boulder, began to pull a wall down to get at it, my admiration was almost blotted out by the familiar apathy, I had to force myself to look interested.

But I had not lived for ten years among archaeologists without learning a discipline. Perhaps I was anxious to prove that the discipline was permanent, perhaps I simply wanted to recapture for a few minutes the habit and practices of the past. At any rate when the sight-seeing party dispersed and Sinclair remarked that he was going to take a look at the slopes to the north of the valley I asked if I might walk with him.

'Pray do,' he said, with possibly a shade of desperation in his good manners.

We set off along the valley and up a track. The sun beat on our backs, the earth glared, the dry grass and the weeds were brittle with heat. And now I was surprised to find myself full of energy. Sinclair, his eyes fixed on the ground with the fanatical gleam which I so well recognized, left the path and began to move slowly across the hillside, stopping every few moments to examine some little object. A respectful camp-follower, I trailed behind. I paused when he paused; occasionally, recovering the vague desire with which my life had once infected me to share in the scholar's passion, I went so far as to pick up one of the fragments of pottery which, thickly scattered over the slope, were engaging him. The hillside grew steeper. Sweating and at a deferential distance I scrambled on, watching the familiar movements, gathering the indistinguishable sherds. I was still taken up with my own tenacity when I became aware that I was embarrassing my companion.

'Please don't bother,' he called down, always with stoic politeness, 'to come up here – do go whichever way you like!'

That the words were a hint he afterwards denied. But as the most civil of hints I took them. For a while I wandered on alone, filling my handkerchief with sherds and reflecting that I was probably giving myself away by including fragments quite modern. Then, putting aside the illusion of the past, I went down to the beach. The divers were far out, bringing up specimens of the scattered amphorai fragments which they had seen in the morning from the surface. They had found nothing of much interest, and I did not go to watch them at work. A pity, Richard Garnett said afterwards, for I missed a splendid submarine landscape: 'It was like Arizona.' I did not regret it. Without mask, fins or schnorkel I waded into the sea. The water was soft and warm. I was content not to be reminded of the secrets beneath it, but simply to swim: to float, leisurely and indolent, with the sun drying the salt to crystals on my face; to be solitary.

The journey back round the nameless headlands was silent. The wind blew cold off the slaty sea, and I was shivering when at nine o'clock and in darkness we came into Emporio harbour. There was an ironic cheer from the yacht. We roused ourselves to answer. But the long day had muted all our spirits, and at supper there were the silences and the spurts of irritability proper to the evening of a holiday. Those who had chosen to stay at home had the sense, I noted, to keep out of our way.

XII

SINCLAIR WAS VERY kind,' said somebody, 'and let her stay in bed.'
We were talking about one of the students who, frayed I daresay by
the sun and the exhaustion of the outing, had developed a temperature. The temporary relaxation merely emphasized the severity of
devotion on a dig; the show must go on. Once or twice I wondered
if my presence was an unintentional goad. Try as I will, I cannot
convince my acquaintances how little, how next to nothing I know
about archaeology and archaeological practice. The bluff, I suppose,
went on in the past too long, and when I insist now the truth is taken
for modesty. At Emporio my detachment was never quite believed
in. Some other observer might have been accepted as aloof and
impersonal. But for me it was difficult to watch and question without seeming to make comparisons.

'At Perachora,' said Sinclair, not as ironically as I should have liked,
'no doubt you worked longer hours.' I could not hope to convey to
him or to anyone else the improvisations, the flippancies, the outbursts
of ribaldry and riotousness which, interrupting the scholar's savage
intentness, went to make up our life at the Heraion.

It was not easy, either, to convince him that I admired the way
in which the excavation party was run. True, Emporio was an easier
place than Perachora to manage. To begin with it was more accessible.
At the Heraion the stuff of our camp, the tents and beds and
cooking utensils, had all to be brought by sea. Water was fetched by
boat from a distant spring; a post-boy brought our daily food by
donkey; we had to build our own camp-kitchen. In Chios no matter
how bad the track which joined the main road between the town and
the village of Pyrghi, a motor-car or a lorry could use it. Equipment

could be transported, supplies brought down it. There were houses at Emporio, a tiny shop, a taverna where we could eat. The fact that the place was the resort of summer visitors meant that a natural traffic went to and fro between the harbour and the village. Above all, there was fresh water on the spot. At Emporio the planner of the excavation did not have to start from scratch.

On the other hand the expedition had to be more elaborately organized. The site covered, as I have said, more than Greek remains; the Roman fortress and the Early Christian church were to be explored later in the summer. The area was large: the Bronze Age settlement down by the sea, the houses of the archaic Greek city on the slopes overlooking the harbour, the temple high on the mountain. And the company was heterogeneous. In 1954 there was not only the archaeological party to be housed, fed and supervised. There were the divers, visitors from another world; to some of them the methods of archaeology were as foreign as the landscape of the moon. And now a third element was introduced into our society: the yacht-party.

The newcomers were to lead a life not merged in ours but parallel with it. They slept on board, they ate on board; they were their own clock. There were hours, at any rate during the first days, when the shipboard company held no communication with the party on shore. Like a pleasure-boat moored off a smart Riviera beach, the white ship lay silent in the empty harbour; only some member of the crew, one of the figures in a singlet always to be seen, in yachts, clattering about with a bucket, looked over the rail to show a sign of life. But even so the presence of the third party could be felt. We turned our eyes to the yacht, we considered the forays to which it might carry us. There would be parleys, a passenger or two coming ashore in a boat, or a diver rowing out to climb on board. And there was an evening when all three parties, archaeologists, divers and sailors, met in the dig-house for a drink before dinner. The shore company wore its best clothes for the occasion, and the appearance of three pretty girls, elegantly dressed, being rowed over the harbour lent to the desolation of Emporio beach the worldly air of the Carlton terrace at Cannes.

Sinclair, as representative of the British School to which the permit both for digging and for underwater reconnaissance had been given, was, I suppose, responsible for seeing to it that all three parties kept the rules imposed by the Greek Government. He was the man in charge. But the owner of the yacht and his wife, his step-daughter and the friends who made up the sea-party could not be regarded as controllable in quite the same way as, say, the students of the British School. Their very presence was a gift, an act of generosity. And for them the Emporio expedition was a summer trip. Not that the other parties took anything but pleasure in it. The archaeological students were volunteers pursuing a subject which fascinated them. The divers had chosen to spend their holidays on a new scientific sport. But both divers and archaeologists had submitted themselves to discipline; they had joined a camp and must put up with its restrictions and its duties. The ship's company were apart. Independent, insouciant, they were the loungers in the heat who had casually taken up diving and might as easily drop it again. They were enthusiastic, they were active. Nobody can be more active than the man who is not obliged to do anything. But at any moment they could – though I am sure they never did – withdraw to the shade of their awning, to their mattresses in the sun. Into our world of frugal living and camp-beds they brought an air of luxury, indolence, good nature and amiable arrogance.

I could not stay in Chios to watch all their services to the expedition, but I was there long enough to see how the presence of the yacht transformed the day's work. After I left for England the divers, by then much increased in numbers, were enabled to explore harbours and sites far to the north of the island. And already while I was still at Emporio the whole party with their gear were being carried in comfort to bays which only two or three divers, laboriously rowing, could have otherwise reached; indeed it was from the yacht that I made my second unsuccessful attempt with an aqualung.

Even if the ship stayed in harbour the motor-launch, towing a dinghy, could go round the point to Komi beach and far beyond. And the launch could help in the search from the surface. For swimmers with mask and schnorkel to cover a large area was slow work. But a swimmer could be towed. A rectangular sheet of metal with handles at each side was trailed at the end of a rope. A man grasping the handles could be pulled flat along the surface; and he could tilt the aquaplane, as it was called, at an angle which would submerge him, give him a closer look at the sea-bed and the rocks, or let him come up to breathe. The first trials were made in the wake of the yacht. But the ship at her lowest speed still moved too fast, water drove into the breathing-tube and the man on the aquaplane, half-choking, had to let go. The movement of the launch could be better regulated, and though even so the swimmer's job was not easy, it was possible. The search went on with less labour and more speed.

But there was work which could not be hurried. At Komi beach, where the fifth-century wreck had spilt its cargo in shallow water, the sherds had to be drawn and photographed as they lay. It was Richard Garnett's idea to divide the area into squares by laying down strips of white plastic in parallel and crossed lines; after the grid had been marked out the draughtswoman of the party lay with mask and schnorkel on the surface and traced on sheets of transparent plastic the shape and disposition of the whole and the broken amphorai. For hours, it seemed, I swam to and fro watching her, or hung over a diver as he loosened from its bed some fragment of evidence; sand-coloured fish crowded round him, nosing at the greenish, frog-footed monster while he struggled to anchor himself against the lift of the water. The sound of his pick floated up, a tiny, remote, metallic tapping amidst the liquid whispering of sea and rock.

And the presence of the yacht, with the touch of fantasy which it brought to our society, could not change the rhythms of life at Emporio. The days went by with the same slow beat. The workmen carrying their spades and picks on the way to the temple went up the path behind my bed in the cool early light. All morning the maze of trenches at the Bronze Age settlement by the shore gathered heat; the pits, deepening, disclosed now and again some blackened, irregular clay vessel, perhaps with the refinement of a handle. In the early afternoon the sun leaned with all its weight; shielding ourselves, we staggered to our tents, our houses, to lie down for half an hour. Sometimes when we gathered for tea on the verandah of the dig-house there was a find from the temple to look at – a painted vase-fragment with an inscription or a tiny faience figure. The archaeologists and the divers went about their business with undeflected looks until dusk, when for an hour or two we became a single party, relaxed and talkative over our drinks and our dinner. Deprived of the screens of formality which life in a town lets us set up against our neighbours; engrossed without affectation in work; living in comfortable simplicity, at close range – in such conditions character unconsciously reveals itself. There among the divers was the practical, inquiring mind, casual adventurousness, a passion for organizing, for making things work; there among the archaeologists was the monasticism which can envelop even the most married of scholars, there was the controlled impatience with the profane world beyond the sanctuary of learning.

I looked on with an enjoyment sharpened by liking for all concerned: the academic jokers; the artists; the rich young men used to having their own way, at first a little discomposed by the strangeness of the Emporio community, then recovering confidence, assuming authority, bustling the girls along. There was even a certain pleasure in recognizing in embryo the fine old archaeological types of the future. Most of the great learned I met in Humfry's lifetime are dead, and I have sometimes lamented the end of a generation of individualists. I was wrong, I said to myself now. As I watched some angular figure in jeans and peasant straw hat, superbly preoccupied, hurrying up the mountain-side with the gait of a don late for a lecture: One day, I thought gratefully, he will be a scholar-eccentric, execrated, perhaps, by a younger generation, but in his own field a celebrity.

Leisurely though the passage of the days, it seemed to me that I had no spare time. I had nothing to do; and I had everything to do. Entranced by a routine to which I was not bound, I longed to look on from a dozen vantage-points. I could not bear to be absent for a minute. One morning from my house I heard a commotion, and looking out from the terrace saw Igor with another of the party stalking something in the field below. Igor was holding the little blue cricket cap he habitually wore; with a sudden throw he sent it spinning to cover the quarry, then pounced with a bath-towel: 'I have it, I have it!' I pelted down to look. The creature, whatever it was, made no struggle. Igor gently lifted the towel: fierce wild eyes, curved beak, mottled plumage – I saw that he was grasping by its pronged feet a peregrine falcon. A salt wind blew, the sun glistened on our hot faces. Igor held the bird at shoulder-level; rippling the liquid surface of the feathers, its neck uneasily twitched to right and left. Somebody ran for a camera; the falcon lifted its noble head and bent on us a savage, bold, fearful look. At last we let it go. Awkwardly, flying low, it skimmed down the field and along the shore, chased by a swarm of little boys; we watched it flapping over the bay until it vanished round the point. Was it hurt, was it ill? We could not tell. There had been a moment of magic: the sun, the wind, the wild creature mysteriously passive in our hands. I might have missed it, I thought.

More than ever I wanted to be everywhere at once. Even when I went to the siesta I lay half-listening for the sound of the compressor, and the hours spent perforce at my typewriter were a misery. Only in the pause after tea did I sometimes stray out of sound of the harbour, and then only to fill in the borders of my knowledge of Emporio.

One evening I set off to walk towards Dotia, the plain to the south frequented in the season by quail-hunters. Go past the Bronze Age pits, somebody had said, and over the hill, walk along the beach until you come to a path up the cliff, climb it, follow the track round by the fort in the plain, and you will join the road from Pyrghi down to the harbour. It was five o'clock when I started: a lucid evening, and on the beach where we had bathed on my first day at Emporio the shingle was still warm. But when I rounded the point southwards to the next cove a wall of land shut out the sun. Everything suddenly was the colour of untouched black grapes: dark cliff, dark arms of rock, dark shingle; the stones, oval, purplish-grey, grinding and cannoning as I walked on them, were the size of a man's two fists. The company of precipice and shadow frightened me, and I stumbled on quickly, round another point, under another minatory cliff, until I saw a track slanting upwards and began thankfully to climb. The path was fringed with the purple and golden flowers of early heat, stonecrop, broom, clematis, cistus, horned poppy; thistles held out ribbon-petalled flat blossoms and long spiny sepals, blossoms like yellow and green stars. I passed a spring, climbed above a dried water-course, and came to patches of cultivation. Once I missed the track, and scrambled on all fours up the terraced cliff until I reached a saddle in the hills and found my way again.

The path took me downwards now, out of sight of the sea and across a plain through olives, masticha-trees and fields of ripe corn. I could see the fort, a square tower with high gloomy walls, and con-fident that I was on the Dotia path I went on. Ahead there were scattered houses. But when I reached them they were empty; there was nobody to tell me how far I was from Emporio. I passed a stone well-head, and there was fresh mule-dung on the path; no other sign of life. The men and women who had been working in the fields had ridden home. The sun, I noticed, would soon slide behind the hills on my right. I began to hurry. Although the fort was behind me by now, I could see no familiar landmarks yet: no Mount Prophet Elijah, no road, no harbour. I crossed a field where the edges of sunlight were already soft. At the far side I came to a stop. I was in a hollow among the slopes at the end of the plain, and the track had petered out.

No doubt Emporio lay behind the ridge in front; I had simply missed a fork in the path. There is nothing like a lost direction for giving one speed, and I went up the stony, terraced slope like a rabbit. At the top, standing once more in full light, I saw with gratitude a valley lying below me. But I could not remember the houses on the opposite hillside. No road was visible. The shape of the mountains was strange to me. And where was the Prophet Elijah's chapel? However, there were houses, and if there were houses there should be people. I could see neither man nor mule, but I could try to rouse somebody. Sound carries like a feather in such clear silent air; I shouted. 'Hullo!' I yelled. 'Anybody there?' Not a stir. 'Emporio! Emporio!' Then, since the words did not matter, 'Help! Help!' The valley was still; nothing moved on the far hillside; only a sundown breeze drove cool into my sweating face as I stared at the fading amber landscape. This was not the Emporio valley, and I was far from the harbour.

There was nothing for it but to turn back the way I had come. It was seven o'clock; I had been two hours on the way. The thought of blundering down the steep cliff path at dusk and clattering along the shingle between black cliffs and black sea was cold. But if I wasted no time I might still have the last of the daylight. I turned and ran down the terraced slope and along the field, until I found the end of the path and came in sight of my landmarks. There was the fort; there were the empty houses; this field I remembered, though with the sun quite hidden behind hills the trodden way through the corn seemed different; and here was the well-head. Somehow the stone blocks looked higher than when I had passed before, and I had not noticed then the twist in the path. I began to run again. I was on a track broad enough now for a mule-cart. I still had, I knew, some distance to go across level ground before I came to the edge of the plain and the slope up to the cliff-top.

With a start I realized that the track was running steadily downhill. For the second time I had mistaken my way.

In full day I should have turned back once more. But the light was fading, the landscape was losing colour and feature. I stood for a moment, before I plunged desperately on, gazing round at hills, at contours which I felt I had never seen in my life. I had no hope of finding my way back to Emporio. Indeed, I had little hope of finding my way anywhere. The best I could expect, since the track was broad, business-like and obviously led to something, was to reach a village, a hamlet where I could spend the night under a roof and not in the open in a cotton dress. Even then I should have no means of letting my friends at Emporio know where I was. Would my absence be noticed at dinner? Would they begin to look for me that night? The

onfident Philhellene who knows the country and has walked back
nd forth over Greece loses her way on an afternoon stroll out of
amp: as if it were not enough, I thought with rage, to make an ass
f yourself with your failure to dive in the sea, you have to make an
ss of yourself on land as well.

At that moment I came to a fork in the path, hesitated, looked up
nd saw the chapel, high on Mount Prophet Elijah, bright in the last
f the sun. I was within five minutes of the harbour.

XIII

I<small>T IS EASY</small> to lose the way in Greece. Hurrying to join the rest of the
party before they went to dinner, I struggled to restore my self-
esteem with the reflection. Days later, retracing the walk in my mind,
I realized that when I saw the sun going down behind the mountain
on my right hand I should have known that I was heading southwards, away from Emporio. But even then I could not think how
missed the Dotia path, or how I hit on it again. Though in imagination I have climbed the cliff, crossed the plain, raced along the track
twenty times, I see no other way to take. In the landscape I picture
there is a single, unmistakable, forkless path.

A path without human figures: it has given the Chian landscape
in my memory an uninhabited look which is quite false, and which
is indeed contradicted by the rest of my experience. At Emporio, of
course, we always had company: the workmen and the local families,
Pandeli and his wife in their shop, the circle at dusk outside the
taverna, talking or listening to the incongruities of the Athens radio
– 'Hey, good-lookin', say, what's cookin'?' came the song over the
darkening shore. Sometimes there were visitors from Pyrghi, women
who picked their way along the beach and stopped to gossip with me
about their children and their pregnancies. And once an old eccentric
came tramping down the hillside by my house and, leaning on his stick,
held me talking in a mixture of Greek and English for half an hour.

'Nestor of the press, they call me.' He took out a decaying wallet
and opened it tenderly to display a bundle of yellow, splitting newspaper cuttings. 'Wait, I will show you.' The roughened fingers
turned over the fragments, dropped one: 'No, that's not it . . . Ah,
here it is; you read Greek? There . . . You see?'

Mystified, I made out enough to understand that it was an account of some duty performed by King Paul of Greece.

'And this, read this . . .' A visit somewhere by Queen Frederica; another royal duty: 'You like your King and Queen?' I asked.

'All of them, I like all the Kings and Queens. The United States, I don't like the United States because they are not royalist . . .'

'You have been in America?'

'Yes, a long time. I worked there, I didn't like it because it was a Republic, I made speeches, they put me in prison, forty days I was in prison. When I came out I couldn't get work. I was quiet, I made no more speeches, but I couldn't get work. So I came back to Greece.'

'You speak English very well.'

'I love the English, I love them because they are royalists. I tell everybody, I should like to see the Union Jack flying over Greece.'

Thankful that there were no listeners to suspect me of inciting him to express such an opinion, I began to edge away.

'Our King, our Queen – I will tell you something,' he said, closing up. 'Look, read this. You see?' He laid in my hands another tattered account of a royal duty, a tour in the islands. 'One day last year it was, in the summer, as it might be now. I will tell you. I was working on my property, in the fields; last year it was. I look up, I see two people coming over the hill, a man and a woman. I look at them. The woman has no hat, no headscarf; she is not a country woman, like a foreigner she is, walking fast, with a stick. "Good morning," I say to them. "Good morning," they say, as if they were laughing, "Good morning." I look at the man.' He lowered his voice. 'The face is, how shall I say . . . But you have seen his photograph in the newspapers, no doubt. I am sure it was . . . Both of them. They did not say who they were. But I looked at them and I knew them. Both of them. "Good morning," I say to them. "Welcome," I say. They ask me about the place, about the village. I show them everything, all morning we walk, they ask me questions, I answer, all morning I lead them. I said nothing, I told nobody, but I knew them, I knew who they were.'

When at last I broke away, 'Perhaps,' he said, 'you have an

English newspaper or a magazine for me? I like to read English.' I gave him an old copy of *The Geographical Magazine*; it was all I had. Gratified, he went off with it under his arm. As he stumped down the path I wondered whether in his imagination I was already turning into some royal personage, travelling incognito in a faded cotton sun-dress.

I never had time to walk to Dotia again. But one other excursion I felt I ought to make. You must, advisers in Athens insisted, go to Pyrghi, it's an extraordinary village; the people are said to be descended from the Saracens, nobody knows who they are. Since the road from the harbour joins the main road from Chios town to Pyrghi I could hardly lose my way, and one afternoon I unclenched myself from sleep and set off in the heat. It is a walk of about five miles, winding, cruel, stony, uphill; I was grateful when a lorry, carrying cement from the caïque which we had mistaken for the yacht, overtook me half-way and gave me a lift.

'Twice I shall make the journey back to Emporio tonight,' said the driver, 'the last time at half-past seven; look for me in the square, I will take you.' Before we parted I had learned that he too, like my taxi-driver in Chios town, had escaped to Turkey in the war in order to fight. 'I travelled everywhere,' he said, laughing. 'Egypt, Palestine, Italy, a regular tour it was.'

Walking in Pyrghi, I thought with respect of the intractable temper which had driven the Greeks from their villages to fight abroad. On the doors which I passed painted scrawls – DDT followed by a date seven years old – showed that post-war hygiene had come this way once. But the village was changeless, living aside from the world in which the men of Chios had fought: changelessly beautiful, changelessly filthy. I went along cramped streets, through tunnelled passages. The Genoese who ruled in Chios before the Ottomans had left their trace in round towers at the corners of dusky alleys, in buttresses and archways; fig-trees rooted high in the walls, balconies were caparisoned with the leaves of vines struggling out of darkness. Looking up from the skyless shadow, I saw at the first-floor level of a house a cemented oven projecting on a platform. On the ground level of the crevasse-street the animals were stalled. A mule stood behind the heavy, broken wooden door in front of me. And from the sepia, steamy gloom of the stables clouds of flies puffed out, screaming in tiny, irritable voices, pouncing, clinging, oscillating, landing, jerking zig-zag on their soft sucker-feet.

In the square, in the airy spaces from which the shadowy, Italianate living-tunnels branched, the houses, the buildings were startlingly decorated. High empty walls of stucco were filled with painted patterns: rows of floral ornament, line upon line of geometric figures, triangles, sail-shapes, stars, chevrons, crowded as in a Victorian sampler; the colours white, grey, blue, excited now and then with red.

'Are they old, the patterns?' I asked, using the word meaning 'embroidery'.

'Old, old!' came the reply. But I could not discover, since I could not make clear what I meant, whether the incised and painted shapes were the restoration of an original already in place or a copy; whether I was looking at a living traditional craft or at a craft artificially revived. I walked on, turning corners, doubling back, as one does in a strange town, to the square, the same street. Old women sat in doorways, staring. Squeamishly I looked away when I saw again and again a festering or an empty eye-socket; the dirt and the flies had marked the people who lived in Pyrghi. In their clothes the women clung, some of them, to a traditional finery. A pinafore dress of blue with exquisitely fine pleating, worn over a heavy, sleeved smock; on the head a wide, cream-coloured cap, pancake-flat, with a fringed kerchief draped over it – faded, dirty, the costume still had an oriental dash. Talking to a group in a narrow street, I was shown the beaded stars, the long silver filigree pins ending in the body of a cock and dangling a glittering ornament with which on feast days the women decorate their head-dress. A girl, demonstrating, stuck the pin at one side of her flat cap, the star at the other; unconsciously her face under the fringed scarf took on a bold, inviting look. The dark eyes shone, the head turned arrogantly on the strong neck; she was the beauty at the fair – or, I suddenly thought, a defiant virgin of the War of Greek Independence.

As I loitered I heard mouse-squeaks behind me, and looking round observed that I had attracted a troop of children. I moved on, and so did they, a tiny spellbound rabble: across the square, down the street, past the village shops. 'Are you not ashamed?' a man in a cafeneion cried at them as we straggled past. But no, they were not ashamed, and I had their silent company until at seven o'clock I decided not to wait for the lorry and set off to walk back. It was the time for coming in from work. All the traffic of the fields was moving towards home: men and their wives, old women and children, riding, walking, silent and singing, they came with donkeys and mules up the road to Pyrghi; the low-slanting sun glowed on their burnished faces and hands and lit with reddish-gold the sheaves of corn swaying on the backs of the pack-animals. For three-quarters of an hour I passed the procession.

'Good evening!'

'Good evening!'

'To Emporio you are going?'

'Yes, to Emporio.'

'On foot you are going?'

'Yes, on foot.' Their well-wishing, and my scramble from side to side of the flinty ruts out of the passage of the burdened mules, slowed me down. All the same I was on the last, level stretch to the harbour when the lorry overtook me.

This time I was too late to join in the nightly drink before dinner. Dusk had fallen; and as I went down the path from my house to the beach and the taverna the pure green light of a glow-worm shone steadily in the dry grass.

XIV

I HAD THOUGHT OF Emporio as an experience I must not refuse. I had gone there as a stranger. Now after a week or two I was absorbed into the place. From the beginning its life had proved familiar. The long, undistracted routine – I knew it all, as I knew the time-table of the dawn wind, the donkey braying in the night, the owls answering one another; even the ants and the spiders which flurried in my house, even the armoured beetles with their helicopter-flight and the jellyfish drifting in the harbour were the same creatures I had known at Perachora.

The day before I left I spoke a few words to one of the workmen. Since my business was not with the excavations I had scarcely talked with the Greeks on the site, but I happened to be standing by when an interpreter was needed for a man who, digging a few days earlier in the Bronze Age pit, had let a heavy rock fall on his toe.

The foot was being dressed. 'The lady,' I said, translating, 'says she will take the nail off tomorrow.'

He looked up from under his sun-bonnet. 'Good, let her take it off.'

'Does it hurt?'

'Eh!' He grinned, baring gold teeth. 'Let it hurt, never mind.'

An hour or two later I was sitting outside the village shop when he came up to the table and laid in front of me a small vegetable marrow. 'For me?' I said, startled.

Radiant with the pleasure of his gift, he turned to go. 'It's nothing, never mind,' he said.

I was accepted; suddenly I was reluctant to leave. That evening at dinner I felt the familiar desire to say goodbye, since say it I must, with a clear finish. I wanted everything to be at the full: the company at its liveliest, the night at its most beautiful; I wanted to part on a moment of elation. Then to drop the flap of the tent, then to pull the shutters to – but as with a few of the party I sat over coffee and Turkish delight on Pandeli's verandah I recognized the vanity of the wish. The moonlight bent its solid shadows, amidst the silent exhalations of the earth the crickets whistled tremulously; our voices were lowered against the overhearing night. Soon we straggled off to our beds. The evening was like every other evening, unfinished.

The next afternoon I stood for the last time at the door of my house, looking down at the stubbly crumbling field and the polished sea. Then I followed the boy with my luggage to the taverna, shook hands all round, kissed Pandeli's wife and bundled into the car.

We were a party of half a dozen, departing visitors and people with errands in Chios town; in their company I shook off the melancholy of leave-taking. I had errands of my own: telegrams to send, my boat-ticket to buy, shopping to do for one of the divers, who had entrusted me with a match-box containing three samples of the boiled sweets he wanted. I had a call to pay on the Nomarch, the Prefect, who received me with kindness and indulged my struggling Greek civilities. At last I had finished. A shade of purple tinged the edges of the evening, and in the regretful light I went back to the harbour to dine with the rest of the party.

The boat for Athens had come in. The café tables on the quayside were filling up; voices expostulated in the anxiety of departure. Since I was to go I longed to be off. But standing at the barrier beside my luggage, or walking impatiently up and down, I found that the goodbyes were not all said. There was the harbour-master, beaming and natty as ever as he saluted me. There was the porter who had volunteered to lead me to the laundry. A man detached himself from a passing group and, dark eyes smiling, hurried to shake my hand; it was the taxi-driver who had taken me to Nea Moni. At the last a hunched old figure came trotting with anxious whispers behind me.

'Kyria, I have some change to give you.'

I looked into his face and saw the red-rimmed eyes of the old porter, the victim of my obstinacy in the tipping shenanigan. Had he been let off his fine? I shall never know, for dumbfounded at the offer of repayment I waved his coins away.

'Bah, never mind. It is well now, have they put thee back in work?'

'Well, it is well. The money, you do not want it?'

'Keep it,' I said grandly as we shook hands. Chios had given me the clear finish I longed for.

XV

In ATHENS THE street-lamps were already lit when I set off toward
Perachora. Arriving in the early morning, the boat from Chios had
given me a long day for work and errands. First I had to go down
to the Agora, the quarter of ancient Athens at the foot of the Acropolis which the Americans had been excavating since the early
thirties, in search of an expert on amphorai. I laid on the workroom
table a sheaf of archaeological drawings I had brought from Chios:
the shapes of the vase-bodies, the curves of the necks, the lines of the
handles. To my relief I was told at once that the type from Komi was
Attic of the late fourth or the early fifth century B.C.; the Emporio
estimate of the date of the wreck was confirmed. I sent off a reassuring telegram to the diving party and settled down in my hotel bedroom to a day at the typewriter. When at last I had finished I took
my rucksack and ran downstairs and into the street without waiting
to eat.

This time I was determined to reach the lighthouse, no matter
what else had to be left undone. There were two possibilities. I could
have another shot at walking from Loutraki, for I knew now where
I had gone wrong the year before. Or I could try to find a boat. In
the thirties when we were camping at the Heraion a benzina – an
engined sailing-ship smaller than a caïque – used to put out from
Loutraki every morning and go past the lighthouse and round the
point of the promontory into the Halcyonic Gulf, there to collect
the fish netted by small boats the night before. Perhaps it still made
its round; if it did I could ask for a lift. A mixture of old habit and
romantic memory prevented me from considering the more con-
venient route used nowadays by most visitors. At any rate it never

entered my head that I might drive from Perachora village down the famous carriage road.

But however I went I should have to spend the night in Loutraki in order to make an early start. I set off, then, by car, for I was too late to catch a train or a bus out of Athens. My chauffeur was a stranger. The old friend who had driven Humfry and me across hundreds of miles of mountains, and who still drove me when I needed him, was ill, and when I went to the taxi-rank a quick-mannered, eager, gentle-voiced man called Thanasi offered himself instead. For company and to while away the two hours' journey I sat beside him in front. Out of the city, over the hill to Eleusis, along the road to Megara – dipping and flashing their headlights the cars and lorries streamed past us on their way back to Athens while Thanasi and I exchanged the traditional questions.

'No,' he said, 'I have no children, that is to say none of my own. But I have baptized several – you understand? You know what it is to baptize a child?'

'Yes,' I said, listening to his stories of standing godfather, 'I understood.' 'I baptize the boys,' he went on, 'the girls my wife baptizes. It is not safe for a man to baptize both a boy and a girl, for who knows, one day the two might fall in love and want to marry, and then they would be prevented.'

'That I do not understand. Why should they not marry?'

'Ah, perhaps with you in England it is different, but here in Greece – I will explain. A story I will tell you. It is like this. A marriage has been arranged: a good boy, tall, strong, with a fine job, and a girl, pretty, modest, of good family. There is a big party, many friends are invited. The guests arrive. The sun shines, there is a little wind – not a cold wind, you understand, a little wind for coolness. The house is beautiful, full of handsome furniture, pictures, carpets on the floor, there is a garden with trees, with flowers. The guests are offered refreshments, all kinds of titbits, ouzo, masticha, wine, everything. Everyone is delighted. "And now," the bride says to the bridegroom, "now I want thee to meet my godfather." "Gladly," says the bridegroom; "I too have a godfather who is kind and good,

I want to introduce you." And he goes to find his godfather, and she goes to fetch hers. Catastrophe! They have the same godfather, it i the same man. What a pity! What can they do? The party is over the marriage cannot take place.'

'I still do not understand. Why cannot they marry?'

'But you see, since they have the same godfather, the boy and the girl are brother and sister. Not really, not by birth, but spiritually let us say, they are brother and sister; for that reason they canno marry, they are spiritual brother and sister. And that is why my wif and I, if we are invited to baptize a child, I baptize the boys and she baptizes the girls, and this way there can be no danger.'

We ran through Megara and on to the switchback coast-road.

'You know,' said Thanasi, 'there are many stories about this region In ancient times a great robber lived here – but perhaps you know the stories?'

'No,' I said falsely, 'no, I didn't know the stories.'

'Perhaps you would like me to tell you?'

'Yes indeed, please tell me.'

'Then I will tell you; it will pass the time. Once, up in those rocks, in those rocks up there a great robber lived. He lived high up there in a cave, and he watched to see who passed. In those days, you understand, the road was not like it is now, it was very narrow. Well, when a traveller came, wanting to go by, that scoundrel stood in the path. "Where art thou going?" he says. "I am going to Corinth," says the traveller, "I have business there, to Corinth I am going." "Thou wilt not reach it today," says the other; "it is late, it is dark; come with me to rest thyself, I will give thee a bed for the night." And he takes the traveller to his house.

'Now when the traveller comes to lie down, perhaps he is a tall man, and the bed is too short for him. "Very good," says the scoundrel who has invited him, "very good, we will arrange that!" And he takes his knife and cuts off the traveller's feet. Or perhaps he is a short man. "That won't do," says the other; and he ties the man with cords and stretches him. No matter what kind of a man the traveller is he cannot escape. And that scoundrel, let me tell you, at last when he has robbed the traveller he takes the wretched man and throws him over the cliff. At the bottom there is a big tortoise – tortoise, you know tortoise? And the tortoise eats the body.'

It was difficult to think of an adequate rejoinder.

'But Herakles – you know Herakles? – a young boy he is, living with his mother. He is growing up, he wants to go to his father in Athens; but his mother refuses. "No," she says to him, "I do not let thee go, thou art a boy still, only if thou canst lift the great rock where thy arms are hidden, then I let thee go." But Herakles has grown up, he lifts the rock, he finds the arms. (Not a gun, you understand, it was too early for that; another kind of weapon it was.) Well, Herakles sets off to Athens. On the way he meets that scoundrel, the one with the bed, and kills him. Then he goes on a little farther and he meets another evil man. This one used to catch anyone who passed and tie him between two pine-trees; he used to bend down the tops of the trees and tie the man to each; then, you see, when the trees were released the traveller, wretched man, was torn in two. This second scoundrel also Herakles kills. Then he goes a little farther, and there is a third danger: a great pig – you know pig? – a pig which eats all the travellers on the road. Well, Herakles kills the pig too, so they say; and this way he comes to Athens and to his father . . . Do you wish me to go on?'

'Please; of course.'

Our headlamps lit up the dusty olive-trees, then left them extinguished in the dark. '. . . to Crete . . . Ariadne,' Thanasi was saying. He was telling the story of the hero returning victorious after killing the Minotaur and forgetting, in his joy, to exchange the black sail for white; like the rest of the tale, it belonged to the legend of Theseus, but Thanasi was still giving Herakles the credit. 'His father is waiting for the ship to come back. Day after day he watches. He sits on the rocks, he looks out to sea. At last, far off, there is a sail. He shades his eyes, he looks. Catastrophe! The sail is black. "He is dead, my boy is dead!" And he throws himself down from the rocks.'

'It is sad, the story.'

'Ah, as you know, it is all mythology, all mythology it is. But I said to myself: we have a long journey, it is night; the stories will pass the time.'

It was a quarter to eleven when we came to Loutraki, and the little spa was shutting down for the night. 'Tomorrow,' I told Thanasi, 'go to Perachora village at midday. If I cannot find a benzina I must walk to the lighthouse and back to the village; stay till I come.' Then I hurried off to the restaurant on the sea-terrace. The waiters were already piling the chairs on the tables. But nobody seemed to bear ill-will when I asked for supper. 'The cook has not gone yet'; I ate fried fish, a salad and apricots, drank spring water, and went to my hotel cool and sleepy. On the way I found a kiosk still open, and bought chocolate and biscuits, provisions for the next day's excursion. The porter at the hotel was definite: no benzina went round the lighthouse point in the early morning. I made my bundle for the trip: food, bathing dress and towel, powder, lipstick, money and a book I was taking to my friends; and asked to be called at six o'clock. The sea clucked and sucked gently under my window, and across the bay I could see the lights of Corinth. I will walk, I said to myself, and this time I will arrive.

XVI

'THANK YOU, THANK YOU,' I called to the knocker at the door. 'All
right, I am coming.' The knocking went on. 'All right, I am awake,
thank you.'

'Kyria, may I come in?'

'One moment.' I dragged the sheet from the bed, wrapped it
round myself, and stumbled to the door. 'My watch says it is only
twenty minutes to six.'

'Kyria, a boy downstairs is asking for you. He says if you go at
once there is a benzina which will take you to the lighthouse. But it
is leaving, it cannot wait, you must go at once.'

Five minutes later, with the dregs of sweet Turkish coffee still
muddy on my tongue, I grabbed my bundle and rushed down to
the hotel entrance. A figure in tattered coat and trousers was standing
at the door: a peasant of about twenty-five, barefoot, smooth-shaven,
with curly hair and the dark, romantic good looks one sometimes
sees in a young Greek shepherd.

'Last night I heard a chauffeur talking about a kyria Payne who
wanted to go to the lighthouse.' He was leading me at a smart pace
to the quay. 'Luckily this morning the benzina is going, so I came
to fetch you.'

'From Perachora art thou?'

'From Perachora, yes.'

'Dost thou know me then, dost thou remember me?'

'No, only the name I remembered. Once when I was little I saw
you with your husband in the village. But that was long ago. Only
the name I remembered. The name Payne I remembered. Many
times I have heard talk about the excavations at the lighthouse and

255

the men from the village who worked there. So I said I would come and fetch you.'

'Art thou also going to the lighthouse?'

'No, here I have work. Only to fetch you I came.'

The benzina was tied up at the jetty; jumping ahead with his strong bare feet, he helped me on board, then stood waving. The captain, a grizzled old sturdy in a hat like an Edwardian child's seaside straw, its wide brim turned up all round, spread a newspaper for me to sit on. His mate disappeared below; there was a breath of hot oil, a rattle, and we bounced off. I was on my way to the lighthouse.

I looked round at my company. The captain and the mate; two youths sitting together, passengers, probably, like myself; a skinny, salty, alacrious little boy, scrambling about, doing this, doing that, learning the sea; and the heavy, water-stained chests full of ice for packing the fish – it seemed to me that nothing had changed in twenty years.

'I remember a long time ago, before the war, a benzina used to go past the lighthouse every morning.'

'Not now,' said the captain, 'not regularly that is to say. Today you are lucky, we are going to collect the fish.'

'Were you here, was it you who made the trip at that time, when there were excavations at the Heraion?'

'Not I, no. But the name of Payne I remember.'

The day was still cool; the sun was only now beginning to look over the flat shores of the Isthmus at our backs. On our right the spur of Geraneia which rises abruptly behind Loutraki was knife-edged in the morning light. A small breeze brushed the water into tiny waves. Across the Gulf the mountains of the Peloponnese were still cowled in mist, but the lower slopes of Kyllene were visible, and presently the outline of Chelmos began to clear. I did not watch it for long. My eyes were on the coast along which we sailed, the shore between Loutraki and the lighthouse: on the road gashed in the mountain-side up to Perachora village, on the pine-woods, the long spine of rock rising and dipping until it reared its dragon-head at the point of the promontory. I could see the lighthouse now, remote, golden as the early sun struck. I tried to make out the way I had walked a year earlier. There was the field with the dried watercourse, there were the huts where I had asked the fisherman if I was on the right path. The lines of the shore flattened, and I knew that behind the low rim was the lake where, realizing that I could not reach the Heraion, I had turned back towards Perachora village. And now a monstrous cliff bristled over us; we were in the shadow of the Heraion headland, and as we skimmed noisily over the tranquil, glass-green water, we could see ahead two or three rowing-boats, and in one of them a man standing up, signalling.

'There,' said the captain, 'there is Vasili; do you know him?'

The engine fell silent; we slid into the tiny, cliff-encircled harbour. The benzina and the rowing-boat swung shoulder to shoulder, hands helped me over the side. 'Goodbye and thank you!' I cried. The captain waved, the benzina snorted, turned and stuttered away; in a moment it had vanished round an arm of rock.

Vasili and I shook hands.

'Welcome!'

'Well have I found thee!'

It was like the meeting of people who see one another perhaps once a month.

The jetty where I stepped ashore was broken, and the masonry of the seaward end tilted towards the water; it had been broken ever since I remembered it. In the harbour the rowing-boats we had seen from the benzina were putting out to fish.

'The boy there, the dark one, he is the son of Pavlo,' said Vasili, leading me up the path which winds high between rocks to the lighthouse. 'Do you remember Pavlo, who was captain of the lighthouse when you were digging at the Heraion?'

I remembered him well: a short, black-chinned man with heavy moustache, taciturn, a solitary drinker, a melancholy outsider in the closely-knit community of Perachora. Now his son, grown up, was one of the three lighthousemen.

'And thou art captain?'

'Now I am captain.'

I looked back, down over the precipitous curve of the lighthouse rock to the harbour. The circle of water was still morning-shadowed by the opposite cliff. There was the miniature valley, running from the beach between steep tumbled slopes to the foot of the crag, highest and steepest of all, where the whitewashed chapel of St Nicholas is niched. And there in the shallow drift of earth I could see the remains of the stoa, the colonnade; the temple blocks, the foundations which we had uncovered; and the fisherman's chapel which we had pulled down to see what lay hidden beneath it and then rebuilt a few yards away. Vasili pointed far off to the floor of the Hellenistic house where once we had given a party for the workmen and their wives. 'Do you remember how we danced and drank, and how your husband fell in the dark into one of the excavation pits?' When we came to the lighthouse enclosure a puppy trotted out, wagging his tail. There had been a dog just like him at the door twenty years earlier.

I went into the lighthouse living quarters. The room, whitewashed and cool, held a bed with a striped woven coverlet, a table and one or two wooden chairs; a woman I did not know, wife of one of the lighthousemen, came to greet me.

'You will take a little tea,' said Vasili; and to the woman: 'Make some tea, quick!'

I drank a cup of the infusion of herbs which country Greeks call tea and ate the hard rusk I was offered.

'It is a long time since I saw thee. Last year when I came to the village thou wast not there.'

'Here I was, here at the lighthouse.'

'I tried to come to the lighthouse, I reached the lake, but I had no time to come farther.'

'I know, I know; I heard. In '45 I saw you, in '45 at our village.'

He had scarcely changed. The broad, easy face with its fair stubble was burned a harsher red, the blue eyes were hazier, the whites more heavily blood-barred from salt wind and, I daresay, ouzo. A shade of discontent, a reproach for the inadequacies of life, had settled over him. But it was still the face I had seen the rst time, a bewildered foreigner, I had come to the lighthouse.

'Do you remember the time we went with your husband to that illage, to Asprocampo, and the old man who said he could tell the me by holding up his finger?' He roared with laughter as he nimicked a peasant who had pretended to use a hand as a sundial.

'Those were good days; it is a long time, it is a long time ago. And ow, now that the war is really over, now that the war with the Communists is over too – how are things with all of you?'

'Bad, bad; nothing goes well. There is poverty, everywhere there s poverty. Nothing goes well.'

'Your government, is it not a good one?'

'I do not think so.' His voice rose to a bellow. 'The Greeks' (using he word which to a peasant means a city Greek) 'are worth nothing!'

A hundred times I had heard the cry. Nobody is more denigratory bout his own people than the country Greek.

'Why dost thou say that? The Greeks are good, the people are ;ood.'

'The people, yes; the people are good. But the great ones eat every-hing and the people are poor; the great ones are all thieves, all hieves they are, they make money, they grow rich and the poor are aungry. Always the same it is, here in Greece.'

'In the village, is there poverty in the village?'

'Always there is poverty. And everything is dear, very dear. Although I am captain now, the money I make is worth less than what I earned before the war. I will tell you my wages for a month; t is not enough, you cannot live on it. I am tired of being a light-nouseman, I am tired of it, I am thinking of leaving the service.'

'But what wouldst thou do then?'

'I should take my pension, whatever is due to me, and go away. But what can I do? I am not trained to do anything else, what can I do? Tell me your opinion, now tell me. Thirty-two years I have done in the service, after thirty-five years I should have the full pension. But I am tired of it, always here in the lighthouse, and the wages are not enough to live on. Tell me, should I stay or should I leave? Tell me your opinion.'

'Is it not a pity to leave now, after working so long?'

'I don't know, I don't know what to do. My children I must think of. Already I live part of the time in Loutraki, I have a room there so that I can send the boy to the school, the gymnasium. When I am not here at the lighthouse, part of the time I live in Loutraki, part in Perachora.'

'And thy daughter, what happens to her?'

'Eh, she lives at home with her mother, what else can she do?'

Listening to his tale, I reflected that of all the Perachorans Vasili had always been the one most given to discontent. Shut in his light-house tower, he had longed for worldly traffic; lighting the lamp, fishing, looking out on the cruel rocks, the windy Corinthian Gulf and the mountains which enclose it, he had fretted for some more abrasive experience. 'A man,' he had said to me when, seventeen years earlier, I had last come to the Heraion, 'a man ought to see the world'; the rough casual manner and the laughter concealed a dissatisfaction which, more articulate than in most country Greeks, sometimes broke out in romantic melancholy. I wondered now what effect disappointment and poverty might have had on his political views, and indeed on the politics of all the village. I still did not know what the Perachorans felt about the Communist rising in Athens in 1944 and the long campaign which was to follow it. When I had seen the village in 1945 my friends, it seemed to me, amidst all the shouting over EAM and democracy had still not committed themselves. And in 1953, though everywhere else I went in Greece people had been free enough with their condemnation, in Perachora the subject of the Communist revolt had been almost pointedly dropped. It was as if the villagers had put a painful experience behind them and refused to be reminded of it.

'What do you say,' Vasili went on suddenly, 'will there be war? Again shall we have war?'

I had not heard the question from a Greek since my travels in the Mornos valley and Epirus a year earlier. 'No,' I said, 'it does not seem likely to me that there will be war now.'

'But that bomb, the atomic bomb; do you not think that the

Americans want war? They do not understand, they are not like us; they have not felt what it is like to have a war in their own country.'

'No,' I said again, 'I do not think the Americans want war. All of us are sick of war. But you have had war in your own country: in the village what happened in the fighting with the Communists? Are there Communists in Perachora?'

'Bah, they have all fled. In the mountains there are a few, not in the village.'

'So there were Communists in the village. Then tell me truly, how did they behave, well or badly?'

'I will tell you. In our village the Communists were organized, they were ready to seize power. They had a leader, Mitso they called him. Often I heard him, much he talked about helping the poor, and some there were who believed him. But what he and the rest wanted, I tell you, was power. Once I asked him, it was in the Occupation: "What are your plans? What will you do?" "We will drive out the Germans and the Italians," he says. "Very good," I say to him; "And then?" "Then," he says, "we will drive out the English and the Americans." "And then?" Then, I say, they themselves would have ruled, and we should have been as wretched as ever.'

'But in the war did they not fight the Germans?'

'Useless it was. They were in the mountains round about, up there they hid; they came down to the villages and took everything people had, food, cattle, everything. Then they ambushed the Germans; but they only made trouble so that the soldiers burned the villages. I tell you, three times our village, three times Perachora was nearly burned.'

'That I never knew. How did it happen?'

'Once the Communists waited by the road – you know, the road from Perachora down to Loutraki. They told nobody in the village, but they waited by the road for the Germans to come: a convoy, I don't know what it was. The German convoy came, the Communists attacked it, they blew up a jeep, they didn't kill anyone but they blew up a jeep. Well, the Germans were going to burn Perachora.

But a man spoke for us, he prevented it. He came up from Loutraki, he called the people in our village together and he made a speech. "I am a Greek," he said. "I am married to a German but I am a Greek like you. Now listen to me and be sensible. Let the Germans alone and they will not trouble you. But if you attack them you will do no good and you will suffer for it. Listen to me: let the Germans alone!" And so our village was saved.'

'What has happened to Mitso now, is he still alive?'

'Alive, alive; in the mountains he is, they have not caught him. Sometimes he comes to a village to get food, he talks a little, then he says goodbye and goes back to the mountains. They have not caught him!' And Vasili laughed without malice.

'Were there not some good men, Communists?'

His voice rose again indignantly. 'All thieves and murderers they were, they did nothing but steal and kill!' And the woman, listening in silence to our talk, burst out: 'All stealing and killing, all stealing and killing – praise be to God, it is over now.'

Walking back down the path from the lighthouse, 'I have a book here,' I said, 'it is a book I wrote about the time when we were digging at the Heraion; thou see'st it has photographs of the lighthouse and of the things we found. It is for all of you at the village; I thought I would leave it with Niko – he can keep it for all of you.' As I spoke I realized my mistake. Foolishly I had thought of the days when Niko and Vasili were lighthousemen together, when, inseparable in our minds, they seemed to us to speak with the voice of all the families of Perachora. Now the partnership was dissolved and Niko had retired; there was no reason why he, more than any other man, should hold something intended for all the village.

Holding his hands behind his back, Vasili looked sulkily at the pages I turned for him. 'I do not know,' he said, 'but if you want my opinion the book should be in the lighthouse. Here it should be, so that when strangers come to the Heraion I have something to show them. They come, they ask me questions about the excavations and the antiquities. Nothing I have, nothing to show them. Here the book should be.'

'So people come to the lighthouse?' I knew the answer; it had always been the same.

'They come, they come; many people come to see the Heraion. They ask me what was found, I tell them bronze, pottery, gold, ivory, but I have nothing to show them. Here the book should be.'

'But now I must take it to the village, so that the others can see it.'

'Very well, I say that you should give it to Yanni at the cafeneion, he will keep it for the lighthouse.'

'Perhaps thou art right. Do many people come to the lighthouse?'

'Many, many: Americans, English, Germans, all kinds. Now we have the carriage road from our village very many visitors come to see the excavations.'

We were standing at the shoulder of the lighthouse rock. Below, the path twisted down towards the harbour; ahead, the spine of the promontory dipped; rose again; flattened into the little pine-covered plateau where we used to pitch our tents; rose once more in the pinnacles where the chapel of St. Nicholas stared tiny and white in the circling sun. The Gulf was flat and empty. At our feet the summer-dried vegetation, meshed and thorny, was lightly brushed with dust. Nothing stirred, nothing breathed; only Vasili's voice, stubbornly insisting on the traffic of the great world. 'Many people come; summer and winter they come, all the year.' I looked at the wilderness, I remembered my lost walk a year earlier, and as I listened to my friend it seemed to me that his words were drowned in a roar of solitude and silence.

XVII

WHAT DO YOU SAY, will there be digging again soon? Will they come to dig once more?' After twenty years Vasili still hoped for the resurrection of the past. On my way down the path to the harbour I reflected on the tenacity of his wishes; once I glanced back, but the stocky, durable figure, trudging to the lighthouse, had vanished over the curve of the rock. By the shore I walked round the foundations of the sixth-century temple; a huge fragment of the entablature still leaned, just as I remembered it, against a shelf of soil. Then I turned past the remains of stoa and triglyph altar and the site of the geometric temple and went up the little valley with its clutter of history: the floor of the Hellenistic house and the carved stone dining couches; the foundations of the eighth-century temple of Hera, the supporting wall, the place of the sacred pool where scores of crushed bowls had been dug from earth which had once been mud and water; the supporting columns and the walls, still smooth-faced, of a cistern, roofless now, where even today at one end a few inches of clouded water tilted. On the slopes the starved olives and pines had scarcely stretched their dwarfish branches; beneath collars of rooting herbs the dressed blocks of walls and foundations were still sharp. Time, at its sexton's job, had idled since my last visit.

Following the streak of pebbles which was the track up to the plateau and the camping-place, I recalled suddenly, with the precision memory spends on worthless detail, the sandals I had been wearing the first time I had come down the path. Bought in some back street of Athens, they were made of strips of white rubber, hot and most of the time slippery with sweat. And at the recollection, at the illusion of their suck against my feet, a hundred summer afternoons revisited me: the Perachorans jovially hacking out the trenches in the valley; the English taking turns to squat round a bowl of acid and water, scrubbing the soil from the sherds; a party of women from the village coming through the woods to visit us; and Yanni setting off with his donkey on the daily trip to bring food and wine, letters and newspapers. At the top of the path I paused on the level ground which had been our home. On the south the rocks which hid the Corinthian Gulf, on the north the ground dropping steeply away in boulders and scrub and desperate pines towards the Halcyonic Gulf; encircling, the pygmy trees crouching from the wind: the very clearing seemed scarcely altered, scarcely overgrown. Here stood the students' tents, the store tent, the improvised kitchen – for a moment I hesitated, looking for the place where year after year the tent in which Humfry and I slept had been pitched. Impossible that I should mistake it: there were the boulders behind which the moon used to rise, there was the path through the woods; only the sapling pines, their pale green tufts wavering into the air, had obscured the patch of familiar earth. Heat and silence, the scent of the wilderness, the sheen of summer on the sea – as I looked across the tumbling slopes, across the northerly Gulf to the faint line of Helikon and Parnassos, my heart turned over. At the Heraion, past and present were the same.

Still, the inconveniences of time had to be taken into account. I set off in the direction of Perachora: through the woods, through the fields where we used to stroll on summer evenings, and towards the lake. The walk to the village takes nearly two hours, but when I looked at my watch I saw it was no more than nine o'clock; I could dawdle over the landmarks, I might even stop to swim in the lake. The fields were bleached, rough with stubble and clods of earth dried hard as stone; short stems of larkspur, their blue flowers faded by sun and drought, grew by the bridle-path. I went past an ancient cistern which had been there to see, open to the air, long before the site was excavated. Then I remembered the system of water-catch-pits beyond the fields on my right: three long, deep gashes in the soil, with a three-forked stone stairway tunnelling into the earth to meet them. I walked across the stubble, the thistles and the stiff haulms

r

scratching my bare legs. There was the first of the pits, the side reddish beneath the topsoil. The mouth of the tunnel had always been hard to find, but a Perachoran had dragged away the concealing brushwood to show it to Humfry, and we had learned the spot. Perhaps in the war it had served as a hiding-place, perhaps it was once more a secret; at any rate I could not find it now. I went back to the path and walked on, through more fields, more pines, to the lake.

In the woods which half-surround the water I could hear far off the sound of an axe, but though I stopped to listen I could see nobody. The fringes of the water quavered, the light blazed; I took off my blouse and, luxurious in the heat, walked on in skirt and suntop. A long way ahead a dog was barking. I was startled by a man's voice quite near, calling to me. I put my blouse hurriedly on again and looked round. The woods rise sharply from the water's edge; food spread on a striped blanket, an oldish man and a boy sat eating in the shade of the bank above me.

We greeted one another; collecting my wits enough to think that in this neighbourhood we were perhaps not strangers, I stopped to talk. 'Do you remember me?'

'Of course, of course. We saw thee coming, at once I knew thee. Dost thou not know me, dost thou not remember who I am?'

'Certainly I remember,' I said, though for the moment I had no idea. I was thankful that, noticing I daresay my hesitation, he spoke his name: Kosta. Then, indeed I remembered: cap pulled flat over a low forehead, black moustache, high cheekbones, a rather sullen expression; lean, youngish, a regular workman at the excavations. 'Well I remember thee,' I said happily. But I should not have known him: deeply wrinkled, his black hair heavily streaked with white, his teeth blackened – twenty years had made him an old man, a witness to the hardships and the meagre diet of the Greek peasant. Today the pair, the man and the boy, were sharing a bowl of vegetables: potatoes, onions, tomatoes mixed together and glistening with oil; there were a few emaciated olives in a screw of paper and a big hunk of black bread.

'Where art thou going, where?'

'To the village. From the lighthouse I come, I went to the Heraion, I visited the excavations once more. Now I am going to the village.'

'Sit down, sit down; eat, we have plenty.'

'I have eaten; at the lighthouse I ate.'

'Eat, eat; thou see'st we have plenty; take some, take.'

A patch of blanket was cleared for me, and I sat down and accepted one or two olives and a piece of bread; it was dry but full of life and taste.

'How didst thou go to the lighthouse, on foot?'

'No, I found a benzina.'

'Ah, with the benzina . . . The captain, didst thou pay him?'

'Yes; ought I not to pay?'

'Thou, to go to the Heraion! Vasili would be angry if he knew.'

The boy – his youngest, Kosta told me – sat eating. He was about eleven years old, a sallow child with a wedge-shaped head and lively inquisitive eyes; a shaven head made him look fairer than he really was. In the presence of his father he was respectfully silent.

'Never mind, I was lucky to find a benzina. They tell me it does not go every day as it used when we were digging.'

'Ah, when we were digging . . . Dost thou remember that time when we had a party? At night it was, we ate, we drank, we danced – near one of the pits of the excavations we were, and thy husband the director fell in.'

'Of course. It is a long time ago, but I remember. And thou, how well thou rememberest!'

'But naturally I remember, for I too fell into the pit at the same time.'

'Thou too? That I had forgotten.'

'Yes indeed, I too fell. Night it was. I fall, I say to myself: But where am I? What has happened to me? Then I hear something near me, something moving, then a voice. The director it is, thy husband!'

'Now I remember. Two or three, I think, fell in that night, with the darkness and the wine.'

Kosta laughed loudly. 'I it was who helped thy husband, together we got out.'

'It was a good party. Just now at the Heraion I saw the ancient house where we sat and ate that night; many years have passed since then. Vasili tells me that he is thinking of leaving the lighthouse service.'

'Vasili! He is always the same. Always he is restless, always dissatisfied. He is always the same.'

'Last year I did not see him . . . And now in a little time I must leave thee and go on to the village.'

'My horse thou must take to ride.'

'It is not necessary. The village is not far, and thou knowest I am used to walking.'

Kosta did not answer me. But I could hear him muttering to the boy: '. . . the horse, she will ride the horse.'

'No, no,' I said again, 'thou art very kind but it is not necessary. Dost thou not remember how my husband and I always walked to the village when we were at the Heraion?'

'I know, I know.' But turning to the boy and speaking gruffly and quickly so that I should not understand, 'Fetch the horse!' he said.

'Last year,' I persisted, 'as I told thee I walked from Loutraki to the lake and then back to the village. I like walking, there is no need for the horse.'

Once more I heard him ordering the boy: 'Fetch the horse!' Then to me: 'How long is it since you dug at the Heraion? The years have passed, the years have passed. And thou, how old art thou now?' While we exchanged ages I saw the boy scramble up and, with a look of mingled irony and eagerness, slip off down the path by the lake.

'We grow old,' I said, 'how can we help it? Tell me, how is Niko of the lighthouse? Last year it seemed to me that he too had aged.'

'Niko! He is always the same. Complaints, all complaints. He says he is ill, with this he suffers, with that – he is always the same.'

'And thy family, thy wife, thy children, are they all well?'

'Troubles I have, many troubles. At this moment I am very anxious about my daughter, she suffers with her tonsils. My wife has just gone with her to Athens, to take her to hospital; I am very anxious.'

268

'Do not worry, in hospital they will take care of her.'

'All the same I am anxious. And the expense, there is the expense. Poverty, that is the great evil!'

We looked in silence at the sparkling water. 'Farther on a little way,' said Kosta, 'there are some Vlachs with their sheep. Thou must look out for their dog, he is savage.'

'I will take care . . . Do not worry about thy daughter, they will look after her in the hospital.'

There was a sound of hooves scuffing on stones. Leaning forward as he walked and pulling on the rope behind him, the boy was coming back with a white horse.

'I do not let thee go on foot,' said Kosta.

The horse was saddled, its girths were tightened; with clucks and admonitions it was backed to a boulder by the lake. Perched sideways on the pack-saddle I spoke my thanks. 'Goodbye!' 'A good journey!' 'Goodbye, goodbye!' With the boy leading the animal I clattered off. I could see Kosta standing for a few minutes in the sun, watching, before he turned his back on us and with drooping shoulders disappeared into the darkness of the woods.

The boy walked without speaking. A stumpy, active figure, pulling steadily on the horse's mouth, looking round now and then to urge the creature, he kept up a brisk pace. Glad of a respite, I watched the well-remembered landscape undulating by. Near the end of the lake, where the woods draw back from the water to leave open ground, I saw the Vlach encampment. It was not yet midday, but there was the feeling of perpendicular heat, and the party, men, women, children and the dog, were sitting in the shade; pressing together to escape the sun, a flock of sheep huddled in a woolly mat round a tree.

'Hot!'

The boy turned to look up at me. 'What did you say?'

'Hot!'

'Eh, never mind.'

We clopped into the mouth of the valley. Grasshoppers sang in the brittle herbs, a few pale butterflies wavered across the track; heat filled the nostrils, and every visible thing, the rocks, the stony soil, the meagre olives, had the colour of dusty metal.

'Art thou not tired?'

'Bah!'

At the point where a year earlier I had first hesitated my guide took the fork I had rejected.

'Last year when I walked to the village I went that way.'

'This way it is shorter.'

We climbed through dappled pine-woods, airless and aromatic. After ten minutes the broken path we followed joined a broad track on the hillside.

'You see! Now we are on the same road again, the carriage road. The way we have come is shorter.' The boy's flat-set eyes widened with triumph. 'We are near now.' Already we were coming out of the pine-woods on to the sloping plateau I remembered; there at the head, a sand-coloured village, its colours fused, its angles flattened by the high sun, stood Perachora. And to remind me once more how still time can stand in Greece, as we crossed the stubble-fields a woman came riding in the opposite direction. She looked at me, just as the woman a year earlier had looked, and after she passed called out her name. I turned in my pack-saddle and shouted greetings after her. But I had forgotten her too.

XVIII

QUICKENING ITS PACE at the sight of home, the white horse jogged into the plateia. A car was drawn up in the shade by a wall, and before I had time to scramble from the saddle Thanasi came running out.

'Welcome!' he said in his eager, encouraging voice. 'Did you find the benzina, did you find it?'

Yes, I said gratefully, yes indeed; without it I should have been in difficulties, I should have been late.

'Last night I was sitting in a cafeneion, we were talking, I said I was driving an English lady, a kyria Payne, who wanted to go to the lighthouse. "Is there a benzina going?" say I. Well, there was a boy listening, a good boy. He says to me, "I know that name," he says; "Listen, tomorrow as it happens the benzina is going; but very early it goes, if the lady wants to catch it she must be there, it will not wait." "Very good," say I; "I will tell thee where the lady is staying, in what hotel. Now, wilt thou have the goodness to go to the hotel early tomorrow morning to fetch her? For tonight it is too late to tell her, she will be sleeping." He says to me, "Very good," he says, "I will go to fetch her." '

'Indeed he came,' I said. 'I was most grateful, and to thee also.'

'It is nothing. Now I will wait for you. They are expecting you in the village, I told them you were coming; how excited they were! You will eat, you will see your friends, I will wait for you; when you are ready you will call me.'

Kosta's boy had tethered the horse and now stood waiting. 'We will go to the home of Niko of the lighthouse,' I said. We crossed the plateia. I noticed at the corner a new house, a square building with clean, fresh stucco; and in the village street I was surprised to see running down the middle where I remembered an open trickle of fresh water, a deep square-cut ditch; two men were busy with tape measures. Everything else was as it had always been: the peeling houses, the stony alleys, the air of indifference. We climbed the steep, winding, stony path to Niko's house. The unpainted shutters of board were closed against the sun, but at the sound of our arrival Niko's wife, pulling her scarf round her head, appeared on the top of the outside steps.

'What a pity, what a pity! Niko went to Corinth this morning, he has business there; he will be very sorry. But come in, come in and rest thyself!'

Once again I sat in the room with the white coverlet on the bed and the fading photographs on the walls; I was offered a spoonful of jam and a draught of cold water. The two daughters in their towny dresses and shoes, their heads uncovered, rushed to kiss me, then sat down ready to fill the gaps in their mother's conversation.

'Where have you come from? From Loutraki?'

'From the lighthouse. This time I found a benzina, I reached the Heraion.'

'Ah, you reached the lighthouse! Last year,' (Theodora turned to the others), 'last year she got to the lake, she looked at her watch, she saw that she had not enough time, so she turned round and came to our village.' She looked at me with slight reproof. 'You are wearing the same dress, from last year I remember it.'

'I wanted to tell thee,' I said to the mother. 'I have a book, I wrote it about the lighthouse and the Heraion and the times when we were digging there. I am going to give it to Yanni at the cafeneion so that it can be for all those I know in the village. But when I am in England again I will send one to thy husband also; it will be for nobody else, it will be for him, since we are friends.'

'He will be pleased, he will be very pleased!'

'We thank you, we thank you,' Theodora echoed. 'But why do you not stay longer in Perachora? Two or three hours, such a short time it is.'

'Perhaps next year I will come back.'

'Next year you must stay, two or three days you must stay here, we will have a party, we will go to Corinth together, we will celebrate.'

Next year, next year: optimism winds itself through the fatalism of the Greeks; there is always tomorrow, next week, next time. And carried on this forward tide, 'Next year!' I promised as I said good-bye to the mother. The daughters walked away with me through a maze of rock-stepped paths. We turned aside to look at the room where the two girls worked as seamstresses for the Perachoran women and their children; we stopped for a moment at the door of a tiny cavernous shop where a bearded old woman, sitting by a few bales of coloured cotton stuffs, gave me a handful of shelled nuts: 'Next year!' High on the village slope we came to the house of a man I had not seen since before the war: Michael Logothetis, staunch workman, good friend in the years of the Heraion excavations. Standing stiffly and respectfully, 'What can we offer you?' he asked. 'Coffee, a sweet, lemonade?' His shy, gaunt wife, sent running to the cafeneion, came back with bottles of the fizzy lemonade which is called gazoza; and talking of twenty years ago we drank.

'We thank you for remembering us!'

'It is I who thank you! Next year, next year!'

And 'Next year!' I repeated, standing and waving goodbye to the sisters. I watched them go, their strong ankles carrying them steadily and quickly, despite their heeled shoes, up the rough street. Yanni was waiting at the cafeneion door. His dark face, as usual, hardly committed a smile, but it was illumined by welcome.

'Did I not tell thee last year that I would come back?'

'So you did; come in, come in.'

The same Government poster, a little yellower, flapped on the wall of the long bare room. At one of the tables two men sat eating; through the window behind them I could see Kosta's boy laughing with his cronies. Yanni's wife came from behind the bottles on the counter to pull out a chair for me; her son, a boy of about fourteen, wearing an apron, went in her place to take the orders. Half a dozen

Perachorans lounged on the boarded verandah outside; inside, th
flies sang their midday song, time loitered.

'Can we offer you an ouzo?'

Yanni watched while I drank. 'What will you eat, eggs, meat
what do you wish?'

'Nothing, nothing; I have eaten.'

'Where did you eat, where?'

'At the lighthouse, with Vasili. And on the way I met Kosta, at th
lake I met him, and he gave me something to eat.'

'Early you will have eaten. Do you want us to fry you an egg?
Refusal would have been out of place. 'An egg then, thank you.

'So you saw Vasili, you saw him?'

'Yes, I went with the benzina, this time I got to the lighthouse.

'Last year you did not get there. You saw the Heraion, you saw it?

'Yes indeed; the first time since the war. The same it looks, only
it needs a little clearing; earth and stones have fallen, plants have
grown over the walls.'

'With the rains the soil comes down, it is not important. Do you
think they will dig there again, what do you say?'

Yanni's wife came from the room behind the counter and put a
plate in front of me. There were two eggs on it, fried in oil. 'A little
wine you will take,' said Yanni, pouring a glass of rhetsina. The boy,
with a long, curious look at me, fetched bread, and I squared up to my
meal. 'A little yiaourti you will take,' said Yanni when I had finished.
Presently: 'How do you take your coffee?' A group of women came
to stand round the table. Some of them I had not seen since my visit
in 1945; some I had forgotten ever seeing; but this I managed to conceal until a broad face under a white headscarf, grinning delightedly
and exposing short, flat, broken teeth, called my bluff.

'Dost thou not know me?'

'But of course!'

'Who am I then?'

'But I know thee well . . .'

'Stasoula I am! Now dost thou remember?' And from the vaults
of time I recalled a smiling young girl, scrambling sure-footed among

he rocks or taking my hand as, at the party after the dig, we danced by torchlight on the floor of the Hellenistic house.

I excused myself. 'It is a long time ago.'

'Time goes, time goes.' Yanni's wife flung out her arm as if to sketch an endless process of annihilation. 'Eh, what can we do?'

'You are changing things here in Perachora,' I said. 'The trench in the road, what is that for?'

'For the water, for the water,' said Stasoula. 'They are laying a pipe, through the pipe the water will flow!' Her voice rose. 'New, new!' she cried, a hand describing a magniloquent spiral.

'New indeed. The village has arranged this, together you have done it?'

'Together,' said Yanni. 'The doctor, whom you know, has helped us – he is Mayor of Loutraki now.'

'Well I know him. I remember the time he and his wife came to the Heraion – we made an excursion together to the islands which they call the Good Islands. Everybody told us we should find gulls' eggs, antiquities, I don't know what, but there was nothing but stones.'

'After that,' Yanni remarked, 'Vasili said they ought to be called the Bad Islands.'

For the third time that day I unfastened my bundle. 'I have a book here which I wrote; it is about the lighthouse, and the village, and all the things which happened when we were digging at the Heraion. I brought it for all of you in the village, all those I know; I will leave it here at the restaurant so that anyone who wishes can look at it. It is a very little present, but perhaps it will remind you all of the days when we worked together, we from England and you from Perachora.'

'We thank you, we thank you very much.' Yanni was almost smiling as he took it. His fingers turned the pages with the awkwardness of a man given a book in hieroglyphics. 'But why is it not translated into Greek so that we can all read it?'

'I am sorry; that does not depend on me. But thou see'st, it has photographs; here is the lighthouse, here are two of the bronze statuettes we found, the lion and the little dove.'

The group round the table had grown. One or two men I did not know had joined us, and the village schoolmaster came to take the book in his hands. The women looked at it from a distance, with incomprehension and respect.

'Who is that?' said one of them, pointing to a figure in a photograph: 'Panaghioti will it be?'

'Bah,' said another, 'Michaeli it will be, the old man.'

'It is a pity,' said Yanni, 'that we cannot read it. What have you said in it, what have you said about us here in Perachora?'

The schoolmaster looked at me earnestly. 'I ask you a favour. I should like very much to have a copy for our school. The children ought to know the history of their region, they ought to know what antiquities have been found here. But I have nothing to show them, if I had the book I could show them the photographs, they would learn about the Heraion, they would be proud.'

'When I get back to England, certainly. I wish it had more photographs. As you certainly know, at the Heraion all kinds of things were found, bronze, ivory, gold, pottery; but this is not an archaeological book, there are only a very few photographs of the finds.'

The lighthouse and the Heraion; the torchlight party in the Hellenistic house, the trip to the Good Islands; the harbour, the broken jetty, the place of our encampment, the unforgotten fields – all day the past had kept pace with me. Not for a minute, since the knock on my door which had called me to the waiting benzina, had I lost from view the landscapes of experience. The very phrases in which we talked, the traditional questions and required answers, the year-after-year-repeated sentences in which my wretched Greek took refuge, everything was a reminder. Smiling, straining to follow, I felt myself a figure in a scene which had been played, which would be played, over and over again.

It was at this moment of re-living – of my fancy that in the Perachoran story there was no time, no change except the cycle of age and leaf-fall – that a spoken question drove into my mind. I turned towards Yanni and looked at him with a frown of bewilderment. He repeated what he had said.

'Have you seen our museum?'

'What dost thou say?'

'Our museum; have you seen it?'

'Your museum?'

'Yes. Have you not seen it?'

'I don't understand. You have a museum?'

'Yes, you will have seen it as you came into our village.'

'Where? I saw nothing. Where?'

'In the plateia; you will have seen it.'

I searched my recollection of the day. 'As I arrived I saw a new white house at the corner of the plateia. Is that it?'

'Yes; we have just finished it. Is it not fine?' And Yanni looked into my face with a pride which, composed though it was, could not conceal the anxiety for confirming approval of a man who has seen the world.

I looked back twenty years and more. On the curtain of my eyes a scene came to life: a patch of dry earth, thistles quavering in a hot gritty wind, and figures long dead walking again. There was Humfry pacing out the length and breadth of the museum site, and Alan Blakeway calling to him across the rectangle; and in the group which watched them the faces were all young; Niko was a brisk fightable lighthouseman, Vasili had not yet married, Yanni was still the dark handsome postboy. The scene which followed it was not so clear. A low wall now ran round the rectangle. It was unfinished, the base merely of an enclosure; looking over it, I could see a tethered goat tearing with hard lips at the thistles. Then nothing; only the empty years of war and death.

'It is true? Truly you have built the museum at last?'

'But of course! Did we not decide with your husband years ago that we must have a museum at Perachora? Now it is finished.'

'But it is a miracle! Never should I have believed, after all this time, that you would build the museum. But how did it happen? Last year when I came to Perachora it was not even begun.'

'Together we did it; the doctor helped us. As you see, we are making our village all new.'

Perhaps there was a shade of irony in Yanni's voice; I could no be sure. But I recognized the confidence as he went on.

'We asked them in Athens, we asked them about the finds from the Heraion. Well, they told us we must build a museum. If we buil a museum, they said, they would give us the things to put in it.'

A second image from the past came into focus: a caïque anchored in the harbour beneath the lighthouse rock, men walking barefoo up a plank from the jetty with packing-cases; the spoils of a season at the Heraion, the bronzes and ivories, the scarabs, the wreckage of a thousand painted vases, all shipped to Athens, out of sight, out of reach of the men under whose fields they had been found.

'And what have they sent you?'

'Nothing yet; we are waiting.'

I thought of the jagged paths, the houses with their patched walls and dipping roofs, the village living its withdrawn, elemental life; and then of the local museums of Greece. Not one I knew but was set in some small town with streets, shops, an inn or two, or had at least the protection of a site with a famous name, a Delphi or an Epidauros. And I had seen some of the best finds from the Heraion already on view in Athens: bronzes, terracottas, a clay model of an early temple, all finely displayed in the post-war rearrangement of the National Museum.

'Occasionally' – I made a hesitant attempt to prepare the way for disappointment – 'Occasionally they keep a few of the most valuable pieces from an excavation in Athens. Perhaps they will not send everything to Perachora; what dost thou say?'

The shutter I knew so well, the shutter of stubbornness which the country Greek opposes to the faint-hearted reasoning of the sophisticated foreigner, came down over Yanni's dark, watchful face. 'They told us that if we built the museum they would give us the antiquities to put in it. Well, we have built it. Now we are waiting.'

XIX

'How much do I owe thee?'

'Nothing.'

'How nothing? I have drunk ouzo and wine and coffee, I have eaten eggs, yiaourti, I don't know what. Nothing how can it be?' Then remembering the rebuke which had silenced me nine years earlier, and thinking to reverse it now, 'This is not a house', I said, 'this is a restaurant.'

Yanni allowed himself the triumph of a grin. 'No!' He pointed to his wife, to the boy, to the children in the doorway behind the counter. 'You see, all the family are here. It is a house!'

The colloquy repeated itself in my ears as we drove down the road to Loutraki and on through the heat of the afternoon back to Athens.

'What good people they are, how hospitable, how good!' Yes, I said aloud to Thanasi, agreeing, yes, indeed they are good. Inwardly I said: they are also indestructible. Around them Europe explodes. Greece is invaded and occupied; Greece starves; Greece cracks and burns in a frightful internal convulsion. The Perachorans are not heard from; they are silent. For they are the unalterable ones. Amidst the general annihilation they hold to their singular dreams; and when the rest of us have forgotten they remember, in their dilapidated village, to build their museum.

This heroic and touching tenacity is threaded with human uncertainty. They are not quite persuaded by their own promises. The vision of wealth, of urban traffic, floats ahead; but when they look around they see only their own straits. 'We cannot read what you have said in your book,' said Yanni. 'If you write again what will you say about us?'

'That we are friends and that you have built a museum. What els must I say?'

'That there is much poverty; that we work, that we are in need Will you tell people? You must tell them about us.'

'I will tell them,' I said.

And that, now I come to write it down, is all I have to pass on. Th Perachorans are poor, and they build a museum; that is the story c the village. With the long faith in Tomorrow and Next Year whicl incessantly wars against the austerity of their lives and the majesti indifference of their landscape, they set up a museum. But on the da it is finished they have nothing to put in it. And so they wait. N doubt enters their minds but that every thing they remember from the Heraion will be returned; that the ivory figurines and the bronz statuettes, the engraved seals, the jewels and the ornaments, th scarabs, the terracottas, that every priceless fragment will come bacl to be enclosed in the square, whitewashed house in the plateia.

They have done their part, and confidently, patiently they wait

THE END